RUSSIAN I
AND REGIONAL

RUSSIAN FOOD is delicious, wholesome and easily prepared from generally available ingredients.

JEAN REDWOOD's cookery book contains a wide selection of recipes in easy-to-use presentation, measured in grams and ounces.

The book is enjoyable to read as well as to cook from. Russian literature provides much 'food for thought'.

There is a complete 'food story' by Chekhov in the author's own translation.

The geographical and historical background to cookery in different areas of the Russian Federation and surrounding countries is fully explained in all its splendid diversity.

RUSSIAN FOOD is based on Jean Redwood's extensive first-hand knowledge of Russia and the Russian language.

➤ Personal Preface and Introduction

➤ Domestic mealtimes

➤ 'The Siren' (Anton Chekhov)

➤ RECIPES

➤ COUNTRIES: where they are, what they grow, what they eat

➤ Maps - Bibliography - Glossary

➤ Index of recipes.

SOURCES OF RECIPES

Principal sources of recipes: countries named in **bold**.
In addition, some recipes come from central Asia and Russia's 'Far East'.

RUSSIAN FOOD

ALL THE PEOPLES, ALL THE REPUBLICS

JEAN REDWOOD

OLDWICKS PRESS

RUSSIAN FOOD
AND REGIONAL CUISINE

Edited by Heinz, Andrew and Alison Redwood
© 2015 Estate of Jean Redwood

ISBN: **978-1-870832-10-6**

First published as: '*Russian Food All the Peoples All the Republics*'
© 1989 Jean Redwood

Front cover and drawings on 'Russian Food' themes
© 1989 David Cooper

Back cover photograph: courtesy Andrew Redwood
'*Author with Poppy seed roll and Borodinskii bread*'

The Estate of Jean Redwood reserves the right to revise the publication from time to time.
01 November 2015

Published 2015 by Oldwicks Press Limited, 5 Links Avenue, Felixstowe, Suffolk IP11 9HD, England

FOREWORD

"My interest in Russian cooking started when I worked in the British Embassy for a year shortly after the war", wrote Jean Redwood in the First Edition of 'Russian Food'.

At the house in Moscow which she shared with other Embassy colleagues "we had an excellent cook and the meals were delicious". It was a view that she confirmed in later years when, after graduating in Russian, she repeatedly visited Russia, Ukraine and Georgia, experiencing and later cooking the food of many countries that were then part of the Soviet Union but are now independent states.

'Russian Food' is classic cuisine with a practical approach to reality for countries where winters are milder than in Russia and where the time available for cooking is far more limited than in the days when many of the historic recipes had their origin. In her Personal Preface, the author remarks:

"I have recommended the less fattening and healthier alternative of yoghurt in recipes where I think an excessive amount of cream is demanded" and "the recipes chosen are ones which do not require exotic ingredients". Moreover, "I have given alternative methods of cooking dishes by modern means for cooks in a hurry."

Altogether, at least one-third of the recipes in 'Russian Food' are from 14 countries in a wide region including the Baltic States, Belarus, Ukraine and reaching Armenia, Azerbaijan and Georgia in the south and as far as Kazakhstan, Tajikistan, Turkmenistan and Uzbekistan to the east.

In re-editing 'Russian Food', all countries have been referred to by their present names as independent states, and the past tense has been used for facts and events that, in the original edition, were described as existing 'today' or 'recently'.

On the other hand, the appealing freshness and immediacy of Jean Redwood's personal observations while living in Russia or visiting it has been retained.

In short:

Since 'Russian Food' was first published there have been dramatic changes in geopolitics - but the recipes are timeless.

Heinz Redwood   Nov 2015

To my friend Vera French
also in memory of her husband John and of
her mother Vera Vladimirovna Terentieva

ACKNOWLEDGMENTS

I am grateful to all my friends and to my daughters for testing and tasting many of the recipes: to my husband who encouraged me and grew the vegetables, especially the beetroot; to my son for his cartographic help and patience; and to my mother-in-law who gave me helpful professional advice as a writer.

I should like to thank especially the friends I made in Pyatigorsk[1] who introduced me to many of the dishes of their region.

My thanks are also due to all who took an interest in my project, and in particular Tony Allen for his unfailing support.

My gratitude above all goes to my mother, a Cornishwoman who cooked with flair. Like the Russians, she knew the art of making a little go a long way and taught me down the years.

---

[1] Pyatigorsk , North Caucasus. The name is derived from the Russian for 'five mountains', whose peaks overlook the city.

TABLE OF CONTENTS

ILLUSTRATIONS on Russian Food 'themes'   Page

MAPS

Sources of Recipes - European Russia and regional overview   Inside front & back cover

About the Author

JEAN REDWOOD lived and worked in the British Embassy in Moscow during the late Stalinist and Cold War Period. She learnt much from her Russian cook who was adept in the use of whatever produce was available.

Subsequent journeys and visits to the cities of Moscow, St. Petersburg and Kiev and to the Caucasus enabled her to make a personal assessment of the people, food and way of life.

Jean was a graduate of Russian; her keen interest in Russian literature both illuminates the recipes and provides cultural context throughout the book.

In later years, living in Suffolk, she worked as a freelance abstractor and translator of Russian economic material, mostly on timber and agricultural products.

PERSONAL PREFACE

My interest in Russian cooking (and I use the word 'Russian' as a general term but include also national dishes from regions outside the Russian Federation) started when I worked in the British Embassy for a year shortly after the war. Then I lived in an old house appropriately named **Stari Dom** (Old House), which once belonged to a wealthy sugar manufacturer, along with six or eight other colleagues.

We had an excellent cook and the meals were delicious after the austerities and rationing in England. I was surprised to find so much fresh fruit and vegetables available. In those far-off post-war days caviar and sturgeon were plentiful and often figured on our menus at **Stari Dom**. You could even buy caviar **zakuski** *(snacks or hors d'oeuvres)* at street corners as well as the creamiest and most delicious ice-creams. You couldn't buy flour in the shops and this was only given out on holidays when long queues would form early in the day; but for most people then anything but the most basic cooking was impossible — kitchens were communal and everyone worked long hours rebuilding after the wartime devastation.

Toward the end of the Soviet era, kitchen and housing facilities improved. Cooking was revived as an important skill, judging by the sudden spate of cookery books that emerged from the different regions. One described how to make the most of breadcrumbs — a drive to avoid unnecessary waste after a series of bad harvests and general food shortage and also a timely reminder to a changing society of the age-old reverence for bread.

At **Stari Dom** I learned to appreciate the many varieties of black bread, **Minskii, Borodinskii, Orlovskii,** and all the little **bulochki** - slightly sweet rolls strewn with sesame and poppy seeds. In the 1980's, bakers' shops in Leningrad *(now St. Petersburg)* and Moscow were still much the same as I remembered them over thirty years earlier - small and dark and usually down a few steps. Bread was laid out on sloping slats behind wooden rails and customers prodded the different rolls with spoons provided to test their freshness[1]. I was told by an elderly shop assistant that the black bread was made from only a small portion of rye and the rest was wheat and some bran was added. The darkness of the loaf comes partly from the use of sour dough leaven and malt.

Our cook in **Stari Dom** used to serve delicious fried sweetbreads, various forms of **kasha** *(porridge made with different grains such as buckwheat, semolina or oats)* beetroot **borshch** and cabbage soup **(shchi)** in all its varieties. We ate all sorts of pies, some stuffed with rice and cabbage or mushrooms or cottage cheese. Soured or fresh cream **(smetana and slivki)** accompanied our sweet and savoury pancakes **(bliny)** with their variety of stuffings, and apples baked in pastry was one of our favourites. All this was very fattening but warming in temperatures which became as low as forty degrees centigrade below freezing when I was there. I have recommended the less fattening and healthier alternatives of yoghurt in recipes where I think

---

[1] Today, a wide range of bread is available. In Moscow, international companies such as *'Maison Paul'* have outlets. Local bakeries chains e.g. *'Khleb & Co.'* still provide traditional breads, cakes and pastries. Shops are modern and brightly lit.

an excessive amount of cream is demanded, thus making them suitable for people on low cholesterol diets.

Many original dishes have survived and remain unaltered over the centuries: **Lepeshki** *(yeast raised flat bread)* made from oat, wheat, maize or millet flour from the north Caucasus. Soup made from **kvas**, a kind of light beer, is still a favourite and so are noodles which came from China and known in Siberia and the Urals as **pel'meni**. Favourite Russian seasonings remain horseradish and mustards. Old recipes are pastries stuffed with cottage cheese, different types of pancakes and fish brawn. Berries were also used with meat dishes and this is no different from the general European tradition.

The recipes chosen are ones which do not require exotic ingredients and which can generally be obtained by people living in or near small towns as well as those living in big cities. It is not expensive to prepare Russian dishes. Most of them require everyday ingredients. Soured cream can be replaced by yoghurt which can be stabilised and thickened, dried mushrooms replaced by fresh. Some old recipes used large quantities of honey, which is now a more expensive item. For economy, a half and half blend of honey and treacle could be used.

I have given alternative methods of cooking dishes by modern means for cooks in a hurry. Everyone pounces eagerly on quick tasty recipes which can be easily memorised and likely to become a family favourite. The aim of the modern cook is to eat well with the minimum of extra work and labour and the minimum of artificial ingredients.

I am not a great lover of fancy presentation of food and as far as I am concerned vegetables should retain their original shapes and the less moulding and handling of food the better. This is generally speaking the English preference, and there we part company with many other cuisines.

How time consuming is it to cook *à la russe*? There are many extremely easy, quick recipes which sound almost too simple on paper but which are really delicious because of the unusual and accurate combinations of flavours. Of course, economic dishes where the mincing and pounding of meat and the stuffing of vegetables is involved do take time. However, most people do possess good food processors or hand-held Mouli slicers and sieves. Many people still prefer a Mouli-baby or grinder to using electrical equipment which sometimes produces too bland and smooth a texture; pressure cookers save fuel, and thoroughly cook food speedily. A blender is ideal for puréeing spinach if some of the water is left in, as it can be drained afterwards and the juice saved for soup.

A real knowledge and understanding of the cuisine of another country can take us one step nearer to understanding the people. It remains a mystery why people, regions and nations, cling to special dishes and particular ways of preparing them no matter what may be fashionable. They are handed down like nursery songs, frequently outlasting myths and cults, and that is why cookery is so fascinating.

RUSSIAN FOOD and Regional Cuisine

INTRODUCTION

Not all ideas cross frontiers happily, culinary or otherwise, and they should stay at home. In this book on Russian cookery I have tried to include those dishes which travel well and settle down in their host countries, taking on local colour and embellishments, and I have therefore excluded some complicated and fanciful nineteenth century and earlier recipes not suitable for modem palates and good health.

What people eat at different periods of history tells us much about their social and economic conditions. Geography also plays a strong part. For instance nothing pointed more to the artificiality of the position of St. Petersburg than the fact that every bit of food had to be imported. The city, created by Peter the Great, was built on marshy swampland. The historian J.G. Kohl, writing in 1842, described Petersburg as standing on a bottomless bog and in spring and autumn the mud oozed up between every little aperture, and to form meadows the grass had to be planted almost blade by blade. He reports that the climate was so ghastly that there was a constant changing of ambassadors and the women were extremely pale and unhealthy looking. Even hay, which was needed in great quantities to keep the fifty to sixty thousand horses of the vast standing army, as well as a further thirty to sixty thousand belonging to the gentry and bureaucrats, had to be brought in from some distance. The Haymarket was an important centre of the city and a good part of the action in Dostoyevsky's **Crime and Punishment** takes place in this area. In **War and Peace** Tolstoy is critical of the importation of unnecessary luxury goods and out of season fruit. Hothouses proliferated in the late nineteenth century, but it was a full-time job for one gardener to turn each plant at intervals so that it could catch every bit of light and vestige of sunshine to produce the small, often sour fruit. It was interesting to read in Soviet newspapers of the new towns being built on permafrost in inhospitable places in Siberia and the plans under way for the building of gigantic greenhouses.

Most of the recipes in this book have been garnered from various solid and reliable cooking manuals with such reassuring titles as **The Book of Tasty and Healthy Food** and many others from the different areas of the Russian Federation and countries it has influenced. I have enjoyed reading nineteenth century cookery books in the British Library and include a number of their recipes, suitably adapted. In comparing modern and older recipes I have been struck by how few changes have been made over the years, allowing for the inclusion in Mrs. Molokhovets' household book (1861-80) **A Present to Young Housewives** of some rather high flown recipes only suitable for someone with an army of servants.

Soviet cookbooks did not give bread[1] recipes so I adapted Mrs. Molokhovets' recipes and reduced the mammoth proportions, adding the appropriate flavourings to produce my version of Minsk and Borodinsk bread.

The variety and technique of food preparation throughout the area covered by this book is considerable. The recipes gathered here are mainly from Central Russia, Ukraine, Armenia and Georgia and some other regional dishes, though not those that have generally passed into

---

[1] In the Soviet era, bread was supplied free to families – no need to bake so perhaps the authorities saw no need for recipes…

'international' cuisine and can be found easily in German cookbooks or in books on Middle East cookery. There are also some 'Empire' dishes from Poland and Finland when these countries were part of the Russian Empire. Of course, there is nothing new under the sun but culinary art evolves like any other.

Recipes from other nations seem to stimulate native originality and creativity. Turgenev illustrates this in his short story **Khor' and Khalinych** from his **Hunter's Notebook** written in 1846, where the landowner Polutykin has introduced French cuisine into his house.

In the Russian cook's hands dishes become unrecognizable —meat dishes taste like fish, fish like mushrooms, while carrots assume weird shapes before appearing in the soup. This may well be a subtle allusion to the cook's slyness in breaking the strict church fasts which united Nicholas I's Empire to such a degree that families ate more or less the same things on the same day throughout the land; on the other hand it could be a social comment to illustrate the inventiveness of the Russian peasant and the Russian love of decoration and carving - skills seen in their folk art and which certainly inspired such painters as Kandinsky and Goncharova and many others.

The Sybarites of ancient Greece were also renowned for altering the taste, texture and aroma of their foods so completely that guests thought they were eating poultry when they were eating fish!! Graeco-Byzantine eating habits were brought to southern Russia when trading relations between Kiev and Byzantium were strong in the years before and after Kievan Rus became Christian in 988.

There are three strongly divided styles of cooking that can be observed:

'Baltic', which is German/Scandinavian influenced;

'Central Russian and the North', which is predominantly Slav and Balkan;

'Transcaucasian' which has a Mediterranean element and has been subject to strong Middle Eastern and Asian influences.

Ukraine and Moldova have a richer, mixed cuisine which is more varied than other regions though not necessarily more imaginative.

For easy reference some factual notes (*Regions and Nationalities*) can be found at the back of the book giving additional information on some of the independent states, together with a number of maps.

The geography and climate of Russia as well as her early trading partners have played a large part in the development of the country's cooking and eating habits. Eastern Vikings travelled down the countless river roads of Russia, which were linked by easy portages which facilitated communication and colonization. They found there the sturdy grains able to withstand the harsh climate, such as rye and buckwheat, staple foods to this day, particularly in the north of the country. Buckwheat also grows in Siberia and Central Asia.

The vast forests provided them with wild honey, mushrooms, berries and nuts, which explains why there are so many recipes requiring large quantities of what are now expensive commodities. Preserving food was an important activity due to the long winters and short growing season. Gogol's short story **Old World Landowners** describes the endless domestic salting, drying and brewing activities of the old wife Pul'kheria Ivanovna, whose husband groaned at night from excess consumption of her products:

'*... jam was made under the apple tree and there was always a fire going, the three-legged cauldron and copper basin were filled with boiling jam jelly or pastila. Under another tree vodka was made from apricot leaves or bird cherry flowers and another from a type of golden headed thistle ... their house was like a chemist's laboratory...except for the flies ...*'

Root storage in winter was no problem. The eastern Vikings (about AD 860) brought the art of preserving fish and their fondness for chilled fruit soups, which is like the Danish **rødgrød** I have served in my own family for years, the recipe for which was given to me by my Danish friend Jytte. Fruit soups are to be found in Scandinavia and Germany.

The main trading route stretched from the Gulf of Finland to the Black Sea where Greek colonies had established themselves. Graeco-Byzantine influences are more clearly noticeable in the cooking of the south and those of Scandinavia in the north, though there is also a mixture of both due to the north-south flow of the great slow moving rivers of western Russia along which the traders passed[1].

The northern shore of the Black Sea and the steppe beyond remained for centuries on the border of the ancient world of Greece, Rome and Byzantium. The Belarusian recipe for Byzantine pork sausage is almost identical to the one I have for Smyrna sausage in my Greek cookbook. Southern Russian cooking was largely influenced by the Greeks through Byzantium. Later influences were the Turks and other peoples of the Near East who introduced a wider use of seasonings.

The Tatars, to use a general term for the Iranian nomadic and pastoral tribes coming from the wilds of then unknown Asia across the open steppeland, also brought their own methods of preparing food and passed them onto the Slavic races who lived in the northern forest regions. They introduced curd cheeses and also brought their different drinking habits and art of fermentation. Unfortunately they also destroyed many of the vines in southern Russia thus halting the development of wine production for centuries. The Tatars arrived before the great Mongol invasions in the twelfth and thirteenth centuries and settled in the Middle Volga and Crimean areas. Rice, tea, dried fruits, nuts, spices and herbs figure largely in their diet as well as milk, soured cream (**smetana**), yoghurt (**katik**), and **airan** (*a mixture of yoghurt and mineral water used as a cooling summer drink*).

Noodles are an early Tatar dish and also pel'meni (small stuffed dumplings). Tatar bread is particularly good and easy to make, and they claim to have known the secret of fermentation for making their sour dough long before it became widespread in Russia. They had a liking for sweet dishes- notably various bread-biscuits based on honey called **pryaniki**, sweet pies

---

[1] The Dniester, the Bug and larger Dnieper, the Don and Volga flow south, but the Northern Dvina and the Pechora go northward. The huge Siberian rivers Ob and Yenisei drain into the Arctic Ocean. The Amur goes eastward.

and strangely mixed sweet-savoury dishes combining black radishes with poppy seeds, carrots with honey and ginger.

Much later on, the expansion and development of Empire reinforced and added to what had already become indigenous dishes, and by the seventeenth and eighteenth centuries Russian cooking was extremely varied. Foreign influence was considerable and in the seventeenth century two-thirds of the gentry were foreigners and a whole dictionary of foreign words was called for.

Pasta dishes made their appearance in the time of Ivan III, and Peter the Great brought western foods from Holland and Germany - white bread, honey cakes, cheeses and sausages. Polish food was also popular, but in the eighteenth century French cuisine was the rage due to Catherine the Great's predilection for things French and this continued in the reign of Alexander I, who had Antonin Carême as chef. Flaky pastry made from wheat flour replaced yeast pastry made from rye and leavened by sour dough. The French connection is seen in the many sauces, salads and garnishes which gradually acquired their own Russian style.

At the turn of the century when the 'World of Art' circle, led by Benois, Diaghilev and other eminent artists exerted a strong western influence, Italian, French and English dishes were fashionable.

After the Revolution cookery and the domestic arts were regarded as bourgeois activities and women 'threw off their chains' alongside the men.

Catering in the Soviet Union had many of the features encountered everywhere - a certain standardisation in an endeavour to please all tastes but which generally satisfies no-one. The acute shortage of fresh fruit and vegetables and shortage of meat so evident in the shops of that era, contributed to the monotony of restaurant dishes[1].

The best things are the cabbage soups (**shchi**) of which there are many varieties, **borshch** (beetroot based soups), mushrooms served in soured cream in individual bowls such as I enjoyed in a converted monastery in Suzdal one cool September morning, and the substantial breakfasts. This should have wide appeal. There are the different kinds of **kashas** *(porridge)* made from oats, buckwheat, semolina or millet, and hot wheat cakes, stuffed pancakes and delicious curd cheese dishes. Other consistently good items of fare are ice-cream and the various breads and rolls. A large chapter is devoted to bread-baking in this book and includes many recipes from the different independent states and regions.

One thing I found I could always buy in the shops was a good assortment of cheeses, yoghurts and kefir milk of high and low fat content and no doubt the ordinary Russian makes full use of these products. In the 1980's various open markets in and around the main cities provided a good supply of fruit and vegetables[2] but at fairly high prices as it was all produce grown on people's private allotments.

Russian eating habits have been regulated and influenced by the seasons and the Orthodox Church's many festivals and fasts. The historian J.G. Kohl writing in 1843 describes some of

---

[1] Much has changed since the collapse of the Soviet Union; cities like St. Petersburg have seen a boom in restaurants, catering to both simple and sophisticated tastes.
[2] Today, a much wider range of produce is available, in common with the rest of the developed world.

the Easter customs and food. On the tables of the rich, butter would be shaped like lambs and even many everyday dishes such as mashed potatoes were in the form of eggs. A large meal was eaten after the Easter Day service and there would certainly be a ham, **tvorog** (*curd cheese*) and hard-boiled eggs. There is an account of a banquet given for the Tsar when all the dishes assumed egg shapes - snipe, pastries, puddings, creams – all emerged from egg shaped dishes. Syrups and preserves glistened through glass eggs and at one course huge eggs of gold paper held raisins, almonds and bonbons. In St. Petersburg alone the consumption of eggs at Easter was estimated by Kohl to be at least ten million (!) as it was customary to put an egg into the hand of every acquaintance.

Fasts were strictly observed for the most part and almond milk replaced ordinary milk, which is why there are so many recipes using it. It makes a pleasant drink and can be successfully used in making puddings and **kasha** *(porridge)*. Herb soups were part of Lenten fare as well as huge pies filled with mushrooms and fish. Large turnips were stuffed and baked in the oven and this is still considered a very tasty dish.

After Easter, according to Kohl, oranges and lemons could be found everywhere. No doubt they were a welcome antidote to the excesses to which Russians were prone in eating and drinking. Kohl writes that the fruit was sold in such quantities and passed off by the vendors as real Petersburg fruit (!) that one would think that "these agreeable fruits must grow in Russia upon the birches and the pine trees".

We celebrated holidays in **Stari Dom** in great style. The oak panelled hall, hung with stags' heads, trophies from the bourgeois past, made an ideal dance hall, and at Christmas we decorated it with evergreens and ate our own traditional Christmas pudding, the mysteries of which defeated our cook, and which we had had imported from Fortnum and Mason. She did make the traditional Christmas **Kutya**, a very simple dish of cooked wheat grain and honey combined with dried fruits which we ate on Christmas Eve. At the beginning of Lent mountains of pancakes stuffed with caviar, smoked fish or curd cheese were served with soured cream **(smetana)**, and at Easter bowls of brightly painted eggs, the high yeast **kulich** - *(a rich brioche type cake)* and the **Paskha** (a mixture of pressed cottage cheese or cream cheese, cream, egg-yolk, dried fruit and nut) decorated the festive table. There are various recipes for this last dish and some include honey and lemon.

The cook's greeting to us on Easter Day was '**Khristos voskresen**' *(Christ is Risen)*, and we replied '**Vo istinu voskres**' *(He is Risen indeed)*. I attended the midnight service the night before in the Cathedral *(Uspenski Sobor)* and as these words ring out people embrace their neighbours. Kohl says that no-one is exempt from the Easter kiss. In the army a general of a corps had to kiss every officer and every commander his own officers and so on down through the ranks. The same thing happened in the civil department. The Emperor had to kiss everyone in his employ at the palace as well as distinguished personages, and on the parade ground on Easter Sunday he would kiss the whole corps and quite a number of selected privates! It must have been a fearsome experience to be embraced by the frosty Nicholas II.

DOMESTIC MEALTIMES ——————————

'People dine ... and meanwhile their happiness is made and their lives are broken'. .Anton Chekhov, from his **Letters**.

'There are no plots in life, everything is mixed up in it, the profound with the trite'. **The Seagull** *by Chekhov.*

The daily gatherings round the Russian table served as an admirable literary device to bring about dramatic denouements and Chekhov made use of it for creating atmosphere and for showing the social positions, divisions and temperaments of his characters.

Bourgeois snobbery, for instance, is seen in a table scene from '**A Dreary Story**'. Here a professor is deprived of his usual simple fare by his ambitious wife when he becomes Dean of his faculty. His favourite cabbage soup and accompanying savoury pies, goose with apples, bream with buckwheat are replaced by refined puréed soups and kidneys in madeira.

Tolstoy also uses this technique at times in **War and Peace**. There is a sharp difference between the smart St. Petersburg dinners with their complicated frenchified menus, and that of country dwellers such as Natasha's uncle, where such typically Russian fare as herb vodka, pickled mushrooms and rye cakes made with butter milk (a kind of scone) are served. In **Anna Karenina** Levin's housekeeper provides all Russian dishes such as nettle soup and smoked goose.

Chekhov had strong ideas on table behaviour and hated the oppressive tyrannical atmosphere created in his own family when his father complained inordinately if the food was not exactly to his taste.

In a letter to his brother he instructs him on how to bring up his small daughter: 'train her in the aesthetics of the stomach ... don't let her nibble morsels of this and that.' I wonder what he would say to our TV snacks today, or street munching?

Mealtimes in 19th century Russian novels seem to have been flexible, especially in Moscow, where they ate at all hours. St. Petersburg was more formal.

Rimsky-Korsakov describes the eccentric Borodin family. Cats overran the house and would hop on and off the tables at mealtimes. So many people, both friends and relatives, came and went, that it is not surprising that Borodin often either went without food or dined twice over. The Tolstoys, on the other hand, had a fairly rigid eating schedule; family chronicles tell *(with half joking exaggeration)* of a Tolstoy day: 10-11 coffee, 11-12 tea on the croquet lawn. 12-1 lunch followed by more tea. Work until five, then bathing. From 5 to 7 dinner followed by croquet and boating until eight. From 8-9 it was 'small tea', 9-10 'high tea', 10-11 supper. Presumably this was in summer and when there were guests. Tolstoy himself used to have two boiled eggs in a glass for breakfast and nothing to eat until five o'clock in the afternoon though in the 1880's he started to take lunch at two or three. Generally the family meal pattern was five o'clock dinner, when kasha was nearly always the first course, and tea at ten in the evening.

One of their early cooks wasn't too good and often drunk and dirty. Small wonder Tolstoy complained of indigestion. For his stomach ache he would take **kvas** with salt. A later cook, Nikolai, would prepare delicious **levashniki** (a type of pie) filled with jam. He would blow into one corner of them so that the crust would not settle; they were known in the family as 'les soupirs de Nicolas'[1].

Tolstoy family favourites seem to have been traditional fare such as **bliny** at Shrovetide when they also kept to a number of prescribed dishes made with lenten[2] oil, and drank their tea or coffee with almond milk. At breakfast freshly baked almond **krendels** were enjoyed and on name days Anke cake, a rich yeast brioche.

 Mealtimes with the Tolstoys could be very oppressive when Tolstoy was out of humour and they would then take place in silence. All this tension within aristocratic and bourgeois circles is in some contrast to the peasant table, where food is life. Manners could be coarse but the meal was usually eaten with great attention and in silence. Isaac Babel describes the ritual and dignity of the Cossacks as they settle to eat their soup around a camp fire, sitting bolt upright, all larking and jostling put aside.

Gogol's descriptions of provincial table manners centre mainly round the **zakuski** table. A chain of dishes are spread out elegantly in a necklace, and everyone helps himself. He describes in hilarious fashion how 'guests would storm the table, armed with forks... some the size of a pitchfork.' Everything is a little larger than life: on one occasion a lady is offered a dish of sauce balanced on the top of a hussar's sword!

Pushkin's family were so eccentric by all accounts that their house had a camped-in atmosphere. Mealtime was somewhat irregular and perhaps explains the way he liked to walk about munching sunflower seeds, peeling nectarines and pacing up and down dining rooms while others ate. When he was working life was more regular, and in exile at Mikhailovskoye he liked to dine early, if somewhat stodgily, on potatoes and kasha.

His grandmother Hannabel kept a more regular household and when he was young his family spent most summers on her estate at Zakharova near Moscow. Pushkin recalls the sight of the round table laid for the noon-day meal in the sunlit dining room, spread with a clean cloth, and on it the symbolic bread and salt of hospitality, the wine glasses filled to the brim, while from the cabbage soup the steam rises. Beside it a pike lies stretched out ... The spell is broken and the guests enter noisily.

The 'new woman' of the 1920's, depicted in Yuri Olesha's story '**Envy**', was supposed to be freed from her kitchen chains. But communal kitchens hardly contributed to improved eating and supplies of traditional cooking equipment were hard to come by.

Babichev, the central figure in this story is an official in the food industry. He is a big, fat man, who blunders into an unknown kitchen with the intention of telling the sceptical women the good news of his plans to 'industrialise the kitchen'; thousands had already 'submitted', and henceforth people would eat in gigantic splendid dining halls. He will put an end to 'make it yourself' and amalgamate all the meat grinders... all the frying pans'. Time

---

[1] 'Nicholas's sighs'. (From 'Reminiscences of Tolstoy', by Iyla Tolstoy, his son.)
[2] Lenten oil: A cooking oil conforming with religious diet restrictions during Lent.

stolen from them by the kitchens will be returned, thus half their lives will be given back. In future, 'potatoes will jump out of their skins as if by magic *(instant mash?)*, whole seas and oceans of soup will be created, there will be mounds of **kasha** like tumuli, and glaciers of **kisel**'. His unwelcome entry disrupts the women and causes primuses to go out, a glass to smash and the soup to be oversalted and they chase him out in fury before he can communicate his 'good news'.

Chekhov's story '**The Siren**' is a splendid account of a meal, summoned up in the imagination of a secretary of a local magistrate's court. Certainly the effect on the reader is a desire to bustle off to the kitchen and prepare something. It is a kind of culinary drama, amusingly strewn with a few phrases of a legal turn. My translation begins on the next page — it is early Chekhov at his amusing best.

THE SIREN

by Anton Chekhov

Trans. Jean Redwood

Before going home to eat after a court sitting of the Justice of the Peace in N—village, the committee members retired to disrobe and to have a few minutes peace.

The Chairman of the committee, a stately man with bushy side-whiskers, who had to give his 'special opinion' on the recent proceedings, sat at the table and hurried to write it out.

The divisional representative of the village court was a young man with a dark melancholy face, named Milkin, reputed to be something of a philosopher, and dissatisfied with the average aims in life. He was standing at the window and gazing mournfully at the courtyard outside. The other more important divisional representatives had already departed. There remained a flabby, fat dignitary, who breathed heavily, and the assistant magistrate, a young German, who looked as if he suffered from catarrh, who was sitting on a small divan and waiting for the chairman to finish writing so that they could leave together to go to dinner.

In front of them stood the committee secretary, Zhilin, a little man with side burns round his ears and with a sweet expression on his face.

He was talking in low tones and looking at the fat man with a honeyed smile.

'We're all longing to eat now because we are tired and it's already four o'clock, but my dear Grigorii Savvich, it's not a real appetite. A real appetite, like a wolf's, comes only after physical exertion as it would when our ancestors returned from hunting with the hounds or after you've covered about a hundred versts[1] round your neighbourhood without stopping.'

'Yes sir, much of it is in the imagination. Supposing let's say, you're on your way home with an appetite and looking forward to eating, then the mind doesn't enter into it; silence and intellect always spoil the appetite. Where food is concerned philosophers and scientists are the bottom, and if I may say so the worst are the ones who don't even eat pork. When you're going home you have to try to keep your mind only on bottles and **zakuski**.[2] Once when I was on the road home I shut my eyes and conjured up a sucking pig with horseradish, which whetted my appetite so much that it brought on an attack of hysterics.'

'Now sir, just when you come into your own courtyard there should be a smell of something good coming from the kitchen, you know what I mean ...'

'Roast goose first and foremost', said the honourable member, sighing heavily.

'Grigorii Savvich, my dear fellow, you can't mean that. A duck is ten times better. The bouquet of goose hasn't the same tenderness and delicacy. You know the strongest is spring onions when they begin to brown, and if you get my meaning, to sizzle, the rogues, drifting over the whole house. Yes sir, when you enter the house the table must be laid, and you sit down, immediately tuck your napkin over your tie, stretch out a hand towards the vodka, taking your time. You don't pour it, our little mother vodka, into any old glass, but into some

---

[1] A verst = 3500 feet or 1.06 km
[2] Zakuski : hors d'oeuvres

old-fashioned silver cup or some such round goblet; and don't drink it straight off but first sniff it, rub your hands, look up at the ceiling nonchalantly, then, without hurrying, raise that little glass to your lips and straight away sparks travel from your stomach through your whole body ... sparks.'

The secretary's face had a blissful expression. 'Sparks,' he repeated, screwing up his face, 'and the very minute you've drunk it you must take a bite.'

'Listen,' said the chairman, looking up at the secretary, - 'a bit quieter! I've already ruined two pieces of paper on your account.'

'Yes sir, I'm guilty, Pyotr Nikolaich. I'll be quiet,' said the secretary and continued in a half whisper. 'Now my dear Grigorii Savvich sir, you must also know how to set about the zakuski. You have to know what to start with. The very best **zakuski** if you must know, is the salted herring. Take a little bite with onion and mustard sauce while you can still feel the fiery sparks; eat the caviar just as it is, or if you like with a slice of lemon; after that a simple bit of radish with salt; again the herring, but best of all, kind sir, are yellow capped saffron mushrooms, chopped finely like caviar (p 22), if you know what I mean, with onion and olive oil - delicious! And burbot's liver - that's a whole tragedy!'

'M-m, yes,' agreed the honourable member, screwing up his eyes, 'fragrant white mushrooms.'

'Yes, yes, yes! with onion, and you know with bay leaf and all kinds of spices. When you open the pot and the steamy mushroom smell rises, it sometimes even brings tears to your eyes. Now sir, the minute the pie is out of the kitchen, then that very minute, as quick as you can, you must take a second drink.'

'Ivan Gur'ich', wailed the chairman plaintively, 'I've ruined the third page because of you.'

'Devil take it – only thinking about eating', growled Milkin the philosopher, showing his contempt. 'Aren't there really more interesting things in life besides mushrooms or even fish pie?'

'Now sir, before you start the pie, take a drink', continued the secretary in a low voice. You're already being carried away, like when you hear a nightingale singing and hear nothing but its voice.'

'The **kulebyaka**[1] must be appetising, shameless in all its nakedness, so that it's a temptation; your eye winks, and you cut out such a big slice, holding it caressingly...You start to eat it and butter spurts out like tears, the stuffing is fat and juicy with giblets, eggs, onion...' The secretary rolled his eyes, his mouth stretching right to his ears.

The honourable member wheezed and rubbed his hands, probably imagining a **kulebyaka**.

'The devil only knows,' muttered the committee member, moving to the other window.

'Two slices have been eaten and the third is saved for the cabbage soup', continued the secretary, sighing. 'To keep your appetite going, order the soup to be served as soon as you've finished the pie. The soup must be burning hot; but best of all, my kind sir, **borshchok** from

---

[1] Kulebyaka — a pie

beets prepared in the **khokhlatskii** manner with bacon and sausage, served with **smetana**[1] and fresh parsley and dill. **Rassol'nik** (p 38.) is also a splendid soup made from giblets and tender kidneys, and if you like soup then it's best made with root vegetables and herbs: carrots, asparagus, cauliflower and other judicious additions of a like nature.'

'Yes, a splendid thing,' sighed the chairman, tearing his eyes away from his paper and, immediately making a mistake, groaned.

'Show some respect. Otherwise I'll be writing the special opinion until nightfall. That's the fourth piece of paper ruined'

'I won't! I won't do it any more. I plead guilty, sir,' the secretary excused himself and continued in a whisper: 'as soon as you've supped the **borshchok** or the soup, order the fish course, kind sir. Of all the fish the best is roast carp with **smetana**, only you must put it promptly in milk the minute you get it, for twenty-four hours, to rid it of its muddy taste and to tenderise it.

'A sterlet is also very good,' said the honourable member, closing his eyes; but to everyone's surprise, immediately heaved himself out of his seat, and looking furious, bellowed across to the chairman: 'Pyotr Nikolaich, are you going to be quick? I can't wait any longer, I simply can't!'

'Let me just finish!'

'Alright then, so I'll go by myself! Devil take you!' The stout man waved his hands, seized his hat, and without saying goodbye, ran out of the room. The secretary sighed, and leaning down to the deputy magistrate's ear, continued in a low voice: 'a pike or carp are also good with a tomato and mushroom sauce. But fish are not filling, Stefan Frantsych; it's not a vital food; the main thing for a meal is not fish, not sauce, but the roast. Which sort of bird do you like best?'

The deputy magistrate made a sour face and sighed: 'Alas, I have to draw the line at that: I suffer from stomach catarrh.'

'No more of that sir, stomach catarrh is something the doctors have thought up; it's more an illness that comes from free thinking or from pride. Pay no attention to it. Let's suppose you don't want to eat, or you're sick, and you ignore it and eat. If, suppose, they serve a couple of the greater snipe with the roast, surrounded by a little partridge or pair of plump quails - the females, then frankly you can forget about any catarrh. And a roast turkey? White, plump, and you know, juicy - rather like a nymph ...'

'Yes, most likely it's tasty,' said the deputy magistrate, smiling sadly. 'I could eat turkey, if you like.'

'But good heavens, a duck? If you take a young duck, caught when the first frosts come, and its been roasted in a dish with potatoes, the potatoes finely cut and allowed to get golden and soak up all the duck fat, and that ...'

---

[1] **Smetana** — soured cream

The philosopher Milkin, with a wild look on his face, evidently wanted to say something, but suddenly smacked his lip, probably envisaging the roast duck; deprived of words, he seized his hat and hurriedly made off, drawn by invisible forces.

'Yes, maybe I could manage a little duck,' sighed the deputy magistrate. The chairman stood up, said goodbye, and sat down again. 'After the roast a man is satisfied and falls into a sweet stupor,' continued the secretary. 'Just at this moment your body feels good and you're in fine fettle. Just to finish off, for a dessert, you might manage three little glassfuls of spiced brandy.' The chairman groaned, and crossed out an entire page. 'I've spoilt the sixth page,' he said angrily. 'It's not conscientious work.'

'Write, write, kind sir,' began the secretary in a whisper. 'I won't hinder. I'll be very quiet, I promise. Stefan Frantsych,' he continued in a barely audible tone, 'home-made spiced brandy is better than any champagne. After the first little glass the smell transports your whole soul - a kind of mirage; it seems to you that you're no longer sitting in your armchair at home but somewhere else in Australia on the softest ostrich ...'

'Oh, very well, let's go Pyotr Nikolaich,' said the deputy magistrate, shifting his legs restlessly.

'Yes sir" continued the secretary, 'when you have your spiced brandy send up a few smoke rings from a good cigar, and then such dreamy thoughts will enter your head. You could be a generalissimo or married to the most beautiful woman in the world who swims all day before your eyes in some pool with golden fish. She swims, and you say to her: 'darling, come and kiss me!'

'Pyotr Nikolaich,' moaned the deputy magistrate.

'Yes sir,' continued the secretary, 'having had your smoke, pick up your dressing gown from the floor and off to bed. Lie on your back, stomach up, and take the newspaper. When your eyes are closing and you're on the borderland of dreams, it's pleasant to read about politics: let's see - they've blundered in Austria; there France has upset someone; there a catholic priest has gone against the rules - you read, and it's very pleasant.'

The chairman jumped up, flung aside his pen, and seized his hat with both hands. The deputy magistrate, forgetting his catarrh and overcome with impatience, also jumped up. 'Let's go,' he cried.

'Pyotr Nikolaich, what about the special opinion?' said the secretary, aghast. 'When will you be able to write it, my kind sir? You have to be in town at six o'clock you know.'

The chairman threw up his hands and rushed towards the door. The deputy magistrate also waved his hands, and seizing his portfolio, disappeared with the chairman. The Secretary sighed, cast a reproachful glance after them, and started to gather up the papers.

RECIPES – General notes

Recipes are for four persons unless otherwise stated

Suggested quantities of fish or meat per person:
Zakuski (hors d'oeuvres): 4 oz /100 g
Main course: 6 oz /175 g

Consider: 'number of courses', 'age and appetite' when determining a serving portion appropriate for your guests and the occasion.

Maps and Regions

Interesting background to the many different countries covered by the cuisine in this book can be found in the section: **Regions and Nationalities**, pp 209 - 231.

Glossary of 'commonly used Russian words and other culinary terms': see page 235.

ZAKUSKI

The Russians entertain informally and the idea of laying out **zakuski,** which can be hot or cold, in a separate reception room, where hungry guests can begin to assuage their appetites at once while they drink their preliminary glass of what is offered *(usually vodka)* is very practical. When homes were more spacious this was a regular feature of Russian entertaining. It is ideal too for early or late comers or for those who don't like to eat late and who can fill up on the first course and take modest helpings of what is to follow at the dining table.

The hot and cold **zakuski** found below are an attractive accompaniment to pre-dinner drinks.

Salting a herring

Easy to do, but directions are rarely given in modern cookbooks. It is one of the favourite Russian **zakuski** and I give it here: the proportion of salt for a medium solution is from 10 to 14% of the weight of the herring.

Big plump fish are best and a 4 oz /100 g one needs 1/3 oz /10 g coarse sea salt and a teaspoon of vinegar or lemon juice.

Cleaning and gutting herring

This is best done by half cutting through the gills near the head and pulling back the head. This normally brings out most of the entrails in one piece. Open the herrings, wash and pat dry.

Pour over the vinegar or lemon juice and leave the fish in a cold place overnight. You need a square plastic box or bread bin if you haven't a suitable stoneware crock on which to lay the fish flat.

Start by putting down a few spices made up of black peppercorns, coriander seeds, a piece of cinnamon stick, a few cloves, a bay leaf, thyme and crushed star anise seeds, mixed with some of the salt and a sprinkle of vinegar.

Next, put in two herrings, side by side, cut side uppermost. Repeat until you have used up all your fish and end with a layer of spices and salt. Cover with foil and a heavy weight and keep in the refrigerator or a very cold place until you need them.

To use, soak in milk and water or in weak tea. As well as figuring in **zakuski** dishes Russians use the herrings for stuffings and potato and herring bakes or form them into cutlets with bread soaked in milk. They even mix them with meat and are the mainstay of the Russian salad.

Soused herrings served with soured cream

4 fresh herrings
1 tablespoon chopped chives, spring onions or fine onion rings
1 tablespoon of milled parsley and parsley stalk
1 finely cut carrot
1 stalk of celery finely cut
2 gherkins (optional)
3 tablespoons white wine or cider vinegar mixed with 1 tablespoon water
6 peppercorns
2 bay leaves
1 teaspoon sugar or black treacle, dissolved in a tablespoon of warm water
salt and pepper.

Clean and prepare the herrings (p 17). Sprinkle the insides of each double fillet with chopped chives, spring onions or onion rings. Salt and pepper them and either roll them up or leave them in their natural shape. Put them in an oblong pie dish with the rest of the ingredients on top. Bake in a very low oven (110-120 C /Gas ¼-½) for a long time until the little bones are quite soft. Add more water during baking if necessary. Serve with soured cream mixed with the cooking juice, or drain them and serve with a vinaigrette sauce (p 108). Another way is to pour a little olive oil over the fish and allow it to mingle with the juices.

Marinated herring salad - rollmops from Estonia.

4 fresh herrings
2 onions, finely grated
18 fl oz /500 ml boiled water, cooled
18 fl oz /500 ml milk
6 tablespoons of chopped fresh dill/fennel and parsley
1 fresh cucumber, sliced and drained
1 large tomato, skinned, deseeded and sliced.

The marinade

1 carrot, cut into fine julienne strips
2 onions, cut into rings
4 tablespoons of vinegar and water mixed
2 chilli peppers used for pickling
2 cloves
2 bay leaves,
salt and pepper
1 teaspoon sugar.

Prepare the fish and fillet them. Pour **half** the cold boiled water and half the milk over the fish and soak for 5 hours. After 2½ hours, replace any liquid using the remaining half of boiled water and milk. At the end of this time shake off the excess moisture and fill the insides of the fillets with the grated onion, and roll them up, and secure with cocktail sticks. Pour over the marinade (method below) and keep two to three days before eating.

To make the marinade, partially cook the carrots, add the rest of the ingredients except the vinegar, and cook until the carrots are tender. Then add the vinegar, boil up and cool.

To serve: remove the cocktail sticks and serve with fresh green herbs, the fresh cucumber and tomato.

Marinated fish

This is a very successful and good recipe. More or less any filleted fish may be used for it. Cut 1 lb /450 g fish into serving portions, having first removed as many bones as possible.

Dip the fillets in seasoned flour and fry lightly in a pan with a knob of butter, a little vegetable oil and the juice of half a lemon. Remove from the pan, cool, and pour over the following marinade which resembles a spicy chutney.

Marinade:
2 - 3 carrots cut up finely into julienne strips
Finely chopped parsley stalks
3 onions very finely sliced
5 fl oz /150 ml of tomato purée
1 bay leaf
3-4 cloves
1 piece of crushed cinnamon bark
5 fl oz /150 ml of white wine or cider vinegar
10 fl oz /275 ml water
salt and sugar to taste

Cook the vegetables for about 15 minutes in the same pan used for the fish, adding a little extra oil. Add the tomato purée bay leaf, cloves and cinnamon bark. Cover and cook for a further 15 minutes stirring from time to time. Pour in the wine or cider vinegar and water. Boil up again for a few minutes. Season to taste with salt and sugar.

Put the fish on a serving dish and pour over the marinade. When it is cold garnish with branches of fennel, dill or with finely chopped spring onions, using the green tops as well. This dish is equally successful served hot.

Herring and apple

Usually a salted herring is used for this (method p 17). Fresh herring is better and healthier. Carefully remove all the bones from a freshly cooked herring (bake as described p 18). Mash the fish with two tablespoons of unsalted butter. Add a little grated nutmeg and a grated apple. It is surprisingly tasty and goes well on slices of black rye bread.

Fish salad with horseradish

This is a good way to make cod interesting. Poach the fish gently, or steam between two buttered plates. Divide into portions after removing bones. Mix horseradish and mayonnaise together, thin with a little vinegar or lemon juice, add some salt and fold this sauce into the fish. Sliced boiled potatoes are sometimes added, and cubed drained pieces of cucumber. Decorate with chopped spring onions and additional grated horseradish and parsley.

Herring Salad

   1 medium herring, boned, filleted and cooked lightly in salted water
   2 boiled potatoes
   1 apple, peeled and sliced
   1 gherkin, chopped
   1 onion, finely sliced
   1 cooked beetroot, finely sliced
   1 or 2 eggs, hardboiled
   3 tablespoons oil
   1 tablespoon vinegar mixed with 1 tablespoon of lemon juice OR water
   1 teaspoon mustard
   parsley or dill
   salt

Cut the cooked herring into serving portions. Slice the apple and keep covered in water and lemon juice.

To make the sauce: mix the hard-boiled egg yolks with salt and mustard, and gradually add the oil and the vinegar mixture. Mix the sauce into the vegetables *(except the beetroot)* and apple and serve with the herring, beetroot and chopped egg whites and parsley or dill.

Crab Salad

   9 oz /250g tin of crab (drained weight)
   1 cooked turnip, cubed
   1 cooked carrot, finely sliced
   2-3 cooked potatoes, sliced or cubed
   1 fresh cucumber, sliced
   1 tomato, skinned, deseeded and sliced.
   a few tablespoons of peas or beans (cooked)
   1 small lettuce
   3 level table spoons mayonnaise (or more, to taste)
   vinaigrette dressing (p 108) to taste
   parsley or dill
   chives

Mix the vinaigrette dressing with the crab juice drained from the tin and pour over the vegetables. To serve, arrange the crab in the centre of a dish surrounded by the vegetables and lettuce leaves. The mayonnaise should be spread over the crab. Thin the mayonnaise with a little top of the milk or yoghurt and sprinkle over fresh herbs and chives.

Fish Salad

7 oz /200 g cod or firm white fish, cooked, boned
2 oz /50 g chopped celery
1 apple, chopped (with or without the skin)
1 bunch of radishes
7 gherkins
lettuce, mayonnaise and vinegar for serving

Mix the vegetables into the mayonnaise, thin this with a little vinegar or vinaigrette dressing, and serve with the fish on a bed of lettuce. Keep a little mayonnaise back for the fish.

A further variation on this theme is to serve the cod with boiled potatoes, gherkins and spring onions.

Kraby zalivnye - Crab with carrot and gherkin set in jelly

2 oz /50 g tin of crab
1 medium carrot, cooked
1 gherkin, cubed
1 potato, cooked and cubed
½ oz /15g powdered gelatine
1 pint /575 ml water

Soften the gelatine with a little cold water, then add very hot water (p 24 has more 'gelatine tips') When cool, pour part of the jelly into a mould, add the crab and vegetables. Put into the refrigerator until half set and then pour over the remaining jelly.

Ikra 'Caviars'

There are a number of 'false' fish caviars in old as well as modern Russian cookbooks. **'Ikra'** is the Russian word for these dishes, which are like a pâté and not confined to expensive sturgeon roes.

A red 'caviar'

1 salted herring[1], cleaned, boned and soaked in a little milk for 10 minutes
2 carrots, grated and lightly fried
1 tablespoon of tomato purée
2 tablespoons butter
1 medium onion, finely chopped and fried
1 hard-boiled egg
1 lemon

Mince the herring, carrot, and onion and mash in the egg, tomato purée and butter. Finish this off in the blender but it should not be too smooth. Serve with lemon wedges.

For a black 'caviar': substitute black olives (stoned) for the carrots.

---

[1] Salted herrings are not easily obtainable. To salt a herring see p 17. I prefer fresh herrings, cooked, boned and filleted.

Courgette 'caviar'

12 oz /350 g young courgettes, deseeded and finely cut
1-2 carrots, finely grated
1-2 onions, finely grated
1 tablespoon tomato purée
1 pinch of sugar
herbs to taste (dill, parsley, coriander or others of your choice)
salt and pepper
black rye bread (optional)

Take the finely cut courgettes, sprinkle them with salt to extract the juice. Pat dry and sauté them lightly, in a small amount of oil. Add equal quantities of finely grated carrot and onion, and the tomato purée. Season well and add the sugar and herbs.

Cook until the vegetables are tender and most of the liquid has evaporated. Let the dish cool. Refrigerate, then serve on black rye bread.

It goes very well with hard boiled eggs.

Mushroom 'caviar'

1 lb /450 g fresh mushrooms, well chopped
4 spring onions and their tops, finely chopped
4 tablespoons butter
5 fl oz /150 ml soured cream
juice of a lemon
salt, pepper and a little cayenne pepper
4 or 5 tablespoons of fresh dill or fennel
1 bay leaf

Lightly soften the onions in the butter, add the mushrooms and lemon juice. Cook over a low heat for 10 minutes. Allow to cool and then stir in the soured cream, dill and seasoning. It's simply delicious! Serve at room temperature. It keeps well in the refrigerator for a few days.

Beetroot 'caviar'

This is perhaps my favourite way of eating beetroot.

2 medium sized beetroots (cooked)
8 tablespoons of vegetable oil
2 tablespoons sugar
zest and juice of 2 lemons.

Make a purée of the beetroot, either in the blender or by mincing it. Add the remaining ingredients. Cook slowly for 5-10 minutes, stirring all the time. Make sure that it doesn't burn. Cool and serve chilled with plenty of freshly milled parsley.

Aubergine 'caviar'

12 oz /350 g aubergines
2 tablespoons of oil
2 onions, chopped
1 tomato, chopped
2 teaspoons lemon juice or white wine vinegar
Salt and pepper to taste

Preheat the Oven to 180 C /Gas 4.

Cover the aubergines with a little oil and bake on an oiled tray in the oven for about 25-30 minutes to loosen the skins. Peel them and mash the flesh.

Lightly fry the onions in some of the oil, add the mashed aubergines and tomatoes, the rest of the oil, salt and pepper and the lemon juice or vinegar. Cook slowly to evaporate the moisture. Serve cold with chopped parsley.

Variation: Add a green pepper.

Herring snack Grenki seledkoi

A 19th century recipe from Mrs Molokhovets and also appeared in more recent cookbooks.

3 fresh herrings filleted, plus their soft roes
2 soft white rolls, sliced across
2 tablespoons olive oil
2 tablespoons butter
4 hard-boiled egg yolks
Russian or Dijon mustard to taste - about ½ teaspoon
1 tablespoon capers

Fry the rolls in the butter. Mix the oil, yolks, mustard, capers and roes together. A teaspoon of boiling water helps mix everything together. Spread on the rolls and add the chopped herring fillets. Bake in a hot oven 200 C /Gas 6.

Ukrainian herring roe pâté

8 oz /225 g herring roe
1 teaspoon boiling water
1 tablespoon oil
1 small chopped onion
1 tablespoon vinegar
salt and pepper.

Remove any skins or membrane from the roe. Pour over 1 teaspoon of boiling water. Add the other ingredients. Blend. Serve with chopped parsley and lemon wedges.

Fish in aspic

The following attractive fish aspic was served to me in Paris by a dear Russian émigré friend, now deceased; I spent many hours with her listening to her fascinating and often humorous accounts of her adventures during the Russian revolution. We also had animated discussions on all topics, including culinary ones, - on jam making and the merits and demerits of cabbage **pirog**.

> 1½ lb /675 g filleted fish, cut into serving portions (hake, haddock, cod)
> 1 carrot, thinly sliced
> 1 onion, thinly sliced
> 1 stick of roughly chopped celery
> A few bay leaves, parsley stalks and peppercorns
> 3 tablespoons of lemon juice
> 3 teaspoons powdered gelatine dissolved in a little water
> salt and sugar
> 1 extra stick of celery and an extra lemon thinly sliced for garnish
> 14 fl oz /400 ml of salted water or fish stock

Poach the fish with the vegetables and herbs in the salted water or fish stock for 10 minutes. Strain the liquid and add to it the lemon juice, salt and sugar, and simmer. Add the gelatine and bring to the boil, stirring all the time. Remove from the heat immediately. Cool the liquid. Put the fish in a suitable dish and decorate with lemon and strips of celery. Pour half the liquid over the fish and place in the refrigerator for 30 minutes. When it is almost set pour over the remaining liquid. Keep refrigerated until ready to serve. Horseradish and soured cream sauce goes well with fish aspic.

Gelatine / Aspic – useful tips

½ oz /15 g gelatine will set 1 pint /575 ml liquid. For acid vegetables or fruit use still more. Alcohol inhibits setting, so use extra. Vegetarians can use agar-agar or carrageen.

To make aspic: follow the instructions on the packet of gelatine. If you plan to turn your fish or meat dish out of its mould use more gelatine. A strong fish fumet or stock will require slightly less gelatine than that required for chicken or meat.

For a really clear jelly take an egg white for every pint (575 ml) of stock. Beat the white and pour in 5 fl oz /150 ml of cooled stock and add a tablespoon of vinegar or lemon juice.

Then pour in the remaining stock, which should be boiling. Put it in a covered saucepan on a low heat and as soon as it boils up take it off the heat.

Leave it to stand for 20 minutes, then strain it very carefully without shaking it, through muslin.

Liver pashtet - pâté

1 lb /450 g of lamb's liver
4 oz /100 g of streaky bacon
4 oz /100 g of butter
1 carrot, finely chopped
1 onion, finely chopped
Parsley
1 bay leaf
Grated nutmeg and a few peppercorns.

Soak the liver in salted or vinegar water or in milk and remove all skin and membrane. Cut into neat pieces and fry it gently with the bacon, chopped carrot and onion, bay leaf and peppercorns until just tender. The liver should be slightly pink and juicy. If the bacon is very lean, use a little oil during frying. Remove the bay leaf and put the mixture through the mincer or in the blender. Stir in the butter, seasoning and nutmeg and smooth the mixture into a serving dish. When cold, decorate with chopped hard-boiled eggs.

Note: I often put all the raw ingredients into a mould covered with foil and bake in a moderate oven (180 C /Gas 4) until it comes away from the sides of the mould.

Variation: Add a dash of sherry or brandy as the Armenians would.

Zalivnye Bluda – zakuski in aspic

An interesting group of **zakuski** found in Russian cookbooks comes under the heading of **zalivnye bluda**, stemming from the verb 'zalit', to pour over.

These dishes containing fish, chicken, meat or vegetables are set in aspic (p 24) and may be served with any of the three sauces that follow, or others to taste. (see pp 184 – 188).

I. Gherkin sauce: to 4 tablespoons of mayonnaise add 6 chopped gherkins

II. Mustard and caper sauce:

2 hard-boiled eggs
2 tablespoons of oil
½ tablespoon Russian mustard (recipe p 187) or use English mustard
1½ tablespoons of white wine vinegar & 1 ½ tablespoons water, mixed
1 tablespoon of capers
½ teaspoon salt
½ teaspoon sugar

Mash the egg yolks, mix them with the mustard, sugar and salt and gradually blend in the oil in a slow stream. Thin down with the vinegar. This part may be done using a blender. Fold in the capers and finely chopped egg whites.

III. Gherkin and onion sauce

For each hard boiled egg:

> 2 tablespoons of oil
> 1 tablespoon of white wine vinegar & 1 tablespoon water, mixed
> ½ tablespoon each of gherkin and grated onion, finely chopped
> ½ tablespoon spring onion including green tops, finely chopped
> ½ tablespoon each of freshly chopped tarragon and parsley

> Season this sauce with a pinch of sugar, salt and pepper, cayenne pepper and a little tomato purée or tomato sauce (p 105).

Mash the yolk(s) with the seasonings and gradually mix in the oil, then the vinegar and remaining ingredients.

Red kidney bean purée with nuts and coriander

> 15 fl oz /425 g of red kidney beans[1], soaked overnight
> 5 fl oz /150 g crushed walnuts
> 2 onions, lightly fried in oil
> vinaigrette dressing made with fresh coriander and herbs
> seasoning of salt and paprika and pepper

Drain the beans and cook them thoroughly in fresh water. Strain and blend them to a purée with a little of the cooking water. Toss with the other ingredients. If no fresh coriander is available, crush some coriander seeds with fresh herbs such as chervil or fennel or use dried tarragon. Chill well. I usually serve the beans in a bowl rubbed with garlic, lined with lettuce leaves, and with a sprinkling of fresh parsley and grated lemon.

Pizza

There are a number of pizza-like recipes to be found in Russian cookbooks. In Belarus they make **kukhon**, which is simply fried onion rolled into the top of bread dough and used as a tasty accompaniment for soup or turned into **zakuski** with various savouries on top.

The Armenian 'pizza' version is more sophisticated. They claim to have invented the pizza despite its Neapolitan connections. They make a light brioche type dough and cleverly avoid the possibility of a tough top by omitting the cheese. Onions and olives are the basic topping.

In Estonia, anchovies are abundant and commonly added to pizza.

For

Burkanu pardeveis or morkovnik - A Latvian vegetarian 'pizza', see page 131.

---

[1] Kidney beans must always be thoroughly cooked.

Armenian pizza - vegetarian

Dough mixture	Pizza topping
2 tablespoons milk 4 oz /100 g strong plain unbleached flour 1 egg, beaten 2 tablespoons olive oil 1 teaspoon salt ½ oz /15 g yeast	3 onions 1 tin (14 oz /400 g) tomatoes OR 7 oz /200 g fresh tomatoes[1], skinned 2 cloves of garlic, peeled salt, pepper, sugar dried oregano olive oil 1 tin (2 oz /50 g) anchovies 12 black olives (optional)

Making the dough

Use a 7-8 inch /18-20 cm baking tin with a loose base. Put the yeast in a cup with the warm milk. Stir well. Warm the flour and salt and then stir in the yeast mixture followed by the beaten egg and olive oil. Knead until elastic and leave for 1½-2 hours to rise.

Preparing topping

Skin fresh tomatoes by plunging them in boiling water. Tinned tomatoes should be well drained. Peel and thinly slice the onions and crush the peeled garlic in a little salt. Heat the oil and gently stew the onions only to soften but not colour them, for about 5 minutes. Add the garlic and tomatoes and raise the heat to evaporate juices. Add the seasoning.. Reduce the sauce, and add the oregano.

Baking

When the dough is ready, brush the tin with oil and press the dough into it, spread over the tomato mixture and then arrange the olives and anchovies on top. Leave the pizza to rise again on top of the stove for ten minutes.

Bake in a hot to very hot oven 220-230 C/Gas 7-8 for 15 minutes. Lower the heat to 180 C/Gas 4; cook for another 15 minutes, covering with foil or oiled greaseproof paper for the last 5 minutes of cooking.

---

[1] Tinned tomatoes are chosen for flavour; fresh 'supermarket' tomatoes are often selected for shelf life instead!

27

SOUPS

Cabbage soup is regarded as *the* Russian soup and there are endless recipes for it.

It is eaten throughout Russia and surrounding areas although it is most favoured by the people in the north and central regions - Archangel, Vologda, Novgorod, the Urals and Siberia, Kursk and Orel.

The southerners mainly prefer beetroot **borshch,** especially in Ukraine and it is their national soup. Cabbage soup or **shchi** is to the Russians what minestrone is to the Italians.

It is eaten by rich and poor and spoken of and longed for by exiles, referred to often in Russian literature and even evoked in poetry.

At the end of Pushkin's poem **Evgenii Onegin** the poet, no longer in his first youth, longs to turn from the sophisticated to the simple life:

> *'My ideal now is a housewife*
> *My desire - peace*
> *Add to this*
> *A bowl of cabbage soup -*
> *A large one.*

Schchi and **borshch** can be made with a sour base, marinated cabbage **sauerkraut** for **schchi,** and a vinegar marinade left from marinated beetroot or marinated cucumbers.

Separate recipes are given for these **rassol** as they are called and their preparation and addition to various Russian dishes opens up a whole culinary vista.

Schchi and **borshch** are thick hearty soups – really a meal in themselves and the good quality meat used to make the stock can be eaten with the soup as a second course or used cold the next day with a sauce.

It is best made the day before to facilitate skimming off any excess fat and it also tastes even better.

To get rid of the cabbagey smell and volatile oils sprinkle salt over the shredded cabbage and pour boiling water over it.

Meat Bouillon (clear meat stock)

'Bouillon' means 'boil'; it is a broth or stock made by straining off the water in which meat, chicken, etc. has been cooked.

General proportions are:

1 lb /450 g meat
1¾ pints /1 litre of cold water

Cook for up to 2 hours or until tender. Better and quicker to use a pressure cooker.
Making the stock the day before it's needed enables excess fat to be easily skimmed off once it is cold.
The following recipe is made with fresh cabbage and not sauerkraut, but the slight sour flavour is achieved by adding lemon juice.

Cabbage soup - shchi

1 lb /450 g meat (can be shin, brisket or stewing steak)
1 lb /450 g fresh cabbage, shredded
½ lb /225 g approx. root vegetables, diced: turnip, carrot, onion
2 tablespoons oil
½ lb /225 g tomatoes or 8 oz tin of tomatoes plus 1 tablespoon tomato paste
Bay leaf and herbs

First, make a bouillon (stock) as described on page 29.

Lightly fry the root vegetables in the oil, put them in a pan with the cabbage and meat bouillon. The amount of liquid needed should cover the vegetables comfortably. Simmer until the vegetables are tender before adding the tomatoes.

If a thicker heartier soup is required put in finely diced potatoes with the root vegetables. Add seasoning towards end of cooking. Some cooks serve the meat separately as cold meat.

It can also be cut in neat slices and served with the soup. Add a spoonful of **smetana** *(soured cream)* to each place of soup and a sprinkling of parsley and dill.

The same soup can be made with sauerkraut and thickened with a flour roux[1] and a little tomato purée before serving.

---

[1] Roux: used to thicken soups or sauces. Make from equal parts of flour and fat. Cook in a pan over low heat.

Borshch - Beetroot soup

There are said to be over thirty varieties of borshch, but the classic basis is invariably:

A good stock, a set combination of root vegetables, the main one being beetroot, and a beetroot ferment.

Before making borshch both a meat stock and a beetroot ferment or marinade need to be prepared. (For a vegetarian version of borshch see page 34).

Stock for borshch

To make 3 pints/1¾ litres of stock use good meat and bones. The meat can be subsequently cut up and eaten with the borshch or served separately at another meal.

8 oz /225 g each of pork ribs and neck of lamb or 1 lb /450 g beef shin or brisket.
1 medium onion
1 carrot
2 bay leaves
salt to taste

Add enough water to cover the ingredients. Simmer to produce the stock and strain before use. The stock can also be made using a pressure cooker or alternatively, if short of time, liquid meat stocks can be found in most supermarkets.

Beetroot ferment for borshch

There are two methods for making the beetroot ferment. The first takes 3-4 days. However, the second, quicker method can be made shortly before cooking borshch.

Method I: 3-4 day ferment

Peel and grate 1 raw beetroot, pour over boiling water to cover the beetroot and put it in a warm place for three to four days.

Method II: Quick ferment

1 raw beetroot
10 fl oz /275 ml meat stock
1 tablespoon lemon juice

Just before making borshch, pour the hot meat stock over the grated beetroot, add the lemon juice and bring it to the boil. Leave to stand for half an hour.

Classic Ukrainian borshch

3 pints/ 1¾ litres of stock, strained
2 medium beetroot, cut into julienne strips
lemon juice
4 potatoes cut into cubes (optional)
1 oz /25 g of bacon fat or 1 fl oz /25ml oil
1 oz /25 g butter
1 carrot, sliced
2 onions, sliced
2 - 3 tablespoons of tomato purée or 2 large tomatoes
8 oz /225 g cabbage
parsley stalks
2 or 3 bay leaves
6 peppercorns and a few allspice berries
½ tablespoon of mild white wine vinegar(3%) and ½ tablespoon water mixed together
2 teaspoons of sugar
salt to taste
2 cloves of garlic, (optional)
5 fl oz /150 ml soured cream and freshly chopped parsley for serving

Prepare the vegetables. Cut the beetroot in julienne strips, and then slice or cube the root vegetables. Use a food processor to save time and plastic gloves to avoid beetroot stains.

Sprinkle the beetroot with vinegar or lemon juice, fry briefly in a little of the bacon fat or oil and then cook separately in a little of the stock until tender. Reserve some of the beetroot juices from this pan as they can be added just before serving to give the borshch a deep red colour.

Lightly fry the remaining vegetables in the rest of the fat or oil, and butter and put them together with the beetroot (plus the potatoes, if used) into the boiling stock. Add the herbs, garlic and seasonings, vinegar/water mixture, sugar and the beetroot ferment. Simmer the soup for 20-30 minutes or until the vegetables are cooked.

Just before serving add the reserved beetroot juice for a ruby red colour. For smoother soup, Ukrainian style, the borshch can be blended before serving. Serve with a spoonful of soured cream in each bowl and freshly chopped parsley.

I have not observed any real loss of quality if some of these stages are 'telescoped', the only thing to bear in mind is that beetroot requires longer cooking than the other vegetables.

I prefer to cook my beetroot quite separately, keeping the lovely ruby juice, and adding it at the very end. Also many cooks use extra beetroot, grate it and cook for a few minutes in a little water or stock, adding it to the soup at the last minute to give it a deep ruby colour.

Ukrainian borshch - regional variations:

1. Add 4 oz /100 g of soaked, cooked haricot beans and a cooking apple.

2. The **borshch** can be made without potatoes but the liquid thickened with one or two tablespoons of flour.

3. Half a head of celery can be added to the basic ingredients.

4. Chernigovski borshch adds a vegetable marrow or two courgettes together with 4 oz /100 g haricot beans and two sour apples.

5. Lvov borshch is made from bone stock, and the beetroots cooked in their skins before slicing and sprinkling with vinegar. They are then gently stewed in the fat or oil with the tomato purée for half an hour. Five potatoes are added to this recipe.

6. Poltava and Odessa borshch's are based on duck or goose stock, the flesh of the birds included when serving. It is also served with small dumplings (**galushki)**, made as follows:

Mix a tablespoon of buckwheat flour taken from 4 oz /100 g of buckwheat flour with about 2 tablespoons of boiling water; cool and add a lightly beaten egg. Beat well and add the remaining flour. If it is too stiff add a little extra cold water. It should be the consistency of thick cream.

Drop teaspoonfuls into boiling salted water. When they are cooked they will float to the top. Put them into the hot borshch about five minutes before serving.

7. Kiev borshch adds chopped celery leaves and two sour apples to the basic recipe.

8. Postn'ye borshch for days of fasting, is a good vegetarian soup. Use the classic borshch recipe on page 31, substituting mushrooms for the meat and adding **kletski** (dumplings) stuffed with mushrooms (see pages 125 & 127). The cream would, of course, be omitted for serving.

Summer borshch

This is ideal when marrows are plentiful and beetroot is young. Leaves and stalks are all used.

    1 bunch of young beetroots
    3-4 potatoes
    1 stalk of celery
    1 carrot
    7 oz /200 g marrow or courgettes, peeled and deseeded
    2 tomatoes
    4 or 5 spring onions, 1 clove and 1 bay leaf
    Seasoning
    1 small carton of soured cream

Cut the beetroot and divide the stalks into sticks. Cook in boiling water or mushroom stock for 15 minutes. Scald the beetroot leaves and add them together with the finely diced vegetables. Cook until tender.

A simpler way is to use a pressure cooker to cook the root vegetables and adding the spring onions and chopped beetroot leaves afterwards. This soup can be eaten cold after putting it through a blender.

Borshch - blended using raw vegetables.

Cut up the vegetables roughly and half fill the blender with them. Blend with sufficient liquid from the recipe. Repeat until all the vegetables are done, except the cabbage, which should be sliced by hand.

A refined borshch for dinner parties can be made from clear chicken stock. The borshch is cooked in the usual way but strained and a little white wine or simple **kvas** added at the last moment. Serve as usual with soured cream and freshly milled parsley.

Cold borshch

Clear chicken broth is used together with the usual vegetables prepared as before. The soup is thickened with two egg yolks. The proportions are as follows:

3 pints /2 litres of chicken stock
2 each of beetroot and carrot, sliced
1 cucumber, diced
1 tablespoon wine vinegar
2 tablespoons lemon juice
1 tablespoon sugar
2 egg yolks
seasoning, chopped dill
1 carton of soured cream to serve with the chilled soup.

To thicken the soup beat the eggs well, add the lemon juice and gradually pour in some of the hot soup, beating well. Do not allow it to re-boil. Add the remaining soup. Serve just nicely chilled but not icy.

Puréed beetroot soup

    1 pint /575 ml stock
    4 large beetroot
    1 tablespoon vinegar
    2 tablespoons butter
    1½ tablespoons flour
    4 oz /100 g smetana (soured cream)

Grate the beetroot and put it into a pan with the vinegar and a few tablespoons of stock or hot water. Add **half** the butter and sweat the beetroot until it is soft. Blend or sieve this and stir in the remaining liquid, adding seasoning and a pinch of sugar. Make a roux with the flour and remaining butter, thin with some of the hot stock, cook for a few minutes and then pour it into the soup and boil it up once more. Serve with **smetana** and freshly chopped parsley.

Bul'on Borshchok

This is a soup based on a clear meat broth. Bring about 2 pints /1¼ litres of clear meat stock to the boil and add about ½ lb /225 g of finely grated raw beetroot, 1½ tablespoons of wine vinegar and a tablespoon of sugar. Season with a little cayenne.

Thick Vegetarian Borshch for winter

    1 stick of celery or leaves, or celery salt if these are not available
    1 onion
    2 carrots
    2 tomatoes
    3 beetroot and the juice in which they have cooked - about 1 pint /575 ml

Additions:
    Frozen broad beans
    Frozen courgettes
    Parsley and parsley stalks
    Bay leaf and seasonings
    Any herbs - fresh ones if available
    2 tablespoons vinegar and a little lemon juice
    1 oz /25 g margarine
    A handful of spinach or sorrel
    Soured cream and parsley for serving

Lightly fry the root vegetables after slicing them. Cook them in the beetroot juice and make it up to about 1 pint /575 ml. Add the vinegar. Cook until all are soft and then add the beans and courgettes and continue cooking until they are ready. Add the seasonings, herbs and finely chopped spinach or sorrel. This soup may be puréed, which is the way I usually make it. Potato can also be added if you want a really thick soup.

Piti from Azerbaijan

This is a thick meat soup, almost a stew, with plums, damsons or prunes. It is also popular in Armenia where it goes under the name of **putuk**.

½ lb /225g of breast of lamb or lamb chops[1]
1 tablespoon of chick peas, soaked overnight
2 onions, sliced
2 potatoes, sliced

 If you want to keep the potatoes whole, add them halfway through the cooking.

Thicken the stew/soup by mashing down one of the potatoes, and add the saffron threads and water and fresh herbs. A tablespoon of **smetana** (soured cream) stirred in with the seasoning at the last moment makes this into a rich and delicious dish.

Chikhirtma - Caucasian soup

This is akin to Greek **avgholemono** and is based on a good light stock, plenty of herbs and is thickened and flavoured with egg yolks and lemon juice.

35 fl oz /1 litre of light stock (preferably chicken)
2 onions, sliced
1 tablespoon of maize flour and 1 of butter for the roux
2 egg yolks.

Herbs and flavourings:

2 tablespoons wine vinegar and water or pomegranate or lemon juice
1 stick of celery, finely chopped
parsley stalks
About 1 cupful (10 fl oz /275 ml) of the following mixed together:
Fresh chopped coriander or chervil and parsley or 1 tablespoon of crushed coriander seeds and 1 tablespoon each of fresh dill, mint and basil
A few peppercorns, pinch of cinnamon, salt.

Fry the onions briefly in the butter and sprinkle in the maize flour. Pour over some of the hot stock and cook through for 3 minutes.

Add most of the remaining stock and the other ingredients except the egg yolks and lemon juice. Mix these together and thin with some of the stock kept back. It should be hot but not boiling.

Add the egg mixture to the soup and test for seasoning. Remove the parsley stalks before serving and sprinkle with chopped parsley. I have found this soup quite delicious cold.

---

[1] Lamb is the traditional meat, but a very good stew/soup is achieved with pork spare ribs.

Moldovan Chorba based on kvas

This is similar to Georgian **chanaki**, **chakhokhbili**, and may be made with meat or chicken.

**1 medium size chicken or
1 lb /450 g lamb or veal[1]
1 lb /450 g green beans, sliced, or white cabbage
5 - 6 large potatoes
parsley and celery stalks
2 onions and carrots, sliced
white part of a leek, sliced
2 tablespoons tomato purée
4 tablespoons of fat
8 fl oz /225 ml kvas (see p 198) or water or light beer and lemon juice seasonings,
plus herbs of dill and parsley**

Cook the meat or chicken in sufficient water to cover. Strain the stock and remove all fat. This is easier if done the night before. Cut up the meat and remove all bones and skin.

Fry the carrots, onions and leeks lightly and put them with the potatoes into the stock to cook through for about twenty minutes.

Add all the remaining ingredients and cook until the beans or white cabbage are tender.

Allow the soup to stand for quarter of an hour before serving with soured cream or thickened, stabilised yoghurt. This is a very refreshing soup.

Kharcho - Caucasian lamb soup

**1 lb /450 g lamb
3 large tomatoes, sliced
2 onions, sliced
2 cloves of garlic
7 tablespoon flour
2 tablespoons tomato purée
Seasonings of salt, pepper, cayenne, ½ teaspoon suneli[2], coriander, basil or celery
leaves and dill, parsley stalks and bay leaves (about 4 - 5 tablespoons altogether).
4 oz /100 g crushed walnuts
5 - 6 cooked prunes or fresh plums or sharp cooking apples and lemon juice.**

A very easy recipe.

Cook the lamb separately in about 2 pints /1¼ litres of water. If cooking in a pressure cooker use half the liquid. Take out the meat, remove any bones and cut it up. Strain and skim the stock.

---

[1] For lamb or veal add thyme, a bay leaf, red cayenne pepper and garlic..
[2] Suneli: see 'spices', page 207.

Fry the onions and garlic separately in a little oil, sprinkle over the flour and gradually pour over a little hot stock mixed with the tomato purée. Add the herbs, walnuts and seasonings. Put this sauce into the soup and finally add the prunes/plums.

Armenian herb soup with eggs and bread

7 oz /200 g wheat bread
35 fl oz /1 litre water
4 medium onions
1 head of garlic
3-4 oz /75-100 g butter
2 eggs
bay leaf, cloves, green herbs to taste.

Chop the onion and garlic finely and soften for a few minutes in the butter in a frying pan; transfer to a casserole.

Heat **two thirds** of the water and pour this over the onion mixture. Add salt, pepper, bay leaf, cloves and bring to the boil for 2 - 3 minutes. Allow to cool. Mix the eggs with the remaining third of cold water and when the onion bouillon has cooled to lukewarm pour the egg mixture in and mix well. Add the bread cut into small slices. Cover the pan and warm the soup gently. Do not allow to boil. When the bread has softened and swollen up nicely strew the soup with finely milled herbs. A good chicken stock instead of water improves this soup.

Onion soup

35 fl oz /1 litre stock from chicken or meat
4 large onions
2 tablespoons of oil or butter
½ tablespoon flour
2 tablespoons of grated cheese - preferably gruyère
1 carrot, 1 stick celery , parsley , bay leaf , herbs cooked in a little water to make a
light vegetable stock and strained as an alternative to the meat stock above or use
vegetable stock cubes).

Wash the onions in cold water and slice them. Fry the onion very lightly and slowly so that it softens but does not brown. Sift in the flour, turn up the heat to medium and stir until the mixture turns golden brown. Pour in the hot stock, gradually, stirring all the time. Season and cook a little longer.

For the traditional croûtons fry slices of stale french bread on one side. Turn them over and spread the grated cheese on top and leave them in the pan until the cheese has melted. Alternatively, pour the soup into heat-proof bowls, put a piece of toast on top, sprinkle with the cheese and brown under the grill.

Russian Onion soup – Dumas version

This 'Russian' recipe is disarmingly simple.

It was made by Alexandre Dumas père, who was a gourmet and capable cook. Though scathing about many of the dishes he ate on his travels through Russia in 1858, he praised much of the home cooking and also had some good things to say about Armenian cuisine.

He gives this Russian version of onion soup made with rye bread:

> **1¾ pints /1 litre boiling water**
> **8 oz /225 g stale rye bread**
> **2 medium size finely chopped onions**
> **2 tablespoons of butter.**

Cut the bread into small cubes and fry them in the butter. Drain well on kitchen paper.

Fry the chopped onion until golden and put back the bread cubes. Cook together until the onion darkens.

Put everything into a deep saucepan, scraping out the frying pan well, and pour the boiling water over and cook for 10-12 minutes.

Rassol'nik – soup based on marinades

Rassol'nik uses up the vinegar waters left from pickling cucumbers, beetroot, cabbage and so forth.

Dill flavoured rassol' was also much favoured for whitening and smoothing hands. In **Dead Souls**, Sobakevich's wife offers her hand to Chichikov and it is redolent of dill and cucumber. Even her elongated shape is likened to a cucumber.

Rassol'nik can also be made using the actual pickled vegetables and there are fish and meat versions.

Principal ingredients are:

> **Chicken stock/ fish bouillon**
> **Parsley**
> **Parsnips or carrots**
> **Celery**
> **Onion**
> **Salted cucumber or marinade**
> **Butter**
> **Smetana**
> **Green herbs**

Fish Rassol'nik

This recipe uses two kinds of fish, spinach and a good many vegetables, making it a complete satisfying meal.

Sprinkle the fish with milk and a little salt and leave for 15 minutes before cooking. This firms it up.

½ lb /225 g cod or haddock or thick white fish
½ lb /225 g sea-bass, plaice or fish of choice (not an oily fish)
2 pints /1¼ litres approximately of fish fumet or water
½ lb /225 g potatoes
2 sticks of celery or celeriac or a handful of celery leaves, finely chopped
2 onions, sliced
2 carrots, cut into matchstick
2 leeks (the white part-finely chopped)
2 bay leaves
1 or 2 salted cucumbers or their brine (in which case use less water).

Several handfuls of spinach or sorrel or a mixture of both, dill, parsley stalks, fennel or fennel seeds, fresh parsley.

Cut the fish into neat portions and poach briefly in the barely simmering fumet or water. Remove from the liquid and put on one side. Make a purée of the spinach and sorrel and keep the juice. Cut the cucumber, remove the seeds and soak in water for 15 minutes.

Boil the potatoes separately. Keep warm. Stir-fry the remaining vegetables in a little oil and add the parsley stalks and herbs. Finish cooking the vegetables in the fish water.

Thicken the soup with a roux made of 1 tablespoon each of flour and butter. Pour on some of the hot bouillon and then amalgamate it with the rest of the soup and bring to the boil. Finally, mix in the spinach purée and potatoes.

To serve, put a portion of fish in each plate and pour over the soup.

Additions: a small parsnip, 1 tablespoon tomato purée and a teaspoon paprika.

Variation:
Substitute mushrooms, capers or olives instead of the carrot and leeks. Serve with chopped parsley, **smetana** or thickened yoghurt. Russians often add chopped hard-boiled eggs.

Sorrel soup

Chekhov made a difficult and hazardous journey to Sakhalin Island where he made notes on the pitiful living conditions of the wretched prisoners and their families. The valuable statistics and highly readable report he produced led to some improvements in their treatment. He was already a sick man when he undertook the voyage by cart and sledge over icy and boggy wastes and which would have taxed the strength of the healthiest. En route, he came across this comforting soup which he praised highly and which I call **Sakhalin soup**.

> **1 pint /575 ml meat stock, or spinach water for vegetarians**
> **14 oz /400 g spinach and sorrel, cooked and sieved**
> **1 carrot, onion and stick of celery, finely chopped**
> **butter and flour for thickening**
> **1 bay leaf**

Fry the vegetables briefly, add the bay leaf and most of the stock (*or spinach water*) and cook until tender. Cook the spinach separately, or stir -fry it adding a little stock if necessary. Sieve or blend to a purée and add it to the cooked root vegetables. Make a roux with the butter and flour (**1 tablespoon of each**) and thin it with any remaining stock and mix it into the soup. Cook together for about three minutes. Serve with chopped parsley and soured cream.

Potato soup with sorrel

> **6-7 potatoes**
> **A few handfuls of sorrel or sorrel and spinach**
> **1-2 carrots**
> **1 onion**
> **parsley stalks**
> **1 tablespoon oil**
> **4 tablespoons of soured cream**
> **salt and pepper to taste**
> **1 pint /575 ml of liquid - stock, milk or water – (milk is my preference)**

Cook the potatoes in the liquid. If using milk alone it is better to partly cook the potatoes first and then cook over a diffuser, or in the oven to save watching it. Lightly fry the onion and carrots, though this is not strictly necessary, and add this to the potato and cook until everything is soft, then add the sorrel or sorrel and spinach. Cook a further five to ten minutes. I usually purée this soup to save chopping the vegetables finely but if you like everything whole then the vegetables need to be cut evenly and the sorrel or spinach chopped and the coarse stalks removed. Serve with soured cream and extra parsley. Cholesterol watchers can use thickened yoghurt instead of the soured cream.

Rassol'nik - kidney soup

> 1 lb /450 g ox kidneys
> 2 gherkins
> 2 or 3 parsley stalks and a stick of celery, cut into strips and sautéed
> 1 onion and 1 leek, sliced and sautéed
> 4 potatoes
> 2 tablespoons oil
> 4 oz /100 g sorrel or spinach, plus a little lemon

Soak the kidneys well, first in salt water, then in vinegar water and then in milk overnight. Alternatively boil up twice in cold water, rinsing them each time. Cook the prepared kidneys in half a pint /275 ml water with the vegetables and potatoes. When tender, add the sliced gherkins and some of the marinade, according to taste. Serve with soured cream or single cream, parsley or dill.

Variation:

Chicken livers may be used and these need little preparation. The soup can also be made with chicken and veal or lamb. Pearl barley or rice can also be added.

Puréed potato and leek soup

> 1 lb /450 g potatoes, sliced and cubed
> 18 fl oz /500 ml of milk and an equal quantity of water
> 2 tablespoons of butter
> 2 leeks

Slice and fry the leeks lightly in the butter, add the cubed potatoes *(do not allow to brown)*. Pour in the water and cook for approx. half an hour. Sieve or purée in a blender and then add the hot milk and stir. Before serving add a little butter and an egg yolk mixed with a little warm milk. Toasted breadcrumbs or fried croûtons or toasted millet flakes may be added for extra body.

Apple and tomato soup

> 1 pint /575 ml stock
> 2 large apples, peeled and cut into rings
> 3 large tomatoes, peeled, deseeded and chopped
> 1 onion and carrot, finely chopped
> 2 tablespoons each of flour and butter to make a roux

Lightly fry the carrot and onion in the butter, sprinkle in the flour; keep stirring while you pour in the hot stock. Bring to the boil and cook a few minutes before adding the apples and tomatoes and some salt. Simmer for half an hour then sieve or blend. Serve with croûtons or garlic bread.

Vegetable soup for vegetarians

    35 fl oz /1 litre of water
    1 pint /575 ml milk
    2 carrots (5 oz /150 g)
    1 turnip (5 oz /150 g)
    3 medium potatoes (approx. 7 oz /200 g)
    2 leeks (use only the white part)
    4 oz /100 g peas
    5 oz /175 g rice
    3 tablespoons oil
    a knob of butter, seasoning, parsley

Cut the root vegetables finely and put them *(except the potatoes and peas)* into a casserole with the oil, cover and let them soften over a low heat for 10-15 minutes. Pour in the water and add the potatoes and washed rice and cook slowly for another half an hour. Sieve or blend the mixture, add the hot milk, salt and butter and finally the peas. Serve with plenty of chopped parsley or fresh herbs and fried croûtons of bread. Rolls crisped in the oven with melted gruyère cheese go well with this soup.

Mushroom cream soup

    1 lb /450 g mushrooms, finely chopped or minced
    1 pint /575 ml hot milk
    4 tablespoons of butter
    2 tablespoons flour
    1 carrot and 1 onion, sliced
    2 egg yolks
    4 fl oz /100 ml single cream or top of the milk

Sweat[1] the mushrooms, onion and carrot in a tablespoon of butter for 10 minutes. Add a cup 10 fl oz /275 ml of water and cook for a further 20 minutes. Make a roux with the. Remaining butter and flour, and gradually stir in the hot milk and any vegetable stock. Discard the onion and carrot-and then amalgamate the mushroom and milk mixtures. Season and then carefully blend in the egg yolks, mixed with the cream. Serve with croûtons. This is a very tasty and useful recipe to have on hand and can be adapted for use with blender to make a completely smooth soup.

Kidney soup follows much the same pattern as above. Soak the kidneys in milk. You will need 1 lb /450 g kidneys, 1½ pints /850 ml of stock or water. Put in the blender before adding the egg yolks and cream.

---

[1] Sweating vegetables: cook very gently in a pan with the lid on. A sweated vegetable should be soft, but not swimming in its own juices.

Carrot and rice soup

Carrots are a favourite Russian vegetable. This turn-of -the century light carrot and rice soup will appeal to vegetarians.

1 lb /450 g carrots, thinly sliced
4 oz /100 g of rice
3 tablespoons butter
9 fl oz /250 ml hot boiled milk
1/2 teaspoon sugar, pinch of salt

Sweat the carrots in the butter with the sugar and salt. Then add 4 fl oz /100 ml of water and continue cooking for ten minutes. Put in the washed rice and a further pint /575 ml of water.

Cook very slowly for forty minutes or bake in the oven if more convenient. Blend or sieve, keeping back a few tablespoons of rice for garnish. Thin the soup with the milk and season. Serve with more butter and fried croûtons.

In old age, Tolstoy was largely vegetarian, though his wife continued to base his soups on meat and chicken bouillon so it is said. The following was Tolstoy's favourite bedtime soup:

Use any good chicken or meat broth, skimmed of fat.

Rice dumplings to go in the soup

4 oz /100 g pudding rice
3 fl oz /75 ml milk
2 eggs
½ tablespoon butter/ margarine
salt to taste
flour

Wash the rice well and cook for about ten minutes in boiling water; then drain. Put in a saucepan with hot milk and stir over a low heat for 15 minutes. You can leave it on a simmering mat or put it in the oven and cook it until it is very thick.

Cool slightly, add butter, salt and beaten eggs and form into balls. Roll them in flour and drop into boiling salted water. When they are ready they rise to the surface.

Before serving, put them into the hot bouillon. The soup is made more interesting with the addition of finely chopped carrots, celery and leeks, first sautéed in butter until soft.

A 'modern' cucumber cream soup

The basis of this soup is a good vegetable stock (p 45), though I prefer it made with chicken. Flavour the stock well with a tablespoon of chopped tarragon, a spring of rosemary, and a teaspoon each of freshly milled chervil, dill or fennel.

(To each 2 pints /1¼ litres of stock you need:

2 large cucumbers, deseeded and roughly chopped. Peel only one.
2 onions, peeled and sliced
2 tablespoons butter
1 tablespoon flour
2 tablespoons barley flour (alternatively make a pearl barley purée)
2 tablespoons of soured or fresh cream
salt and pepper, cloves

Make a roux of the flours and butter and gradually mix in half of the hot stock and simmer for a few minutes. Add the unpeeled, chopped cucumber with the onions and half a dozen cloves. Simmer for five minutes, sieve or blend. Add the remaining stock *(If using barley purée add it at this juncture)*.

Mix the yolks with the cream and a little more butter. Blend into the soup which should be just off the boil. Season. Blanch the other, peeled cucumber in boiling salted water, drain and refresh in cold water and pat dry. Chop it fairly finely and add it to the soup. Serve with parsley, dill or fennel. Coriander and mint are pleasant alternatives as used in some Armenian dishes.

Mushroom stock for vegetarian borshch

1 oz /25 g dried mushrooms
1 pint /575 ml water
1 onion

Soak the dried mushrooms for a few hours. Boil them up in the same water and leave them in a vacuum flask overnight.

Make up the liquid to 1 pint /575 ml, add the onion and simmer for half an hour. They may also be cooked briefly in a pressure cooker to speed things up.

To make the mushroom borshch, see recipe on the next page, adding the cut up mushrooms.

Plum or prune borshch variation:
Instead of mushrooms, add 7 oz /200 g of soaked, chopped prunes or fresh plums towards the end of the cooking period.

Vegetable stock for borshch

35 fl oz /1 litre of water
1 small carrot or turnip
parsley stalks or half a parsnip
1 stick of celery or more
Mushroom stalks (optional)

Simmer the chopped vegetables in hot salted water for 30 minutes. Leave to stand at least 10 minutes before straining the stock. Add any suitable fresh herbs for variety.

Mushroom borshch

2 oz /50 g dried mushrooms OR 8 oz /225 g fresh open mushrooms
1 lb /450 g beetroot
2 stick of celery, finely cut
1 large onion, finely sliced
parsley stalks and tops for garnish.
salt, pepper and herbs for flavouring, 1 bay leaf
a little vinegar and a teaspoon of sugar
4 tablespoons of smetana (soured cream)

Cook the beetroot as directed on page 31. Cut them into julienne strips, sprinkle with vinegar, and pour over the hot mushroom stock page 44. Add the rest of the ingredients, except the cream, and simmer. Towards the end of cooking when the vegetables ale just tender, stir in the cream and chopped parsley and serve at once.

Puréed fish soup

1½ lb /675 g fish (cod or haddock)
2 tablespoons flour
4 tablespoons butter
1 pint /575 ml milk
1 carrot
2 onions, sliced
parsley stalks and tops for garnish
seasoning
hard -boiled eggs, optional

Make a fish fumet from the head and some root vegetables as described on page 57

Fillet the fish and cut into good bite size portions. Stew gently with the sliced onions and half the butter. In a separate pan make a roux with the remaining butter and the flour and gradually stir in the hot fish fumet. Bring to the boil and add the fish and cook gently until just done. Then sieve or blend your soup/ season, adding the hot milk or milk and cream. As a refinement, mash two hard boiled egg yolks in a little milk and add it to the soup. Serve with croûtons and freshly milled parsley.

Fish soup from tinned crab

1 large tin of crab
2 tablespoons butter/ margarine
1 tablespoon of flour
18 fl oz /500 ml of milk
1 egg
4 tablespoons cream or milk (hot)
seasoning, nutmeg

Set aside some firm white pieces of crab for garnish. Flake or mince the rest of the crab and put it in a casserole with 10 fl oz /275 ml of cold water or fish stock and heat through for about ten minutes. Make a roux with the fat and flour in a separate pan and gradually stir in the hot milk. Add the crab mixture and cook briefly. Remove from the heat, add a knob of butter, seasoning and the egg whisked together with the cream or milk. Finally add the reserved crab pieces.

Shellfish borshch

8 oz /225 g prepared frozen crayfish, shrimps, prawns, mussels or squids or a mixture
5 oz /150 g cooked grated beetroot
8 oz /225 S fresh cabbage, finely cut
1 carrot and 1 onion finely cut or grated
parsley stalks, chopped
1 oz /25 g butter or oil
1 tablespoon tomato purée
35 fl oz /1 litre (use water in which the beetroot and cabbage have been cooked)
salt, sugar, peppercorns, a few peas, bay leaf , vinegar, smetana, fresh green herbs

Defrost frozen shellfish. Cook them in a little salted water or fish stock for 5 minutes.

Steam the cabbage in a little water with the parsley stalks and a bay leaf. Sauté the carrot and onion in the butter. Add the fish and tomato purée and the cooked cabbage *(remove the parsley stalks and bay leaf).*Pour in the water, add the herbs and bring to the boil. Lastly add the vinegar, sugar and serve with **smetana** and freshly milled fennel or parsley.

Karelian fish soup made with milk

1 lb /450 g fish - whiting, haddock, cod
2 big Spanish onions, finely chopped
5 potatoes, finely sliced, salt and a little water
35 fl oz /1 litre milk

Cook the fish and vegetables as above but in very little water. Remove all fish bones and skin from the cooked fish before adding the boiling milk to the fish, vegetables and fish liquid.

Season to taste and strew freely with parsley and fennel, or try thyme and tarragon for a change.

Simple fisherman's soup

1 lb /450 g fresh fish fillets with all bones removed
6 potatoes, finely cut or cubed
2 sliced onions or leeks
35 fl oz /1 litre water
parsley, dill, salt, peppercorns, 1 bay leaf

Put everything together in a casserole or pan, and cook on a low heat for approximately 30 minutes. Serve with any available herbs.

Fish and celery soup

2 carrots, cut finely
1 medium size onion, chopped
1 or 2 stick of finely chopped celery
1 oz /30 g butter or margarine
2 tablespoons washed rice
6 cloves, salt
12 oz /350 g raw fish fillet, boned and cut into large pieces
35 fl oz /1 litre water, parsley, lemon juice

Sauté the carrot and onion in the fat, add the remaining ingredients except the lemon juice.

Cook gently, and before serving add the lemon juice, parsley and a pinch of sugar. Chopped celery leaves can be added as a garnish and for extra flavour.

Thick fish soup

14 oz /400 g fish — cod, haddock, whiting or other firm fish (not oily)
35 fl oz /1 litre water
1 carrot grated
1 leek or onion finely chopped
salt, peppercorns, 1 bay leaf
2-3 potatoes, finely cubed or sliced
1 tablespoon flour, 1 egg yolk, smetana, fennel, parsley, tarragon

Clean the whole fish, trim and put into cold salted water, bring to the boil and cook very gently in a fish kettle until just tender, pearly and juicy- approx. 10 minutes, depending on the thickness of the fish. Add the herbs towards the end of cooking.

Fry the root vegetables separately in the fat and thicken with the flour. Cook gently until almost soft.

Lift the fish out of the kettle and put on one side. Boil the potatoes in the fish water until tender. Pour some of this hot bouillon over the carrot and onion mixture and bring to the boil. Check the seasoning.

Remove any bones from the fish and flake or divide into bite sized pieces.

Beat the egg yolks and put this, the fish pieces and **smetana** into a soup tureen and pour over the hot soup, stir lightly and strew with plenty of freshly milled herbs.

Botvin'ya - cold fish soup with kvas

This is a Russian classic soup — essentially a simply cooked fish dish with a green sour sauce. It is quite thick and may also be eaten hot.

The **kvas** element in it is said to have a beneficial effect on the digestion according to one Russian cookbook, because of the presence of lactic and carbonic acids. In Ukraine they add finely cut up beetroot and the leafy tops of young beets. These are high in Vitamin A.

The historian Kohl enthused over **botvin'ya** describing it is as the most delicious and completely original in concept of all soups; however, the slightly sour fermented taste of kvas may not please everyone, in which case substitute lemon juice mixed with a little soda water.

Good fish such as salmon or sturgeon is the classic requirement, but firm white fish such as halibut, turbot or haddock may be substituted, with the addition of crab meat or shrimps. Purists insist on the spinach and sorrel being finely chopped and not puréed as in the recipe below. Sometimes young nettles are used instead of spinach - similar to Greek nettle soup.

Additions may be grated lemon or soured cream, added when serving, At the height of summer finely cracked ice is served with it in a separate bowl.

> ½ lb /225 g fish, lightly steamed in a fish fumet/stock with bay leaf, onion and a few black peppers
> 18 fl oz /500 ml kvas (p 198)
> 5 oz /150 g spinach and a good handful of sorrel leaves
> 1 fresh cucumber, finely chopped, salted and drained
> A few finely chopped spring onions
> A tablespoon of grated horseradish
> dill or fennel
> salt and pepper
> a little French mustard (optional)

Bone the cooked fish, cut into portions, put on one side. Pour over a little fish stock to prevent it from drying.

Cook the spinach and sorrel in a small amount of water. Purée it in a blender or cut up finely. Press out excess moisture, add the remaining ingredients. Chill well, serve the fish separately or spoon over the soup, as you please.

If you find the soup too thin thicken with some flour mixed with some of the spinach water and cook it for a few minutes before adding it to the soup.

Vegetable and herb soup from Tajikistan

About 4-6 handfuls of sorrel and/or spinach, chopped
3-4 potatoes, cubed
4 onions
2 tablespoons sunflower oil
4 oz /100 g flour
1 tablespoon of green basil[1]
1 tablespoon green coriander[2]
5 black peppercorns
¾ cup (8 fl oz /225 ml) of thickened drained yoghurt, kefir or half yoghurt and soured cream
2 teaspoons salt
2 pints /1¼ litres hot water

Fry the onion until opaque - do not brown. Add the flour and cook together on a low heat for a few minutes before gradually adding half the hot water (or you can use well-flavoured stock for variety), stirring all the time. Use a whisk to ensure smoothness and pour in the rest of the water in a slow steady stream. Bring to the boil, add the salt and put in the raw cubed potatoes. After twenty minutes add the sorrel/spinach, and ten minutes later the green herbs and cook this for a further few minutes. Let the soup stand for ten minutes for the flavours to develop. Then add the yoghurt/**smetana** mixture before serving. Health watchers and whole food addicts might like to try this recipe using different flours - rye or barley for instance.

Brinchoba - vegetarian soup from Tajikistan

4 onions
1 cup (10 fl oz /275 ml) of washed and drained rice
2 carrots, sliced
4 tomatoes, cut up and deseeded
2-3 oz /50-70 g butter or oil
1½ lb /675 g potatoes
10 fl oz /275 ml soured cream
4 tablespoons each of green coriander and basil
4 bay leaves
2 pints /1¼ litre of hot water

Preparation is much the same as above. The vegetables are lightly fried, all the water added, brought to the boil and the washed rice thrown in with the salt.

When the rice is half cooked, add the cubed potatoes, etc. Check the seasoning and add more salt if necessary.

---

[1] Dried basil plus some parsley may replace the fresh herb.
[2] Fresh coriander can be replaced with crushed coriander seeds plus some green melissa.

50

Thick bean soup

11 oz /300 g of dried beans (soaked overnight)
1 carrot
1 onion
1 stick of celery
1 tablespoon tomato purée
2 tablespoons butter or oil
1 carton of soured cream (5 fl oz /150 ml)
parsley root, dill, fennel
bay leaf and seasoning

Cover the beans with plenty of water and bring them to the boil and simmer until nearly done. Alternatively, cook in the Pressure cooker, following instructions. Chop the vegetables and fry in the butter and then stir in the tomato purée. Add these to the cooked beans which should still be firm. Season and put in the bay leaf. Cook until quite tender and serve with the soured cream, fresh green herbs and plenty of black pepper.

This is a very tasty and satisfying dish.

Lobio is a famous Georgian soup, made with kidney beans[1].It can be made using the recipe above.

Okroshka – cold kvas based soup

This is a cold, kvas based soup; I like it instead mixed with kefir or yoghurt and a little soda or mineral water. The soup is thick - half liquid and half vegetables and should be a little sharp.

The following is a **Tatar** recipe from **Kazan**:

12 fl oz /350 ml of kvas (recipe p 198)
4 oz /100 g cooked meat - lamb, veal or ham or a mixture or poultry or game or fish
1 medium onion
½ a fresh cucumber
1 egg, hard-boiled
4 fl oz /100 ml thickened yoghurt (see recipe p 149)
salt, a little sugar, dill, smetana for serving

Steam the root vegetables and cube them finely or make into julienne strips. Add the liquid and finish off by adding the fresh chopped herbs, finely chopped spring onions and sliced hard-boiled egg. There are meat, fish *(a good way of using cod)* or purely vegetable versions adapted to suit seasonal supplies.

A similar cold soup is made in the Central Asian countries as a refresher with extra kefir and yoghurt added to make it more of a drink, and the **Urals version** uses sour cabbage instead of cucumber **rassol**.

---

[1] Kidney beans: must always be well cooked.

Vegetable Okroshka

10-11 fl oz /300 ml kvas
2 medium potatoes
1 carrot
A little turnip or swede for flavouring
A few radishes
3 or 4 spring onions
½ fresh cucumber
2 tablespoons of smetana
1 egg, hard-boiled
dill, a little mustard , sugar , salt

Various doughs for making the noodles, pasta, little stuffed pies and other accompaniments to Russian soups are found in the pastry section.

Ukrainian cold borshch with apples and cucumber

1 lb /450 g beetroot
2 apples, peeled and chopped
2 fresh medium size cucumbers, deseeded, drained and chopped
6 finely chopped, blanched spring onions
2 eggs, hard-boiled and sliced
4 fl oz /100 ml smetana (soured cream)
Salt, vinegar, sugar, freshly chopped parsley, dill or fennel, boiling water and a slice of rye bread.

Cook the beetroot in the usual way with a little vinegar added to the water. Grate them, pour over enough boiling water to cover and add the bread. Leave for 24 hours or overnight in a cool place. Drain off the liquid and season with salt and vinegar and sugar to taste. Put the apples, cucumbers and onion into the liquid, stir well, then put the sliced eggs on top. Serve with the **smetana** and chopped dill, parsley or fennel.

Variation:
Replace the apples with cooked diced potatoes, and add 2 oz /50g of grated horseradish.

Cold Armenian chick pea & dried apricot soup - chirapur

3½ pints /2 litres water[1]
4 oz /100 g chickpeas, soaked overnight
8 oz /200 g apricots, soaked overnight
2 oz /50 g sugar

Rinse the chick peas, drain them and cook them in sufficient water to cover until they are soft but not mushy. They take a fairly long time to cook — up to two hours. A pressure cooker will save a lot of time or buy canned peas. Add the apricots and sugar, cover and cook until tender. Cool with the lid still on the pan. The soup may be puréed or left whole.

---

[1] If using a pressure cooker you will only need half the given liquid.

54

FISH

> *"On (the table) lay a large white sturgeon, other lesser ones, salmon, black pressed caviar, fresh caviar, herrings, stellated sturgeon..."* There was a pie made of the head and cheeks of a three hundred pound sturgeon; in addition to these fishy delights were pies of all descriptions and *"vodka of dark olive colour..."* Nikolai Gogol from **Dead Souls**

Of all the Russian Literary figures it is to Gogol that one turns to learn what was served at 19th century provincial parties. I don't imagine that sturgeon, ordinary or otherwise, is going to occupy much of the time of the average-cook today, but if it should chance your way the simplest method of cooking it, providing it is not such a gigantic one as described above, is to steam it over some fresh herbs in a fish kettle, or cook it as you would a beautiful salmon or salmon-trout (recipe p 62).

Russian folk tales abound in stories of fish and **rusalki** (mermaids), and well they might, for once the great rivers teamed with so many fish that the waters seemed to heave. All that is in the past, for rivers nearly everywhere have become polluted and it is only in recent years that conservation is being taken more seriously. Even so, industrial plans often conflict with environmental ones and inconvenient filter plants hold up production and rules are flouted.

Fish life has suffered also since the Stalin era when the "transformation of nature" schemes began. Dams in the Volga have reduced the number of river fish, slowed the river's flow, which has resulted in longer periods of icing and more rapid silting. There is little point in enumerating all the types of freshwater fish once available in Russia and the fish recipes included here make use of fish easily obtained from the average fishmonger.

Russian fish cookery books nowadays obligingly say 'fish' for most of their recipes and merely distinguish between the oily, the white and the flat fish.

River fish have always been greatly preferred in Russian kitchens and recipes give tips on pre-preparation of sea-fish to get rid of the 'fishy' taste and smell. The fish may be either rubbed with salt or marinated briefly in lemon juice or mild vinegar just before cooking. If no 3% vinegar is available use half vinegar and water.

Fish needs careful handling to retain its full delicate flavour and it is a good idea to buy fish last when out shopping. Some fish only need to be put in a little salted water shortly before cooking and some cooks recommend cooking the fish in water to which some lemon juice or vinegar has been added to keep the flesh firm.

Toward the end of the Soviet era, several 'meatless' days were introduced in Moscow, due to shortages. Fish cookery books were also printed to encourage fish eating. Most of the fish obtainable[1] in the big towns was tinned, salted or smoked. Live fish were said to be transported (costly); I never saw any.

Even in St. Petersburg which is close to Lake Ladoga and the lakes of Karelia where fish is plentiful, fish was served only once a week in the hotel I stayed in.

I find most cookery books give far too long a cooking time for fish. Generally it only needs to turn opaque. It should be pearly and juicy and therefore when it is fried or grilled needs some 'outer protection' such as egg and breadcrumbs or to be lightly sautéed on a bed of onions or finely cut vegetables. Accompanying sauces for fish in most books tend to be creamy and based on a flour roux.

Fish accompanied by separate vegetable sauces and purées such as are to be found in many Russian recipes are better and healthier. Spinach is a softener and fish can be wrapped and steamed in the leaves. All the **'plaki'** Byzantine-derived fish dishes are baked in protective layers of vegetables — onions, tomatoes, celery and so on and often covered with a layer of finely sliced lemon. This is suitable for most fish; for very fine fish where the flavour should not be masked, these vegetables can be cooked separately.

In our family we eat all vegetables with fish including parsnips and cabbage— it all depends on the glut in the garden. It is in this way that one discovers affinities. The possibilities of 'parsnip with almost everything' was brought home to me when a whole row of them was inadvertently dug up and we ate them in salads, soups and with fish.

Some bases for simmering fish are liquid from marinated vegetables such as cucumber **rassol'** and flavoured with onion and saffron. This is suitable for white fish and improves the flavour of cod. It is good for a cold fish dish. The liquid should just cover the closely packed fish. The fish can be simmered first in the **rassol'** with herbs before adding any other liquid to finish the cooking. Dill and onion or horseradish sauces are traditional favourite accompaniments. Mushrooms in **smetana** *(soured cream)* turn it into a much richer dish.

Baked fish is usually lightly coloured in butter or oil before being covered and baked in **smetana** and lemon juice in a moderate oven (180 C/Gas 4). The cover is removed for the last few minutes. This is a way favoured by Ukrainians.

---

[1] Fresh fish is now widely available..

Fish fumet or stock

A general useful fish fumet or stock to serve as a basis for fish sauces and a poaching liquid:

18 fl oz /500 ml approx. of water
1 teaspoon salt
2-3 peppercorns and a raw fennel seeds
1 bay leaf
1 onion - finely chopped
1 carrot - finely chopped
1 stick of celery or leaves or a fan parsley stalks
thyme and savoury to taste

Boil all these ingredients together for ten minutes, then add off cuts of fish and simmer gently for another ten minutes. Cool and strain. This stock can be frozen.

A little vinegar or lemon juice can be added to the stock if using it for poaching and this helps to keep the fish firm.

Cod with potatoes and onions –Treska s kartofelem i lukom

A simple dish using cod.

1 lb /450 g fish
3 potatoes, medium sized
3 fresh tomatoes
3 tablespoons butter
3 onions
parsley stalks and a stalk of celery
herbs - dill, fennel and parsley, salt, pepper
1 dessertspoon of wine vinegar

Cut the fish into suitable portions and sprinkle with the vinegar. Leave for 5-10 minutes, pat dry, dip in seasoned flour and fry lightly. Chop the onion and cook lightly in the oil.

Layer the fish and onions, season, cover with tomato rounds, pour over fish bouillon or water *(4 tablespoons)*.

Edge the dish with rounds of cooked potatoes, pour over melted butter, cover and bake for 25-20 minutes 180 C/Gas 4.

Note:
A very similar recipe adds fried mushrooms, **smetana** sauce plus grated cheese and breadcrumbs which are put over the fish before baking. The **smetana** sauce is made by using any fresh vegetable water thickened with flour and **smetana** stirred into it.

Cod Orlov

Which Count Orlov this dish is named after is uncertain. It is a 19th century French/Russian dish and is basically cod steaks covered in a Mornay sauce to which finely chopped onions and mushrooms are added.

> 4 cod steaks (about 6 oz /175g each)
> ½ lb /225 g finely chopped onions
> ½ lb /225 g finely chopped mushrooms
> 2 oz /50 g grated cheese, butter for frying

Mornay Sauce

This sauce has many variants. 'Fish liquor' and 'soured cream' are not generally found in Western recipes.

> 2 oz /50 g butter
> 4½ tablespoons flour
> 1 pint /575 ml warm milk or milk with fish liquor
> 2 oz /50 g gruyère or Parmesan cheese
> 2 egg yolks
> 2 tablespoons fresh or soured cream

Poach the cod gently with a few herbs. Put on one side and keep warm. Soften the onions in a pan with the butter but don't allow them to brown. Add the chopped mushrooms. Simmer until most of the liquid is reduced. Put the cod into a well buttered dish and cover with the onions and mushrooms. Coat this with the sauce made in the usual way by mixing a roux from the butter and flour. Gradually add the hot milk, bring to the boil and simmer for 5-10 minutes. Stir in half the grated Gruyère or Parmesan. Mix the egg yolks and cream and add to the slightly cooled sauce. Do not re-boil. Sprinkle over the remaining cheese and brown under a hot grill or in the oven.

Baking and steaming fish - variations:

i   Cook **Cod with horseradish** in a fish fumet or in a mixture of lemon juice, vinegar and water. Spread the fish with grated horseradish and cover with sufficient liquid. Season and add a bay leaf and fennel.

To finish the dish pour over **smetana**, thinned with some of the liquid. Bake or grill a further ten minutes.

ii   A Russian favourite is **Fish with onion.**

The fish is nearly always lightly browned beforehand, and certainly in Ukraine. It is first dipped in flour and seasoning before frying.

Layer the fish with finely chopped onions. Cover with sufficient boiling milk and bake in a moderate oven (180 C/Gas 4).

iii   Fry the fish as above and put it in layers in a casserole with cabbage cooked as per recipe (p 98). Bake in a moderate oven (180 C/Gas 4). and serve with a tomato and onion sauce.

iv   As above, but make a thick cheese sauce, adding caraway seeds and pinch of sugar.

v   Bake, steam or fry fish with a little onion and serve with a nut and mustard sauce: Crush a few walnuts and the yolk of a hard boiled egg together.

Add a tablespoon of mustard *(either English or Russian (recipe p 187).*

Slowly pour in 1 fl oz /25 ml of oil and equal quantities of weak vinegar and fish stock.

Add a tablespoon of fresh or dried breadcrumbs. A blender would do the job in a few seconds.

Stuffed grey mullet (kefal') baked on vegetables and onion skins

If you can set hold of the above excellent fish, well and good. Otherwise the stuffing mixture does for any large fish. The fish may be cut up or left whole. If it is kept whole, you will need another smaller fish for part of the stuffing. I suggest lightly cooked flaked whiting.

> 1½ lb /675 g fish (mullet and whiting)
> 2 oz /50 g bread
> 1 lemon
> 4 oz /100 g onion (some grated; some peeled carefully)
> 1 beetroot
> 2 medium carrots
> 1 egg
> ½ - 1 teaspoon of sugar
> 2 teaspoons of oil and chopped fennel
> salt and pepper; a little milk
> spinach and sorrel leaves (optional)

Proportions of fish to vegetables can be varied to preference.

Sparkle the fish with lemon and rub in salt on both sides. Take a piece of fish or the whiting and mix with enough breadcrumbs previously soaked in milk and squeezed, to stuff your fish. Add a tablespoon of grated onion, raw egg to bind and season with pepper, salt and half a teaspoon of sugar. Add 2 teaspoons of oil and chopped fennel. Stuff the sections of fish or the whole fish with this.

Grease a casserole and lay rounds of cooked beetroot and parboiled carrots on a bed of carefully washed onion skins. Put in the fish and add another layer of vegetables. Pour over enough cold water to cover. Cook 1½ 2 hours in a low oven (140 C /Gas 1), basting from time to time. The recipe recommends this long cooking but if it suits your schedule cook in a moderate oven at 180 C F/Gas 4 for three quarters of an hour.

The proportions of ingredients for this dish are left to the cook's resources:

I like to bake mullet tightly wound in spinach and sorrel leaves which impart a lovely flavour and keep the fish firm.

Sakhalin fish pie

This is a simple fish, potato and onion pie. Raw or cooked fish may be used. Potatoes are cooked in their skins, mashed, mixed with an egg a few tablespoons each of flour, butter, soured cream and seasoning. Half the resulting purée is used to line a pie dish, and the fish and sliced onions are layered up inside, finishing with the remaining Potato which forms a 'lid'. Leave an opening for steam to escape. Bake in a moderate oven 180 C F/Gas 4.

Trout

Lake Sevan in Armenia is famous for its trout and the locals often stuff the fish with raisins and rice mixed with butter, and finely cut up ginger. The fish is then baked whole in the oven. It is quite delicious. In the absence of fresh ginger, grated ginger root mixed with the rice provides the flavour. Even nicer are a few pieces of crystallised or preserved ginger with the sugar and syrup removed.

Herb butter stuffings used in Armenia and also in the Caucasus and Azerbaijan include a mixture of tarragon, basil, coriander, mint and parsley. To add sharpness, a few radish leaves and zest of lemon may be added and spring onions.

Herrings also benefit from such treatment and can then be grilled in the usual way.

Before **steaming or simmering trout** to go with sauces etc. place them for a few minutes in hot vinegar water to retain their bright colours.

To grill trout clarify some butter by melting it in a pan and pouring it through some muslin.

Brush the fish with this and grill approximately four minutes each side. Use moderate heat at all times for trout. Any stuffing for grilled trout should be cooked separately and heated, otherwise it is better to bake the stuffed trout in the oven.

Grilled trout

Grilled trout is delicious wrapped around in fennel branches. If you have no special fish grill to facilitate turning the fish, grill one side and then transfer the fish into a frying pan ready with a thin layer of hot oil, fennel and chopped tarragon and cook that side for about four minutes.

Baked trout between layers of vegetables

Onions, skinned tomatoes, finely cut sweet red pepper may be used, and tarragon plus seasoning and a little white wine to cover. Bake this for about 30 minutes, covered lightly with a piece of foil. Alternatively, you can wrap the fish in a paper parcel of double thickness greaseproof paper.

Ishkan style trout from Armenia

Take some fresh breadcrumbs and bind with sufficient butter. Add a few chopped apricots and three tablespoons of fresh tarragon, shallots or finely chopped onions. Add to this the juice of a pomegranate and some of the crushed seeds *(or substitute grapefruit/lemon juice and zest)*, pepper and salt. Make a fairly firm stuffing. The 'Ishkan style' trout is then usually poached in a little white wine for about ten minutes.

Stuffed trout with almond sauce

An Armenian recipe.
> **4 trout**
> **4 oz /100 g of ground almond**
> **2 lemons, juiced**
> **seasoning**
> **1 teaspoon of ground cumin**

Preparing the stuffing: Mix the ground almond, lemon juice, seasoning and ground cumin. The stuffing should be firm, but add water if necessary.

Preparing the sauce: Mix the ground almond and a little white wine or water, plus sufficient top of the milk to make a thin pouring sauce. Simmer for about five minutes.

Baking and serving: Stuff the fish, oil on both sides. Bake in a moderately hot oven (190 C /Gas 5) for approx. 20 minutes. Pour the sauce over the fish just before serving.

Variation:

An easily made stuffing is to soak a little bread in milk with 2 tablespoons of fresh tarragon[1]. In winter, dried tarragon may be used together with fresh parsley or coriander.

Salmon

My method is to sprinkle a little salt on both sides of the salmon and wrap it in a double thickness of well greased *(with butter)* greaseproof paper, folding the ends well. Lower your parcel into gently simmering water and cook for ten minutes. Lift it out carefully. With luck your parcel will not have lost the natural fish juices. Cover it and cool rapidly if it is to be eaten cold as you would do for meat.

This way of cooking the salmon without herbs or lemon juice keeps it a beautiful colour. Serve on a white plate in its own juice with lemon wedges and sprays of fennel.

---

[1] Tarragon is a favourite Armenian herb.

Armenian Fish Plaki

2 lb /900 g of white fish (cod, haddock or plaice)
2 large lemons
2 medium onions, sliced
3 tomatoes peeled and chopped
2 carrots thinly sliced
2 stalks of finely cut celery
5 fl oz /150 ml oil
3 tablespoons chopped dill, fennel, chervil or parsley or coriander and tarragon leaves or thyme.
½ clove of garlic

Sauté the onion and garlic in the oil just to soften. Add the tomato, carrots and celery. Cook five minutes and then season. Put the fish into a greased baking dish and cover with the vegetables; or you can sandwich the fish between two layers. Put thinly sliced lemon over the whole surface and sprinkle with the herbs. Bake at 180 C /Gas 4 for about 20 minutes — depending on the thickness of the fish.

Variation:

The Armenians also add a red pepper to the vegetables and cover the dish with a layer of thinly sliced, blanched potatoes.

Po evreiskii - Pike or Perch

A 19th century recipe; the fish is cooked is the Jewish way.

1½ -2 lb /675-900 g pike or 1 perch[1] (or similar firm white fish)
1 leek
1 stick of celery
a few finely chopped nuts - walnuts or hazelnuts
1 bay leaf
A few black peppercorns
3 cloves, pinch of saffron
1 teaspoon of honey and a few raisins

Make a fish stock (p 57). Cut up the vegetables and lightly cook them in a little water. Pour in the fish stock and poach the fish briefly until just opaque. Remove the fish onto a serving dish, thicken the remaining liquid with fine breadcrumbs to which a little honey and a few raisins are added. Scatter the finely chopped nuts over before serving.

---

[1] Adult perch may weigh 2 lb /900g; a fully grown pike could weigh 35 lb /16 kg or more.

Plaice or Flounder steamed à la Grecque

A 19th century recipe from Mrs. Molokhovets.

1½ lb /675 g fish fillets
2-3 tomatoes skinned and seeded
1 garlic clove
1 small onion and 1 spring onion
bunch of spinach and a handful of sorrel leaves, finely shredded
½ lemon
dill and parsley, salt and pepper to taste
butter for frying - about 2 tablespoons

Chop the onions and tomatoes and fry lightly in the butter until just coloured. Add the spinach and sorrel. Stir-fry for a few minutes before adding the seasoning and herbs. Put in the fish, then add sufficient water to cover. The fish will cook in a few minutes, remove and put on a serving dish. Blend or purée the sauce, which should be fairly thick, and serve with slices of lemon.

Tefteli - Fish patties

These are made basically from minced fish, with some bread or breadcrumbs added which have been previously soaked in milk and excess moisture squeezed out. It is then seasoned and bound with egg.

Fish cutlets, **zrazy**, **tefteli**, **roulettes**, **frikadelki**, **kneli**, **bitkis**, generally have this basis.

Tefteli are usually first steamed then baked. If **steamed** coat the fish balls in flour; if **baked** or **fried** coat in egg and breadcrumbs. A sauce may be baked with the tefteli or prepared and served separately.

The Russians, as do the Scandinavians, generally mince the raw fish together with the other ingredients to produce a smooth mass and eliminate small bones. I have tried making them with very lightly poached fish, which is then flaked and boned and mixed with finely grated onion or its juice and found them every bit as good as well as saving time and washing up. These can be briefly fried, steamed or baked with or without sauce.

The cooked tefteli freeze well.

I often make these tefteli with cod cheeks, the most delicious part of cod *(but curiously sometimes sold as pet-food in the UK!)*. Grated cheese and nutmeg may be added for variety.

Fish balls – quick recipe

Two medium sized fresh haddock fillets or cod
1 tablespoon of grated suet
1 small onion, finely grated or chopped
2 tablespoons potato flour
2-4 tablespoons milk
salt and pepper

Method I - Mince fish and onion twice, season and gradually mix in the milk. Form into balls and rest them in the fridge for half an hour to firm up. Drop into boiling water and cook for approximately 5-10 minutes.

Method II - Lightly cook fish, remove bone and skin, then proceed as above.

Kneli – Fish balls

Kneli are slightly more refined than fish balls, going through the mincer 2-3 times, and the egg white is folded in separately and the mixture chilled before gradually adding cold milk or thin cream and salt and pepper. A test of their lightness is that they should float on top of a bowl of cold water!

Proportions: (for 4-5 persons)

2 lb /900 g of fish fillets
18 fl oz /500 ml of milk and cream together, part for moistening the bread and the remainder added
salt and pepper to taste
4 egg whites

These delicate creations should not be prepared much in advance. A good food processor would be useful.

Fish balls - Moldovan

These are not traditional, but as celery is grown widely in Moldova it has crept into many modern recipes.

1½ lb /675 g fish fillets (a mixture of cod, bream or haddock)
1 small onion, grated
3 tablespoons each of finely chopped celery and parsley
3 tablespoons of corn (maize) flour and 1 tablespoon of breadcrumbs
2 eggs
fish fumet made from fish trimmings, 1½ pints /850 ml of water, a large onion and a carrot.

Lightly poach the fish in the hot fumet. Cool, flake and remove any bones and mix with the other ingredients. Form into balls. These should be fairly firm. Simmer them gently in the fumet serve with a tomato sauce.

Crab and rice tefteli

6 oz tin of crab meat (175 g)
2 cups (20 fl oz /575 ml) of cold cooked rice
4 eggs separated
2 oz /50 g flour
2 oz /50 g breadcrumbs
sufficient oil for deep frying

Mix the crab juice with the rice. Pound the crab meat and add to the rice mixture with the butter and egg yolks. Season - not too much salt. Form into small balls or oval patties and dip into the flour, then the beaten egg whites and the breadcrumbs and fry in the hot oil for approximately 4 minutes. An electric fryer is ideal for this. Sprinkle with chopped fennel or parsley, or incorporate the herbs in the tefteli.

Fish cakes

For cooks in a hurry, using canned salmon and tvorog *(curd cheese)*. You can use cottage cheese but then you will be slowed up by having to sieve it.

8 oz /225 g tin of salmon and its liquid
3 tablespoons of curd cheese
1 medium onion, finely grated
3-4 tablespoons of bread crumbs
½ egg white, beaten lightly
1 tablespoon of fresh chopped dill or fennel OR parsley, tarragon or thyme.
seasoning

Remove the bones from the fish and mash the flesh down into part of the liquid. Add the cheese, onion, breadcrumbs, egg white and herbs and seasoning. Allow the mixture to stand for 10 minutes to absorb the liquid. The mixture should be firm enough to form into patties. Add more breadcrumbs if necessary.

Shape into patties and fry briefly in hot oil for two minutes a side. Drain well, then serve them with mayonnaise mixed with lemon juice or soured cream or yoghurt.

Baked fish with yoghurt and cabbage Kazakh style

1 lb /450 g fish, haddock or cod cut into portions
1 tablespoon of flour
½ pint /275 ml yoghurt or kefir
3 eggs
1 lb /450 g cabbage, finely chopped
1 lemon
Fennel, dill, parsley, salt and pepper

Brown the fish on both sides in a little hot oil and season it well.

Steam the cabbage but don't overcook it. Put the cabbage into a greased casserole, lay the fish on top and then pour over a custard made from mixing the yoghurt/kefir with the beaten egg. Bake at 160 C /Gas 3 until just set and serve with lemon wedges and fresh herbs.

Balyk - bozbash from Azerbaijan - steamed fish with cherries or plums

Azerbaijanis like to steam their fish slowly either on the stove or in the oven. This is suitable for whole fish or thick steaks. The fish is usually marinated beforehand in pomegranate juice. You can use a mixture of grapefruit and lemon juice to tenderise and firm your fish. It adds extra zest, while the small plums add colour.

1 - 1½ lb /450-675 g fish (cod, haddock, hake, turbot or any large fish)
2 large potatoes or more to suit numbers, thinly sliced
3 onions, thinly sliced
4 or 5 plums (prunes may be used in winter)
2 tablespoons of pomegranate or lemon juice or a mixture
8-10 peppercorns, salt, 1 tablespoon of chopped parsley

Prepare the fish as you like, either keeping it whole or cutting it into fairly large pieces. Marinade in the juice for at least ten minutes, longer if possible, or even overnight. Butter an oven-proof dish suitable to stand inside a steamer or casserole. Put the fish, vegetables and plums in alternate layers with the seasoning, ending with a layer of potatoes. Strew over the parsley. Put the dish into the steamer a quarter filled with boiling water. Cover the steamer with a lid or foil *(not the dish itself)* and cook slowly for 4-5 hours in a very low oven 120 C/Gas ½ . Add more boiling water about half way through the cooking time. A wet towel over the lid will slow up evaporation.

The addition of fennel is very pleasing.

Odessa - style stuffed fish

This southern fish dish from Ukraine can be simplified by using method II below.

Recipe for 2-3 persons.

> **1 lb /450 g thick white fish**
> **2-3 tablespoons breadcrumbs soaked in a little milk and squeezed out**
> **4 small onions, fried lightly in oil**
> **2-3 tablespoons oil**
> **1 egg**
> **3 cloves of garlic or to taste**
> **1 bay leaf**

Method I The fish is skinned and the skin used to provide a covering for the stuffing. Remove as many bones as possible before mincing the fish, breadcrumbs, half the garlic and half the fried onions together. Season. Mix in the egg and form into four patties; divide the skin into four pieces and stuff them. Fry briefly to crisp them. They will finish cooking in the onion sauce that follows the recipe.

Method II Steam the fish lightly between two plates after removing the skins. Flake the fish and add the other ingredients as above and form into four patties. If the skin has been broken or it is inconvenient to spend time skinning the fish beforehand, remove it after poaching. Coat the patties in egg and breadcrumbs and fry them in the usual way.

Onion sauce

To finish the dish put the remaining fried onion into a little water, add any fish fumet/stock and cook for about ten minutes. The patties are then added with the remaining garlic, bay leaf and more seasoning. These patties are served with fresh tomatoes or with gherkins in winter.

Fish Kazakh style - baked in pastry with nuts

Any pastry may be used but the proper Kazakh way is to make a yeast dough using:

11 oz /320 g flour
1 teaspoon sugar
1/3 oz /8 g yeast
2 eggs
3 fl oz /75 ml water or milk
4 oz /100 g butter

Mix flour in a bowl, add the liquid, egg and yeast and sugar and salt. Stand in a warm place for 1-1½ hours. Knock back and cool and then proceed as for making rough puff pastry. Roll out thinly before using.

I often use frozen puff pastry bought in thin sheets and make up 'fish envelopes' by placing a frozen fillet of sole or plaice in each square with the nut filling on top.

Fish filling

1-1½ lb /450-675 g fish, cut to fit pastry squares
1-2 onions, finely chopped
2-3 tablespoons of chopped nuts.

Fry these ingredients together, add salt, pepper and parsley and any herbs to hand such as fennel or dill, plus a tablespoon of soured cream added to give extra richness and juiciness.

Fill the pastry squares, turn them into envelopes, paint with a little egg or milk and bake in a hot oven (220 C /Gas 7) until well risen and golden.

This is a very light and delicate stuffing and could also be used in the same way with meat, chicken, cooked rice or eggs, in which case a little gravy would be needed.

A slimming way would be to cook the stuffed fish in paper parcels or foil.

These fish pies are equally good cold and can be satisfactorily frozen.

Monastery stuffed fish

Russian Orthodox priests and their families were least likely to be influenced by foreign cooking and may provide a fairly reliable source of information of what ordinary people ate in the 19th century.

The country priests' diet was often a peasant one and they relied on produce from their own gardens, which they had to dig themselves, and any food offerings they received from their flock in return for services rendered.

Priests the world over seem to maintain a lively interest in food and are often very knowledgeable on its preparation. Chekhov noted the extraordinary good rye bread and excellent fish **shchi** he ate when he joined pilgrims on a visit to the Holy Mountain near Taganrog. Many notable literati were priests' sons or grandsons and Chernyshevsky came from a long line of priests.

The following recipe seems to have come from a well-to-do monastery as rum is included in the original ingredients. I have omitted this as the operation recommended sounded hazardous and inflammable. As a compromise, liquor of your choice could be added to the liquid and boiled for a few minutes.

Recipe for 6 persons.

> **2 lb /900 g fish**
> **6 oz ham**
> **3 tablespoons chopped parsley**
> **3 tablespoons butter**
> **¾ lb /350 g mushrooms**
> **4 tablespoons olive oil**
> **1 lemon.**
> **liquor such as rum, vodka or brandy, optional**

Stuff any large fish with well chopped ham and parsley. Wrap the fish in buttered paper and then tie it in a cloth with string to keep the flesh firm. Foil would be a good and easier alternative. Make a fumet as described on p 57 with about 1½ pints /850 ml of water plus 2 tablespoons vinegar and peppercorns and simmer in this until just tender. Time taken will depend on thickness of fish.

Fry the mushrooms in the olive oil. IN A SEPARATE PAN warm the rum etc. and set aside. Add some of the fish stock to the mushrooms and boil well to reduce and concentrate the flavours. Serve the dish with lemon wedges.

Baked cod with apple and celery

Recipe for 2-3 persons.

> **1 lb /450 g cod fillet**
> **3 oz /75 g celery**
> **1 onion, chopped**
> **2 cooking apples, peeled and sliced**
> **4 tablespoons tomato purée**
> **5 fl oz /150 ml milk**
> **2 tablespoons butter**

Butter a dish, make a layer of the mixed vegetables, add the fish and season.

Mix the tomato purée with the milk and pour over the fish. Dot with butter and bake at 220 C/Gas 7 for 30 minutes.

Fish Plov from Turkmenistan

Recipe for 2-3 persons.

> **1 lb /450 g haddock or hake**
> **12 fl oz /350 ml water**
> **1 tablespoon oil or butter**
> **1 carrot cut into matchsticks**
> **1 finely chopped onion**
> **1 parsley root or stalks**
> **4 oz /100 g rice**
> **Juice of half a lemon/grapefruit or pomegranate**
> **1 tablespoon finely chopped parsley and dill fennel**
> **some saffron threads[1] soaked in 1 tablespoon boiling water**
> **2 bay leaves**
> **seasoning**

1. Cooking the fish

Bring the water to a boil with the parsley root, bay leaves and seasoning and lower the fish into the gently simmering water and cook until opaque.

Transfer the fish to an oven-proof greased dish and add half the finely chopped or grated onion and the herbs; pour over the saffron and its liquid, the **smetana** and seasoning. Cover with foil and put into a low oven (140 C /Gas 1).

Serve the **plov** in a deep dish with the lemon or pomegranate juice poured over the fish separately.

---

[1] Turmeric can be used as a cheaper alternative to colour rice, but it won't have the same taste, of course.

2. Cooking the rice

Prepare as described on page 80. Make sure it is very dry and fry it in the oil or butter. In Turkmenistan they would use the fat from the tail of a special breed of sheep. Travellers' tales relate that the sheep's tails were so heavy that they had to be supported. However, I have no way of verifying this. Remove the rice from the pan and drain. Fry the remaining onion slices and carrot, pour over strained fish bouillon, bring to the boil and tip in the rice. Cook on a low heat, using a diffuser mat underneath, until all the liquid has evaporated. Add the remaining seasonings and herbs. Cover tightly and put in the oven for twenty minutes.

Baked fish - Plaki

This is my favourite way of eating fish. It is Byzantine in origin. Any type of fish may be used, but not oily ones such as herring, and mackerel.

> **4 fish steaks or flat fish fillets (1-1½ lb /450-675 g)**
> **2 medium onions, sliced in rings**
> **2 tablespoons of oil**
> **2 cloves of finely chopped garlic**
> **½ cup of chopped celery, including the leaves**
> **½ cup of thinly sliced carrots**
> **1½ cups of chopped, peeled tomatoes**
> **½ cup of water**
> **lemon slices and chopped parsley**

Season the fish with salt and pepper and cover and leave in a cool place. Fry the onions and garlic gently in the oil with the celery and carrots.

When they are soft, but not browned, add the tomatoes and water, cover and simmer for 15 minutes. Some of this sauce can go under the fish in a greased casserole and the remainder on top. Cover the top layer with a very thinly sliced lemon so that it sinks in nicely during cooking and acts as a protective barrier.

The fish comes out beautifully white and juicy, after baking it for approximately 30 minutes in a moderate oven (180 C/Gas 4). The time depends upon the thickness of the steaks. Thin plaice fillets will only needs 15-20 minutes.

The great thing about this dish is that it can be served hot or cold and looks very pretty with the lemon slices on top, garnished with parsley.

A Ukrainian dish - Herring baked in an egg custard

4 herring fillets (1-1½ lb /450-675 g)
1 tablespoon flour
4 eggs
4 tablespoons of oil
4 oz /100 g of spring onions
4 tablespoons soured cream
seasoning
green dill or fennel and parsley

Remove as many bones as possible from the herring fillets, if necessary using tweezers. Season, toss in flour and fry a few minutes in the hot oil until each side is a light golden brown. The fillets can be placed in individual greased, heat-proof dishes or in one large round dish with the tails in the centre.

Mix the soured cream and the eggs with the chopped spring onions, season and bake in a moderate oven (180 C/Gas 4). When baking any custard-type dish, and particularly when other dishes are in the oven requiring greater heat, place a thick newspaper in a baking tin and pour over warm water before standing your custard dish in it. This ensures even cooking of the custard. Bake on the lowest shelf.

Serve with plenty of milled herbs.

Fish in parcels

8 fish fillets (1-1½ lb /450-675 g)
3 tablespoons of butter/margarine
½ teaspoon mustard powder
½ clove crushed garlic
2 tablespoons chopped parsley
salt and pepper

Prepare the fish by seasoning it and pouring over the lemon juice. Blend the fat with the remaining ingredients.

Take four large pieces of cooking parchment and oil them. Put a fillet on each, spread with a quarter of the filling and top with another fillet. Repeat for each parcel. Fold the paper over and close the edges firmly, turning over the ends several times so that no juices escape. Bake at 190 C /Gas 5 for 15 to 20 minutes, on a baking sheet.

Foil can be used instead of paper. Allow an extra five minutes cooking time.

Fish bake - zapekanka with buckwheat

Dip the fish in seasoned flour and fry lightly. Put it into a greased casserole in layers with buckwheat (cooked as per recipe p 115) and hard boiled sliced egg. Pour over soured cream. Finish the dish by covering with toasted breadcrumbs and grated cheese. Bake in a moderate oven 180 C /Gas 4 for twenty minutes.

Red wine sauce for fish

18 fl oz /500 ml of fish fumet or broth of vegetable water with parsley stalks, bay leaf and a few herbs
2 tablespoons each of flour and butter
2 onions, 1 carrot, 1 celery stalk or leaves, finely chopped
6 tablespoons each of tomato purée and red wine
2 teaspoons sugar
Seasoning, parsley
4 tablespoons soured cream

Cook the fish in the broth, simmering gently until opaque. Remove the fish and keep warm.

Fry the sliced vegetables; then add some of the warm fish and broth and cook until vegetables are soft. Sieve or blend them and add the tomato purée and red wine. Thicken the sauce with a roux made by mixing the flour and butter together and add a little more broth or water as necessary. Cook for a further five minutes and then stir in the soured cream and parsley.

Pour over fish and serve.

If sauce is to be made before the fish itself is to be cooked, small slivers of raw fish could be added to broth instead. Cutting into fragments will help transfer flavour to the broth.

Nut sauces (p 184 - 186) also go well with fish.

Meat

The most typical Russian meat dishes in this section are the ones calling for ingenuity in making a little go a long way - the **kotletki**, **bitki** and various meat and vegetable bakes. In the past meat did not play a great role in everyday peasant fare, except when the pigs were slaughtered on feast days and holidays. These were numerous, at least eighteen days plus the great feasts of Easter, Ascension, Whitsun and Shrovetide.

In St. Petersburg in winter the historian Kohl describes the ghostly ranks of cattle 'frozen on the hoof' for cooks to choose from. They were unceremoniously and haphazardly hacked into blocks by the sellers. Fish were dealt with in the same way and little fish **'snitki'**, set in great lumps of ice, were chopped off in splinters.

If this was the style of butchery, I can understand the proliferation of marinades and household tips given on how to soften meat. A favourite method is to soften meat in milk for a few hours. I do this to liver and kidneys, but I had not considered it for other kinds of meat. Dry mustard rubbed into lamb the night before also acts as a softener. Wash it off the next day in cold water before cooking the meat

Marinade for Roast Pork

Marinade your joint or chops overnight or even for two or three days in the following:

Equal quantities of vinegar, water and red wine with half this amount in vegetable oil. Add herbs such as bay leaf, tarragon, parsley stalks, plus onion rings, peppercorns and salt. Cook your joint or chops in the usual way with the marinade. To finish off, press grated toasted rye breadcrumbs, mixed with the zest of a lemon, into the meat and brown for a further ten minutes. Remove the fat from the gravy, using a separator, or put a bowl of the gravy in the refrigerator for it to harden before removing. Add the lemon juice to this, and if you like a thicker gravy mix cornflour into a few spoonfuls of cold water and then boil it up with the meat juices. This pork dish is traditionally served with redcurrant sauce flavoured with cinnamon.

There are many recipes for meat stuffings, going under a variety of names according to region.

I have set out some specific recipes below together with a list of possible alternatives, seasonings, spices, herbs and covering sauces.

The method of cooking many of these forcemeats is also interchangeable and the cook can always find a recipe suitable for the moment and the ingredients to hand.

Golubtsy - Russian stuffed cabbage rolls

1 firm green cabbage
1 lb /450 g lean minced beef
4½ fl oz /125 g of uncooked buckwheat or long grain rice
1 teaspoon salt
1 finely chopped onion
4 tablespoons butter
½ teaspoon crushed coriander
black pepper and a pinch of ground ginger to taste
1 tablespoon of lemon juice

Blanch the cabbage leaves for 1½ minutes in boiling water, pat dry and leave to cool. Heat the oil or butter and fry the onions until soft. Add the beef and remaining ingredients stirring thoroughly. Cook gently for 10 minutes.

Stuff the leaves with the mixture, roll up and pack closely in a buttered dish.. Then pour any one of the given sauces on page 186 over the cabbage rolls, cover the dish with foil and bake in the oven at 180 C/Gas 4 for 1¼ hours. For the last 30 minutes, remove the foil to allow the golubtsy to brown, basting regularly with the sauce to keep them moist.

If you intend to eat the golubtsy later or to freeze them, omit the last half an hour of browning. To re-heat from room temperature, cook under foil for 30 minutes and then remove the foil for a final 30 minutes, again basting regularly.

Kotletki – meat cutlets

General proportions for these meat cutlets are:

1 lb /450 g meat to
4 oz /100 g white bread, soaked for 10 minutes or so in milk
fresh breadcrumbs for coating the kotletki
1 beaten egg for mixing

The reason for using the bread is to absorb the meat juices instead of allowing them to escape into the gravy. Flour may also be used. My Danish friend has a good system of putting her two kinds of minced meats in a bowl and then leaving a quarter space for tipping in the flour to eliminate fussy weighing.

Generally speaking, the Russians use bread crumbs or bread soaked in milk and this does make the kotletki juicy and light. The Armenians are not above tipping in a little of their famous brandy. Grated onions are usually added to **kotletki** to make them more interesting, as well as crushed garlic and any herbs to hand. I also add a teaspoon or so of tomato purée and a grating of nutmeg.

Soviet restaurant **kotletki** were generally very indifferent to put it kindly, but the home produced article was juicy and tender.

Armenian Meat Balls

1 lb /450 g minced beef
1 large tomato or two teaspoons tomato purée
3 tablespoons chopped parsley
2 medium onions
1 tablespoon oil or butter
½ cup (5 fl oz /150g) of whole-grain wheat or bulgar wheat soaked overnight
salt and pepper and a little mint
a teaspoon of brandy may be added.

Fry half the quantity of meat and onions. Cool. To the other half add the wheat, tomatoes or purée and seasoning and herbs. Flatten the first half and round them in the ball of your hand. Stuff them with the second half. Alternatively mix all together in the blender, form into walnut sized balls and fry.

Baked Moldovan meat balls with celery, in tomato sauce

½ lb /225 g minced lean pork
½ lb /225 g minced beef or you can mince your own
2 stick of finely chopped celery
3 tablespoons finely chopped onion
1 egg
salt and pepper – about ½ teaspoon
1 cup (10 fl oz /275 g) of tomato juice for the gravy

Mix everything together *(except the tomato juice)* form into balls, place in a greased dish, pour over the tomato juice and bake, covered, for 1 hour in a moderate oven 180 C /Gas 4.

Lithuanian Liver Dumplings

½ lb /225 g cooked minced liver
4 oz /100 g bacon cooked and crumbled
6 oz /175 g fresh breadcrumbs
2 eggs
2 tablespoons oil or softened butter
1 tablespoon chopped parsley
½ teaspoon each of fresh herbs: savory, marjoram, thyme, chives or a little onion juice
¾ teaspoon salt
a little mushroom or meat sauce to moisten.

Combine all together. Add flour or more breadcrumbs if mixture is too floppy. Drop small balls of the mixture into hot soup, simmer gently and cover for twenty minutes. Keep the lid on all the time.

Bitki - Meat balls with mushroom s from Ukraine (Bitki po-selyanski)

¾ lb /350 g liver
3 small onions, chopped
1 tablespoon flour
oil for frying
4 oz /100 g mushrooms
5 potatoes
1 tablespoon tomato purée
salt, pepper, dill or parsley

Mince the liver with some of the onion, add seasoning and form into balls. Dip into the flour and brown lightly in the oil. Put alternate layers of onion, liver and mushrooms into a greased casserole with a heavy base, finishing with the vegetables. Scrape out the juices from the frying pan, add a little water and pour over the liver. Finish cooking over a low heat or bake in a moderate oven (180 C/Gas 4).

N.B. In all liver dishes I soak the liver overnight in cold salted water or in milk. Milk tenderises and rids the liver of any bitter taste.

Ukrainian Pork Rissoles Mirgorod style

   1 lb /450 g pork
   3 onions, sliced
   3 cloves of garlic
   3 stale slices of white bread or rolls, soaked in milk and squeezed
   ¼ pint /150 ml milk
   2 tablespoons flour
   2 tablespoons tomato purée
   3 oz /75 g vegetable or other fat
   9 fl oz /250 ml stock or use a stock cube and water, salt pepper, dill and parsley
   and fresh thyme soaked in a little water

Cut the meat into neat slices and put it through the mincer with the garlic, soaked bread, and one finely cut onion. Season and add the thyme mixture. Beat it well and divide into eight patties, dip in flour and fry in the fat until golden on both sides, drain and put in a greased shallow casserole. Mix the remaining onion with the tomato purée and fry briefly in the pan juices, gradually stirring in the stock. Simmer for ten minutes, and serve with the patties. Butter beans are the usual accompaniment.

Shaslyk – skewered lamb

This Caucasian dish is much like Greek **souvlakia** and is very simple. Take enough lamb for four people. The recommended cut is the front fillet from a leg of lamb. Understandably, most cooks are reluctant to cut into a fine piece of leg. Lamb fillet if you can get it, or carefully trimmed chump chops or boned shoulder will do and the remainder can be used for soup or some other dish.

Trim the meat, keep some of the white firm fat for threading on the skewers and to act as basters. The onions should be sliced downwards from the top so that you have thickish pieces for threading onto the skewers, which should be flat. Sprinkle meat with fresh marjoram or fresh thyme *(failing this, dried thyme)* add salt and pepper, the juice of a lemon and/or grapefruit *(if pomegranates are out of season)* and about four tablespoons of olive oil. The meat and onions can be left to marinade until you are ready to cook.

Rub the skewers with fat. Thread on a few pieces of meat, one of fat, a small bay leaf and a piece of onion until the skewer is half full. The meat and onions, etc should be close together leaving the ends clear. If liked, halves of tomatoes cut crosswise can be added with the cut end facing the skewer point. The grill should be heated beforehand and the meat turned at intervals unless you are the lucky possessor of a spit.

A favourite flavouring for **shaslyk** in the Caucasus is barberry. These are hip-like berries rich in Vitamin C, but not easily obtainable in Britain. A sprinkling of **Adzuki,** or **Khmeli** herb mixture may be added to the marinade.

Brown Rice for Plov (Pilau)
Method I
Soak the washed rice in warm water for at least one hour Eastern cookbooks often recommend the rice to be soaked overnight. Wash the rice well until the water runs clear. Have boiling salted water ready - two parts water to one part rice. Add a little butter or oil Io the water, tip in the rice and cook very gently on a low heat until the rice has absorbed the water. Do not stir. Then add in more oil or butter from a given recipe and continue cooking for about another 30-45 minutes[1].

Method II
Wash the soaked rice in cold running water. Boil in plenty of boiling salted water for a short time. Remove while it is still firm in the centre. Wash in cold running water. Drain well. Put half the given amount of oil in a saucepan with a thick base, add the rice, stir well to warm through, then cover and leave in a warm place for another half an hour or so.

Plov from Uzbekistan
   1 lb /450 g lamb
   2 pints /1¼ litres warm water
   2-3 cups (20-30 fl oz /575-850 ml) of rice plus twice the amount of warm water
   2 or 3 carrots, cut into matchsticks
   2 onions, sliced
   oil or lamb fat
   seasoning

Heat the oil in a heavy saucepan, lightly fry the finely cut lamb pieces, add the onion and carrot and fry together for five minutes. Then add the warm water and seasoning and bring to the boil. Add the well washed and drained rice. Smooth the surface and make two or three holes right down to the bottom of the pan with a wooden spoon handle. Pour the warm water for the rice into these holes and cover the saucepan with a lid wrapped in a serviette or foil so that it fits closely, and leave it for about half an hour over a very low heat or in a low oven (140 C/Gas 1).

---

[1] White rice requires far less cooking time.

Azerbaijani meat plov

Basic ingredients:

> 8 oz /225 g long grain rice
> Two parts water to rice
> 1 lb /450 g lamb - preferably fillet, trimmed of fat
> 2-3 onions, chopped finely
> salt and pepper
> saffron soaked in a little boiling water (use the filaments and liquid)
> oil or butter for frying

Main additions:

> Fruit approx 4 oz /100 g of any of the following:
> Sharp plums
> soaked cooked prunes
> soaked, cooked dried apricots, or fresh apricots
> fresh melon, morello cherries
> and a handful of raisins fried in a little butter or plumped up in boiling water and
> drained

or

> combinations of chopped cooked chestnuts and almonds, or walnuts or peppers
> and aubergines, other vegetables such as carrots and spring onions and spinach/
> sorrel (used in plov sabza kourma).

Herbs and spices: - flavouring variations

> Coriander (*fresh or crushed seeds*), mint, thyme, tarragon, cloves, caraway seeds,
> garlic.
> Fruit juices to moisten: lemon, pomegranate (keep some seeds for decoration)
> apple, apricot.

> Yoghurt is served with fruitless plov or the meat sauce is sharpened with sorrel.

Method 1 - Simmer the meat separately either whole or cut up, using the stock to cook the rice. When cool enough to handle, cut up the meat if cooked in one piece, brown it in a little oil or butter, add the onion and gently stir-fry before adding the remaining ingredients, (except the fresh herbs) in a little stock or water.

Method 2 – Chop the raw meat into small pieces, brown it and the onions and cook until tender with the other ingredients. The best way is to cook it as if for a stew in a moderate oven 180 C /Gas 4 for approximately 1 hour, depending on the cut of meat used.

Method 3 - Involves the addition of making a pasta-dumpling type dough known as the **kazmag,** designed to go on the bottom of a well greased pot to stop the rice sticking during cooking. I usually dispense with this.

Moldovan Moussaka

This adaptable moussaka can be made entirely of vegetables or with the usual meat and vegetable mixture.

The meat mixture

9 oz /250 g of fresh lamb or pork
1-2 small onions
1 large potato and carrot
2 cloves of garlic
1 tablespoon milk, cream or smetana
1 tablespoon flour
2 tablespoons sunflower oil
dill or parsley

Put the meat through the mincer with the onion, potato and carrot and season well. Lightly brown it in the oil and then add the milk or cream. This makes for a soft juicy layer of meat in the middle of the **moussaka**.

Vegetable Moussaka

2 aubergines and/or 2 courgettes, sliced, salted and drained
½ a small cabbage, shredded and blanched (optional)
3 tomatoes or drained tinned tomatoes or purée
2 onions or two leeks
1 tablespoon each of chopped parsley/fennel/dill
4 cloves of garlic, crushed in salt
a few black peppercorns
1 bay leaf
celery[1], finely chopped is sometimes added to Moldovan moussaka (optional)

Custard Topping
2 eggs
2 tablespoons milk or cream or stabilised yoghurt or soured cream
seasoning

Instead of the custard the moussaka may be covered with fresh breadcrumbs or a thinly sliced raw potato, dotted with butter and smoothed over with more soured cream.

Line a greased casserole with strips of the blanched cabbage *(if used)*, or start with the sliced aubergines or courgettes. Layer up the rest of the ingredients, sprinkling the herbs and seasoning between layers ending up with a layer of vegetables. Cover with foil and bake for 45 minutes at 180 C /Gas 4. Remove foil and finish baking for a further 15 minutes.

---

[1] Celery has become abundant in Moldova

Kidneys baked in spinach leaves

Buy your lambs kidneys a day or two before needed. Soak overnight in vinegar water, rinse and then soak further in milk after having opened up the kidneys and removed the central core and any fibrous threads. Pat the kidneys dry, roll in seasoned flour and wrap in several layers of spinach leaves. Pack them tightly into a greased dish, pour over as much **smetana** *(soured cream)* as you like and bake in a moderate oven 180 C /Gas 4 for half to three quarters of an hour. Cook in a low oven (140 C/Gas 1) for longer if it suits your cooking programme. The kidneys are deliciously soft and free of all bitterness. The liquid may be thickened with a little flour to make a sauce.

Variations are:

a tablespoon of marsala, fried mushrooms added lo the sauce or spring onions.

Kidneys in soured cream

This is a much favoured Russian recipe and they prepare kidneys in this way:

Cut them in half, remove the central cores and leave them to soak in lightly salted water for 2-3 hours *(or overnight)*. Strain them and put them into a pan and cover with cold water and bring them up to the boil. Pour the water away and repeat the process.

Then put them into more cold fresh water, bring them to a boil and simmer until only just tender *(it won't take long)*. Strain, wipe them and cut them finely and then lightly colour them in butter for a minute or two and remove to a casserole.

Cut up root vegetables such as carrots, potatoes, turnip, swede into matchsticks and cubes and parboil them and then fry them. Put them into the casserole with the kidneys, add some sliced salted cucumbers, a bay leaf, a few herbs and add three tablespoons of **smetana**, a tomato and a crushed clove of garlic. Simmer together or bake in the oven.

Don't overcook or the kidneys may toughen.

I prefer my own method of preparing kidneys as in the recipe above, as there is less risk of them getting tough.

Liver Stroganoff

I have been frying liver in thin strips for years and now realise this turns into a liver Stroganoff dish when mushrooms and the inevitable soured cream are added.

1 lb /450 g liver
2 tablespoons butter
2 tablespoons each of chopped onions and mushrooms briefly fried
1 tablespoon flour
Parsley/dill
seasoning

If using lambs' or liver other than calves', soak first in salted water or vinegar, then in-cold milk overnight. This rids it of any bitterness. Remove all threads and skin - if necessary scraping it away. Pat the liver dry in kitchen paper, dip in seasoned flour and fry briefly to seal in the hot butter - a minute each side will suffice depending on how thinly you have managed to slice the liver. Add the fried onion and the flour and cook for five minutes before pouring in the soured cream, which should be slightly warmed.

2 tablespoons of tomato purée may be added to sharpen the flavour (optional).

Grilled Mititei - beef sausages Moldovan style

It is also a popular dish in Romania and just the thing for a barbecue -

1 lb /450 g beef - skirt or shin
1 clove of garlic
bacon or ham fat for the grilling or frying
pinch of soda
4 salted gherkins or 4 fresh tomatoes
2-4 tablespoons mujdei (garlic) sauce[1]
salt, pepper, fresh dill and parsley

Mince the meat with the garlic or buy good quality minced meat and crush the garlic with salt and add it to the meat. Thin with a little stock or water (about 1 tablespoon), add the seasonings and the soda and leave in a cold place-for ten to twelve hours. Flour your hands and form the meat into sausages and brush with melted fat or oil and grill, or fry in the usual way.

---

[1] Mujdei sauce: 1 head of garlic mixed with a little salt and then thinned with a little meat or chicken broth or boiled cooled water.

Zrazy - minced meat bake

Now that one can get good minced meat at the butcher's it's not so much bother to make the many tasty forcemeat and hamburger type dishes found by the dozen in most Russian cookbooks. It's still better to make your own, of course, especially if you have a food processor or electric mincer. I usually use half minced beef and pork to make a juicier dish.

The following is a Lithuanian one, also much liked in Poland, and different from most of its kind in the free use made of horseradish and herbs, especially marjoram.

Lithuanian zrazy

> 1 lb /450 g minced beef
> 2 teaspoons each of marjoram and chives
> 1 egg
> ½ teaspoon black pepper and salt to taste
> 2½ tablespoons each of flour and softened butter
> 2 oz /50 g rye breadcrumbs or fresh wholemeal crumbs mixed with crushed dark rye crispbread
> grated root of horseradish or ready grated or creamed horseradish
> 1 large Spanish onion, finely chopped
> 9 fl oz /250 ml stock or water
> 1 tablespoon oil
> 8 fl oz /225 ml of smetana or thickened yoghurt with added lemon juice

Mix the meat and herbs and add the beaten egg and seasoning and form into flat cutlets, roll them in flour and fry briefly over a high heat to seal the juices. Put them into a buttered low-sided casserole and cover with a forcemeat made of the breadcrumbs, flour and softened butter and horseradish. Add a layer of onion and then the **smetana** or thickened yoghurt and lemon juice. Pour over the stock/water, mixed with the oil, cover with foil and bake for three quarters of an hour in a moderate oven - 180 C /Gas 4.

Variations:
Layer the meat with hard-boiled eggs and thinly sliced blanched turnip.

Georgian lamb stew Chanaki

This is a simple and easy to prepare casserole dish[1].

1 lb /450 g lamb fillet or chops
1½ lb /650 g potatoes
18 fl oz /500 ml water
½ lb /225 g tomatoes or an 8 oz /225 g tin of tomatoes plus a tablespoon of tomato purée)
½ lb /225 g each of sliced aubergines and prepared sliced green beans
1 large onion, sliced
1 bunch of parsley or fresh coriander or crushed coriander seed
seasoning

Try also using different herbs such as basil, rosemary, dill, mint and tarragon or sharpen the stew with cayenne pepper and paprika.

Remove as much fat and skin as possible from the lamb fillet and cut it into neat pieces. Add all the other cut up vegetables and the herbs. Pour over the cold water, cover and cook in a moderate oven 180 C /Gas 4 for 1½-2 hours.

A "twin" Georgian stew is **chakhokhbili** made from beef, lamb or chicken. Here the meat-is fried first before casseroling. Omit the aubergines and potatoes and double the amount of onions, tomatoes and herbs and add four or five cloves of crushed garlic.

Variations:

For the lamb version add mint and tarragon and thicken the stew with ½ lb /225 g potatoes. Sometimes lemon or pomegranate juice or while wine is added. The chicken version is the same with the addition of a teaspoon of suneli (p 207) and a pinch of saffron.

Armenian lamb stew is on similar lines with the addition of soaked, cut up dried apricots. Here the meat is cooked first, then cut up and fried with the onion before combining with the strained stock and other ingredients. This has the advantage of ridding the stock of any fat.

Russians make a simple lamb stew using easily available root vegetables of turnip, onion and leek and serving it with a caraway or cumin sauce, thickening the cooking liquid with a roux of equal quantities of flour and butter and adding 2 teaspoons each of cumin or caraway seed, seasoning, a pinch of sugar and dash of vinegar or lemon juice.

---

[1] Can be frozen for a short period of up to a month

Galya - Azerbaijan stew

This is usually made with veal, but lamb is a good substitute.

1 lb /450 g stewing veal or lamb fillet
½ lb /225 g chestnuts, shelled and cooked
4-5 oz /100-150 g lentils, (brown or green) soaked overnight
3 oz /75 g mixed chopped nuts
6 oz /175 g dried chopped apricots, soaked overnight
4 large onions
1 whole bulb of garlic, chopped or 4 cloves of garlic and 4 spring onions chopped, including the green part
2-3 oz /50-75 g butter
1 tablespoon fresh thyme or 2 teaspoons of dried
1 tablespoon fresh mint
7 tablespoon chopped parsley and stalks
9 fl oz /250 ml boiling water

Remove most of the fat from the meat and any skin. Beat it out slightly and cut it into neat squares. Fry it briefly in the butter with the onion and chopped garlic, pour over the boiling water and add the lentils and simmer for 20 minutes before adding the remaining ingredients, except the parsley. Finish cooking for a further 30 minutes in the oven.

I usually cook this dish entirely in the oven after browning the meat or in the pressure cooker to save watching it. If using veal for stewing it is certainly better cooked slowly in the oven at 170-180 C /Gas 4.

POULTRY

Chickens, especially small poussins, were once consumed in such large numbers at Easter Time that they came to be called 'The Great Martyrs'. I suppose they still are if one considers current intensive rearing practices.

Recipes from the Caucasus are varied, relying on regional nuts and fruit to provide contrasting texture. The purely Russian recipes are simple to prepare and chickens are either carefully simmered with a few vegetables or roasted and simply stuffed with an apple to retain moisture in the breast. They are also often just lightly parboiled and simmered before browning in the oven.

Boiling/braising a large fowl the Ukrainian way

Choose a bird of 4-7 lb /2-3 kg and remove the extra fat skin on the back.

First simmer the giblets and wing tips in plenty of water - about 3 pints /1½ litres with a few carrots, stick of celery and tops, parsley stalks and a few soft tomatoes. Bring to the boil, skim, then put in the bird. The water should come three quarters of the way up. Cover, and either cook in a low oven (140 C/Gas 1) or simmer slowly on a mat on the stove.

Test the thick part of the thigh for readiness. A clear almost colourless liquid should come out. If you intend to finish the bird off in the oven, only parboil it and stuff it with forcemeats chosen from pp 127-128. If cooking in the pressure cooker cut off the thighs so that the heat penetrates completely and the whole bird is ready at the same time. Cook the bird breast down to keep it moist. This is the best and easiest way I know of cooking a chicken or fowl for serving with white and other sauces.

A lovely garnish for braised fowl or chicken or turkey joints is fresh pomegranate when they are available here in late autumn. Armenians thicken the gravy with a few spoonfuls of stabilised yoghurt flavoured with cumin and scatter the pomegranate seeds over the sauce and chicken before serving.

Roast chicken - low fat method

For those avoiding extra fat in their diet, ease the skin from the bird by pushing your fingers between the breast and skin and gradually slipping it off. You can get most of it off whole in this way. Then sprinkle the bird with a little seasoned flour and pour over beaten egg mixed with dill and bake in a little water or wine, breast side up, until the egg dip has firmed, then turn it over and cover with foil to finish cooking.

Stuff with a really large quantity of chopped parsley and lemon zest.

Georgian chicken tabaka

This colourful chicken dish is presented with typical Georgian flair. One can eat it hot or cold and it has the advantage of cooking through quickly on the stove in a heavy pan without the need to use the oven or joint the bird.

Only small chickens are suitable. Cut along the underside of the bird, lengthwise, turn it over and beat it flat with a mallet. You will need to remove the breastbone for it to lie flat. Make slits in the skin to tuck in the legs and wings.

Salt and pepper the bird on both sides and add a little cayenne and paprika pepper before brushing it all over with walnut, peanut, safflower or olive oil. The bird can be conveniently prepared in advance and left in a cool place.

Heat a heavy griddle or frying pan, put in the chicken and put a heavy heat-proof flat plate or cover on top, weighted down with a 2 lb /1 kg weight, or as many weights as you can conveniently use. The chicken must lie completely flat during the cooking. It will take roughly 30 minutes each side

The Georgians usually serve a Spanish type omelette with this dish. Beat your eggs and set them in an omelette pan with previously cooked spinach and onions or aubergines. This is served with a yoghurt based sauce spiced with herbs and coloured with a few threads of saffron. The whole effect is striking, with the dark golden chicken, green omelette and saffron yellow sauce.

Armenian Chicken Amich stuffed with apricots and raisins

    2 oz /50 g parboiled rice
    5-6 apricots and a few raisins soaked overnight
    2 oz /50 g each of blanched almonds and hazelnuts
    Cracked plum/prune, apricot kernels if available
    2 teaspoons fresh basil or 1 of dried
    2 cloves and ½ teaspoon of cinnamon

Lightly stir-fry the ingredients in about 3 oz /75 g butter and stuff the chicken. Rub the skin with olive oil and sprinkle it with salt. Put a little water in a roasting pan, put the chicken on its side and turn it over once during cooking and baste.

A turkey may be treated the same way, though I always cover mine and cook it breast down to keep it juicy.

Guruli - spiced chicken from Georgia

This recipe includes the usual walnuts plus an interesting mixture of herbs and hot spices.

1 medium sized chicken
2-3 onions, chopped
2 tablespoons crushed walnuts
1 teaspoon each of: freshly grated ginger, cayenne pepper, crushed coriander, salt
5-6 cloves
1 teaspoon of grated cinnamon
2 tablespoons each of parsley and chervil or fennel and tarragon
a little butter of cottage cheese

Thyme vinegar: Steep some fresh thyme in 4 tablespoons of hot vinegar and water *overnight*.

The next day, thoroughly mix together all the herbs and spices with the thyme vinegar.

The chicken can be cooked whole or cut up. Brown it in butter with the onion, then add the well mixed herbs and spices.

Whole chicken: Ease away the skin at the breast bone and put some of the herb mixture with a little butter or cottage cheese between the skin and breast meat.

Chicken pieces: Press the herb and spice mix well into the chicken pieces.

Cook in the usual way.

Chicken stewed in the Megrelski style - from Georgia

1 medium sized chicken
6 oz /175 g walnuts, chopped
5 onions, finely chopped
2 raw egg yolks
3-4 tablespoons butter
2 tablespoons wine vinegar and water mixed
1 tablespoon freshly milled mint
4 tomatoes or 2 gherkins
seasoning and dill

Brown the chicken and put it in a baking dish with the onions, walnuts and mint and a little water or stock. Cover and cook in the oven or on the stove in a deep dish until tender, basting occasionally. To make the sauce, mix the yolks with the vinegar, add the strained gravy with the fat removed and cook gently without allowing it to boil. Serve with dill, the tomatoes and gherkins.

Variation:

Cook the chicken with a carrot, onion, parsley and celery. After straining the gravy add to it 4 tablespoons of raisins, a little sugar and salt and slewed prunes/plums or cherries.

Turkey - cooked the Ukrainian way

Prepare by rubbing the inside of the bird well with a teaspoon of grated ginger. Stuff simply with two whole apples and a handful of plumped up muscatel raisins. Bake your turkey in the usual way. The juices may be thickened with a little cornflour and well seasoned.

The apple stuffing keeps the turkey breast moist. Roast the turkey first on one side and then on the other to ensure that the breasts don't dry out.

Moldovans cook turkey with a stuffing of parboiled rice and raisins bound with egg. The turkey is roasted with carrots and onions, parsley, celery, bay leaf and seasoned with black pepper.

Turkey joints with apricots

    1 lb /450 g turkey
    3 onions, chopped
    2 tablespoons butter or walnut or other light oil
    1 oz /100 g apricots, previously soaked and cut
    ½ tablespoon flour[1]
    4 tablespoons each of tomato juice and white wine
    2 tablespoons sugar
    pinch of cayenne
    ½ teaspoon cinnamon
    2 cloves of garlic
    2 bay leaves
    1 teaspoon each of vinegar and hot water mixed together
    1 tablespoon parsley and tarragon
    smetana (optional)

Skin the joints, brown them in the butter or oil and put them in a casserole. Fry the onion which has been tossed in flour. Pour in the liquids, apricots, sugar, seasoning, spices and herbs and cook a few minutes. Pour the sauce over the turkey and either bake it in a moderate oven or simmer on the stove until tender. Serve with fresh herbs and stir in a little **smetana**.

The Russians, like the Chinese, eat more parts of animals and poultry than in many western countries. Stuffed goose neck is a speciality and it is also a Jewish dish.

It makes all the more poignant Isaac Babel's story "My First Goose". The central character, a novice Jewish recruit, finds himself alien and hungry in a Cossack unit during the revolution. Cossacks were the traditional enemy of the Jews and they tease the bespectacled new recruit unmercifully.

---

[1] Cholesterol and 'weight watching' tips: Omit the flour and **smetana** (soured cream). Use a gravy boat designed to separate excess fat.

In desperation he kills a harmless goose crossing the yard, stamping its neck underfoot and handing it on the tip of his sword to the half blind Jewish landlady to cook.

The Cossacks then accept him and invite him to sup with them. They, of course, were experts in butchery and took pride when decapitating either an animal or the enemy to avoid spilling much blood.

Stuffed goose neck

Bone the neck, clean it and take out the fat. Mince the fat with goose liver and a few chicken livers or a little veal and some onion and bread which has been soaked beforehand in milk. Season and add either a little mixed spice or grated apple and caraway seed. This tasty stuffing can be used to stuff the main part of the bird if preferred.

Bind the stuffing with one or two eggs and stuff the neck. Ideally the ends should be sewn but this is a bother, and a piece of string, toothpick or foil may serve the purpose. The neck should not be overstuffed. Prick all over and simmer in salted water for 50-60 minutes. Serve with prune sauce (p 186) in apricot.

GAME

Even dogs dream of delicious dinners in Gogol's story **'Memoirs of a Madman'**. In it, two dogs 'correspond' and the letters, ostensibly 'love letters', inevitably turn to thoughts of food:

*'Ah, ma chère', sighs one, 'I feel sorry for my mistress returning so pale from the ball.... very likely no-one has fed her... I couldn't live without my game sauces - excellent with **kasha**, so long as there are no carrots, turnip or artichokes...'*

Théophile Gautier observed game marinated in juniper berries, but which smelt disconcertingly of turpentine. Always an adaptable traveller, he ate and liked it, though had some reservations about bears' paws, bear hams and elk.

Generally game needs a little marinating before cooking to offset any dryness and bitterness. The best and simplest is milk.

A basic spicy marinade is made from equal quantities of vinegar and water flavoured with chopped celery and leaves, onion, carrot and parsley and the following herbs and spices: bay leaf, cloves, cardamom, garlic, Jamaican allspice berries, juniper berries and a good pinch of salt.

Marinade the birds overnight if possible.

Variations:

1. Lemon juice, mint and marjoram added to the basic root vegetables.
2. A sweet marinade of sugar, soft fruit berries and lemon juice'
3. Bran or beetroot based kvas (p 198)
4. Vinaigrette with added herbs.

Russians often roast their game, but I prefer just to brown mine first in oil and butter on the stove and then cook it covered in a low oven (140 C/Gas 1) with a few of the above vegetables and herbs and dry wine. This usually takes an hour.

A traditional recipe is to bake the game in soured cream, thinned with a little milk (thickened yoghurt is a good substitute). I would always cover the dish and cook the bird breast down to avoid dryness.

Any of the following can be served with game: soured cream & mayonnaise, red cabbage, celery and marinated fruits.

VEGETABLES

Reading through Russian cookbooks I realise more and more that many present day vegetarian and health food recipes owe their origin to eastern Europe. The Russians have always liked ragouts of vegetables, rather than have them served boiled and unadorned.

Russian cookbooks devote whole sections to garnishes, and many sauces consist completely of vegetables, without flour to thicken them, and often appear more like a ratatouille and provide interesting texture to dishes.

Jerusalem Artichokes in white sauce

The Russians call these 'earth pears' and they are quite popular. The name comes, not as one would suppose, from Jerusalem, but from the Italian word **Girasole** (sunflower).

The artichokes are scrubbed well and cooked in their skins in half milk and half water over a low heat. A white sauce is made from this in the proportions of 1 tablespoon flour to 9 fl oz /250 ml liquid. Add a knob of butter and plenty of salt and pepper. Serve with fresh parsley.

Aubergines

2 aubergines
2 onions sliced and lightly fried
3 tablespoons flour
4 tablespoons soured cream
1 tablespoon tomato purée or use fresh skinned tomatoes

Cut the ends off the aubergines and blanch them in boiling water. Slice them and dip in seasoned flour and fry. Transfer them to a casserole together with the fried onions. Warm the **smetana** in the frying pan in which the vegetables have cooked and mix in the tomato purée or fresh tomatoes. Bring to the boil and pour over the aubergine mixture. Serve with parsley.

The same recipe can be used for courgettes or young marrows.

Red Kidney bean purée with onions and nuts (Krasnaya fasol's orekhami)

4 oz /100 g beans (soaked overnight)
1 oz /25 g walnuts, finely chopped
1 onion, finely chopped
salt and pepper
parsley

Cook the beans in fresh water until tender and sieve or mince them *(using a pressure cooker would save time)*. Keep back two tablespoons of the cooking liquid to mix with the chopped pounded walnuts.

Mix all the ingredients and season. Strew with chopped parsley and serve with a green salad.

Beetroot

Russians, and especially Ukrainians, make an unusual and wide use of this vegetable. It is said to be rich in potassium and other minerals. One Russian cookbook claims that it aids the digestion and improves the blood; another claims that it can lower blood cholesterol. Without vouching for this I would say that there is a case for using beetroot more imaginatively than we do.

The Tatars like to steam beetroot and turnip separately and serve them together. The beetroot juice is kept to serve as a drink mixed with milk and chilled.

Hot grated beetroot as an accompaniment to a main meat dish

8 oz /250 g beetroot
1 tablespoon butter
2 tablespoons soured cream
salt, pepper, sugar, vinegar to taste

Cook and prepare the beetroot in the usual way. Peel and slice it into matchsticks or dice it and put it into a pan with the melted butter. Add a little water or bouillon and all the seasonings and cook for a few minutes. Add the soured cream, stir and cook another five minutes. This is good with lamb, goose or game. It is a Tatar recipe and the Kazakh version is with an added grated onion and with yoghurt instead of the soured cream, which is served separately. This is a good, delicious recipe.

Variation:
Finely grate the cooked beetroot and mix it with a lightly fried onion and a sliced tomato. Cook briefly and add a few drops of vinegar or a tablespoon of blackcurrant or blackberry juice, one or two tablespoons of sugar, and salt and pepper to taste.

Baked beetroot

Speedy method: wash, skin and grate beetroots and put them into a buttered dish. Sprinkle the layers with salt, pepper, lemon juice or vinegar and a little sugar and dot with butter. In Ukraine they stir a white sauce into sliced beetroot. Vinegar and lemon juice is added to give the dish a sharp piquant flavour and two tablespoons of butter are added at the last moment to give the sauce a glossy look.

Ukrainian way with young beetroot is to stuff their leaves with partially boiled rice or buckwheat. Scald the leaves and stuff them with cooked rice flavoured with fried onion or cooked buckwheat with fried onion or mushroom. For method of cooking rice, buckwheat and other grains see page 115.

Grated beetroot with apple

6 raw beetroot
1 tablespoon each of flour and butter
1 tablespoon soured cream
2 apples, grated
seasonings of salt, pepper, sugar, vinegar or lemon juice.

This is most successful with young raw beetroots. Scrub them well and grate and put them into a casserole with a few tablespoons of boiling water and partly cook them on a low heat. Add the apples and the soured cream and continue cooking until tender. Mix the flour with the vinegar or lemon juice and add the remaining ingredients and cook through for five minutes. Serve with chopped parsley.

Beetroot and onion bake

6 medium beetroot
1 large onion
1 tablespoon butter
3 tablespoons soured cream
1 tablespoon flour
2 tablespoons cider vinegar or 1 tablespoon wine vinegar and
2 tablespoons water, well mixed
salt and pepper

Bake the beetroot in the oven until tender. Skin and slice them and gently fry for a few minutes in the butter. Add the onion and fry for a further five to ten minutes. Mix the soured cream with the flour and add it to the beetroot and onion. Season, and lastly add the vinegar and bring the mixture to a boil. Put all into a greased casserole and bake in a moderate oven 180 C /Gas 4 for 15-20 minutes.

This is a good accompaniment to game or roast beef and provides a lovely bright contrast to the brown meat.

Beetroot Cutlet

4 medium sized beetroots
1 tablespoon of semolina or 2 tablespoons of dried breadcrumbs
1 egg
salt
oil or butter for frying
seasoned flour and extra breadcrumbs

Cook the beetroot in the usual way, or bake in the oven; skin and grate them finely. Fry them in the oil and butter for a few minutes, then sprinkle in the semolina slowly, stirring all the time. Cook gently for 10-15 minutes. Cool the mixture, mix with the egg and salt and divide into oval cutlets. Dip in flour and breadcrumbs and fry until golden. Serve with melted butter and soured cream with parsley.

Cabbage

The modern recommendation for cooking this vegetable is as fast as possible and in very little water to retain as much vitamin C as you can. The Russian way is the opposite. The cabbage is first cooked slowly -in a little water and butter - the process taking up to forty minutes, until all moisture has been absorbed.

Usual additions **combined during the cooking process** are: lightly browned onions, tomato purée and favourite seasonings of caraway and dill. The finish is achieved with toasted or fried breadcrumbs and soured cream and/or grated cheese.

Stewed cabbage and apple

1 cabbage
2 apples — finely cut
2 tablespoons caraway or fennel seeds
1 teaspoon of vinegar
4 fl oz /100 ml soured cream
1 tablespoon flour
1 teaspoon sugar
1 tablespoon butter

Remove coarse parts of the cabbage and cut the leaves into fine strips. Put it into a pan with a close fitting lid and add the butter and enough boiling water to come roughly 2 inches /5 cm up the pan. Bring back to the boil and put in the two finely cut apples, caraway or fennel seeds and vinegar. Cook until almost soft, stirring from time to time. Mix the soured cream with the flour and some of the juices from the pan. Stir this into the cabbage with the sugar and seasoning. Cook over a low heat for a further five minutes.

This dish may also be baked in the oven with an egg custard mixture poured over - in a sense turning it into a cabbage and apple moussaka. (See next recipe).

Cabbage and apple bake

1 cabbage
4 apples, sliced
4 tablespoons soured cream
2 eggs
1 tablespoon flour

Prepare the cabbage as above and cook on its own in a little water and butter. Then add the apples. Coat the mixture with softened butter. Beat together the soured cream with the flour and eggs. Season and fold into the cabbage mixture. This makes it into a soufflé type dish.

An alternative is to pour the custard over the cabbage and have it more as a moussaka. Bake in a greased tin lined with breadcrumbs at 350 F/Gas 4 for 25-35 minutes. Dot the top with melted butter. Cut into slices before serving and pour over more melted butter! Delicious!

Steamed Cabbage with onion and tomato purée

1 medium cabbage, finely shredded
5 fl oz /150 ml water or stock
2 onions, sliced and lightly fried
2 tablespoons tomato purée
1 tablespoon vinegar
1 tablespoon sugar
1 tablespoon flour
3 tablespoons butter/margarine
1 bay leaf
salt and pepper

Put the cabbage and water or stock into a casserole with 1 tablespoon of butter or margarine and cook slowly for 40 minutes. Then add the vinegar, sugar, salt and pepper, bay leaf and cook for another ten minutes. Make a roux with the remaining butter and the flour, add it to the cabbage and bring to the boil.

Fold in the fried onions and tomato purée and cook for a few more minutes.

Carrot Cutlets/Carrot Bake

6 medium carrots
5 oz /150 g sieved cottage or curd cheese
3 tablespoons of semolina
8 fl oz /225 ml milk
1 egg yolk and egg white
1 teaspoon sugar
2 tablespoons breadcrumbs
2 tablespoons butter or margarine
3 tablespoons soured cream

Cook the thinly sliced carrots until tender in sufficient hot milk to cover, with a knob of butter and pinch of salt and a teaspoon of sugar[1]. Sprinkle in the semolina and cook another ten minutes. Add the egg yolk, sieved cottage or curd cheese. Mix well to a firm consistency and when cool form into cutlets; dip them in the beaten egg white and breadcrumbs and fry for a few minutes on each side until golden brown.

Alternatively smooth the mixture into a greased shallow dish or casserole, sprinkle over the breadcrumbs and dot with butter and soured cream. Bake at 350 F/Gas 4 for 25-35 minutes.

Kohlrabi in milk sauce

Use only young non-fibrous kohlrabies. They have a lot of vitamin C and it's a pity they are not always to be found at the greengrocers. Peel and slice the kohlrabies and cook in a little water with a few tablespoons of butter and salt. Serve with a white sauce and slices of hard-boiled eggs and parsley.

Kohlrabi with carrot

1 lb /450 g kohlrabies
1 lb /450 g carrots
2 tablespoons butter
1 tablespoon flour
sugar, salt, dill to taste

Clean and finely chop or grate the vegetables and put them in enough boiling milk to cover and cook gently until soft.

Make a roux of the butter and flour in a separate pan and then pour over some of the hot liquid from the vegetables and cook thoroughly.

Mix all in together and add the seasonings.

---

[1] Preferable to bake carrots with milk, etc. in oven to avoid stirring or possible burning.

Zapekanka of potatoes and vegetables

1 lb /450 g potatoes, boiled and mashed with a beaten egg
2 hard-boiled eggs, sliced
2 carrots, cut into matchsticks and cooked
2 onions, sliced and fried
2 tablespoons bread crumbs
2-3 tablespoons of soured cream
6 tablespoons of white soured cream sauce made with the following:
1 tablespoon each of flour and butter and
2 tablespoons of soured cream and seasoning

Layer up the vegetables alternately with the sliced eggs, beginning and ending with potato. Cover with the soured cream, or you can use thickened yoghurt. Bake for half an hour in a hot oven ((220 C/Gas 7).until browned. Serve with the soured cream sauce.

Potato cakes or potato bake from Belarus

There are many recipes for this from other parts of Eastern Europe and they are similar to the Swiss **rösti**.

4 large potatoes, grated, drained and squeezed as dry as possible.
2 beaten eggs
2 oz /50 g self-raising flour
1 level teaspoon salt
1 medium onion, grated

Mix the potatoes with the eggs and other ingredients and drop spoonfuls of this batter into hot fat and dry over a medium heat for 5-10 minutes a side.

Or heat some fat in a baking dish in a hot oven 220 C/Gas 7 and put spoonfuls of the mixture into this and finish baking at 230 C /Gas 8 for 15 minutes then lower the heat to 180 C /Gas 4 until the potato is crisp and well risen which takes about three quarters of an hour.

Belarusian Pampushki

These are made from a mixture of raw and cooked potato - a quarter of puréed potato to three quarters of raw grated Potato. Other ingredients are finely diced and fried ham or bacon, lightly fried onion, **smetana** and seasoning.

Squeeze out the raw potatoes as above and mix with the sieved cooked potato. Season. Form into little cakes and fill with any of the mixtures given on pages 127-128. Seal the edges carefully and drop them into boiling salted water and cook for about twenty minutes. Serve with the bacon and onion and pour over the soured cream.

Gul'bishnik - Belarusian potato dish with curd cheese.

1 lb /450 g potatoes
1 onion
2 oz /50 g butter/margarine or a small carton of soured cream
1 dessertspoon of rye or wheat flour
1 small carton of cottage cheese (well drained)
4 tablespoons milk
1 egg
salt and pepper

Boil the potatoes, mash them and keep them warm. Fry the onion in the fat, and add the flour. Cook for a few minutes. Mix in the cottage cheese. Boil the milk and beat the egg. Fold the onion sauce into the potatoes and then slowly add the hot milk and egg mixture. Bake in a moderate oven (180 C/Gas 4) until golden.

Spinach and eggs Borani - a Georgian recipe

1 lb /450 g spinach with sorrel mixed in if possible
5 small finely sliced onions, fried in butter/oil
15 fl oz /425 ml yoghurt or kefir or buttermilk
3 eggs
3 tablespoons fresh basil or 2 teaspoons dried
2 tablespoons fresh thyme
2 tablespoons fresh coriander or 1 tablespoon of crushed seeds plus parsley
1 teaspoon of cinnamon

Blanch the washed spinach for 3 minutes to soften. Blend to a purée or chop finely. Drain and season. Mix it with the fried onion and herbs. Re-heat and add the beaten eggs and cook for a few more minutes to set the eggs.

The Russian version of this is to take the cooked drained spinach and stir-fry it in 2 tablespoons of butter. Then put it into a casserole with a custard poured over, made from 3-4 eggs and 6 tablespoons of warm milk.

Vegetable Cutlets

1 lb /450 g mixed vegetables - carrots, swede, marrow, cabbage and spring onions, all finely chopped
½ pint /275 ml milk
2 oz /50 g semolina
2 eggs separated
4 tablespoons breadcrumbs
2 tablespoons butter/margarine

Put the carrots and swede into a pan with the hot milk and a tablespoon of butter, the sugar and salt; and stew gently for 15 minutes. Then add the cabbage and marrow and spring onions and cook for a further 20 minutes or until tender. Sprinkle in the semolina and cook another ten minutes, stirring all the time to avoid lumps. Remove from heat, cool slightly and add the egg yolks and salt. When the mixture is cool form into oval patties, dip in the beaten egg whites and breadcrumbs and fry until golden. Serve with a white sauce or with soured cream and chives, or any other combination of fresh herbs.

Vegetable sol'yanka

1 small head of cabbage, finely cut
2 carrots, thinly sliced
2 onions, chopped finely
2½ tablespoons of margarine or butter
2 tablespoons of tomato purée and a chopped gherkin
1 tablespoon of cider vinegar or wine vinegar and water
1 root of parsley
½ tablespoon of white flour
1 tablespoon of capers
1 tablespoon of grated cheese
2 tablespoons of breadcrumbs
seasoning, pinch of sugar

Cook the cabbage separately in as little water as possible or steam it. Fry the vegetables lightly in the butter or margarine, add the tomato purée, the gherkin and the flour. Mix the cabbage and root vegetables together with the herbs, capers and seasoning and cook altogether for another 10-15 minutes, stirring from time to time. Transfer the vegetables to a greased baking dish, cover with the breadcrumbs and cheese, dot with butter.

Vegetables baked in smetana (soured cream)

    3 small turnips
    3 carrots
    1 cauliflower, divided into florets
    1 small marrow or 2 courgettes
    1 lb /450 g new potatoes, sliced
    3 tablespoons butter, softened
    1 tablespoon flour
    5 tablespoons soured cream
    1 teaspoon sugar and salt and pepper to taste
    herbs for flavouring
    breadcrumbs
    3 tomatoes, fried, for garnish

Cook the root vegetables together, and the potatoes and cauliflower in separate pans. Add the marrow or courgettes to either pan after twenty minutes. Drain the vegetables and put them into a greased casserole lined with breadcrumbs. Mix the flour, butter, soured cream and seasoning together and pour over the vegetables. Dot with more butter.

Grated cheese may be added to make this an ideal vegetarian dish. Bake in a hot oven (220 C/Gas 7).until golden. The tomatoes are fried and served as a garnish together with freshly chopped parsley and chives. I always add an onion to this vegetable bake.

If you like garlic, squeeze a clove and mix it into the sauce.

Givech - a Moldovan vegetarian stew

    4 potatoes, sliced
    1 carrot, sliced
    3 onions, sliced in rings
    1 marrow, peeled, deseeded and sliced
    1 aubergine, sliced, salted and allowed to drain
    4 tomatoes, quartered
    4 oz /100 g green beans, lightly cooked
    4 oz /100 g peas
    4 tablespoons of oil or butter
    salt and pepper
    1 bay leaf
    dill and parsley, optional garlic

Lightly fry the root vegetables in the oil until golden brown and put them into a casserole. Pour over a thick tomato sauce and continue cooking them for ten minutes. Dry the aubergines and fry until golden and then add them to the casserole with seasoning and the remaining ingredients. Bake at 160 C /Gas 3 for fifteen minutes.

Vegetarian Sauce

15 fl oz /425 ml of stock
2 tablespoons flour
3 tablespoons butter
5 tablespoons of tomato purée
1 small carrot
parsley root or piece of parsnip
1 stick of celery
2 onions

Slice the vegetables finely and fry with the tomato purée. Add the flour which has been mixed smoothly with some of the stock, season and cook until thick and then add remainder of stock. Sieve for a perfect smooth finish. A quick way: put all the ingredients into the blender and then cook over a medium heat until the vegetables are soft.

Turnips and swedes

Both vegetables are still very popular in northern parts of Russia. Most recipes consist of the plain boiled vegetable with a fairly elaborate sauce.

For 8 oz /200 g swede or turnip
2 eggs, separated into yolks and egg whites
3 teaspoons sugar and
4 tablespoons cream.

Thicken the yolks with the cream and sugar in a double saucepan and when it has cooled slightly, add the beaten egg whites.

An easier sauce is the usual white milk sauce thinned with the hot liquid from the boiled turnips and sprinkled with parsley.

The turnips and swedes should be boiled in unsalted water. Russians are also prepared to go to the trouble of stuffing their swedes with any of the stuffing given on pages 127-128, or with rice and onions or semolina. Baking or frying them is an easier alternative. Parboil the sliced turnip/swede. Transfer to a greased casserole. Season, Pour over **smetana**, strew with breadcrumbs and bake in a moderate oven (180 C/Gas 4) until tender.

Golubtsy from Ukraine

Beetroot leaves as well as cabbage can be stuffed with rice and buckwheat or other fillings.

Scald the leaves first by plunging them for a minute or so in boiling water. Cook rice or buckwheat in the usual way (p 115), add some finely chopped onion and cabbage lightly fried in butter together with a tablespoon of tomato purée or fresh tomato and salt and pepper.

Fill the leaves with this mixture and put them into a buttered dish and cover in breadcrumbs. Dot with butter, sprinkle with lemon juice and bake at 180 C /Gas 4 for 45 minutes.

Mushrooms

The Russians, as most people know, are passionate mushroom gatherers and find infinite varieties in the woods adjoining towns and in the vast forests.

When I travelled by train to Yasnaya Polyana, Tolstoy's former country home, the railway carriage was crowded with people clutching baskets and haversacks full of mushrooms of all shapes, sizes and colours. The earthy smell in our compartment was overwhelming.

Like other families the Tolstoys liked to go out looking for mushrooms, and a mushroom gathering expedition is the scene of a hoped for proposal in Tolstoy's **Anna Karenina**. In her nervousness the girl talks only of mushrooms, her suitor is annoyed, and instead of the prepared proposal finds himself responding by asking what the difference is between white and birch mushrooms. The proposal never takes place.

There are a great number of mushroom recipes, and pickling and salting them ensures a year-round supply. We cannot hope to achieve the same flavour with our ordinary field mushrooms or the small commercially produced button kind, but a few dried field mushrooms mixed in with them, plus a dash of mushroom extract enhances the flavour.

The simplest ways are the best. Russians usually fry them, often with a little spring onion and usually they are blanched beforehand. Then a soured cream sauce may be added and the mushrooms baked in individual dishes in the oven. Grated cheese over the top is a variation.

Marinated mushrooms are easily prepared and make a pleasant and unusual **zakuski** or accompaniment to cold meat.

The proportions for the marinade are half wine or cider vinegar and water, a teaspoon of salt, and the usual flavourings of dill seed, peppercorns and a bay leaf. Flavoured vinegars *(tarragon for instance)* may be used.

Boil up the marinade, allow to cool while preparing the mushrooms. These should be of a high quality and very fresh. Discard the stalks, wipe the caps and put them in cold water and a little salt and bring to the boil and simmer for 15 minutes.

Drain well and pack into clean jars and pour over the cooled marinade. Cover the top with sunflower oil and close the lid. Keep in a cool dark place for three to four weeks.

Mushrooms in soured cream

A classic Russian dish and very simple.

Fry 1 lb /450 g mushrooms in butter, thicken with a teaspoon of flour, cook five minutes before adding the soured cream and seasoning. Allow to bubble a moment and serve with dill and parsley.

Mushrooms are often served in little individual earthenware pots and finished off in the oven.

Variations:

I   Cover with grated cheese and grill or bake.

II   Fry mushrooms and onions separately, before amalgamating them. No flour thickener is added.

III   Steam mushrooms in concentrated meal stock and butter for thirty minutes.

IV   Steam them first then fry in butter as before and finish by simmering them in soured cream.

Mushroom and cabbage sol'yanka

Cook a cabbage, finely sliced, in a little water and butter for 15 minutes then add two tablespoons of tomato purée, sugar and salt to taste, pepper, a bay leaf and a teaspoon of vinegar and continue cooking for another half hour.

Meanwhile, simmer 8 oz /225 g of mushrooms in salted water for ten minutes. Drain, chop and fry them together with a few finely sliced spring onions. Mix cabbage and mushrooms together, add a chopped gherkin and serve with fresh herbs and a tablespoon of soured cream.

SALADS

Vinaigrette dressing (or sauce)

The classic French dressing is usually for twice the amount of oil to vinegar or other acid used. It is a matter of taste how sharp you like your salads and how bland the vegetable to be dressed. Vinegars vary, but use only wine vinegar and vegetable oils purchased where you know there is a fast turn-over in sales.

I usually make a mixture of lemon juice and vinegar and blend in almost twice the amount of oil, adding caster sugar, salt and pepper to taste. Herbs and a clove of garlic are added an hour or so before use. A pinch of mustard improves the vinaigrette when using it for bland vegetables. Herbs are a good salt replacement if you cannot take salt in your diet and some Russian recipes replace it with soft berries and grated apple.

Coleslaw - Alma-Ata salad

1 lb /450 g white cabbage you need 2 tablespoons wine vinegar mixed with 2 tablespoons of water and ½ tablespoon of sugar. Vinaigrette dressing (as above).

There are several methods of preparing the cabbage for coleslaw and which makes it much more digestible and less bitter.

Method 1 — Cut cabbage finely, salt it lightly and squeeze it between your hands to soften it until the juice begins to run. Drain for a few minutes before adding a vinaigrette dressing.

Method 2 — Blanch the shredded cabbage for 2 minutes, drain, cool under cold water to refresh, drain well before adding the vinaigrette.

Method 3 — Heat some weak vinegar and an equal quantity of water and a pinch of salt and soften the shredded cabbage in this. Drain. Add only oil and sugar, not a full vinaigrette dressing.

The coleslaw is completed by adding:
1 apple, chopped
1 stick of celery, chopped
1 tablespoon of mayonnaise
1 tablespoon yoghurt
1 tablespoon top of milk.

Stir thoroughly to evenly distribute the ingredients.

Unsalted salad for one

3 oz /75 g white cabbage
1 oz /25 g each of beetroot and berries (blackberries, raspberries, blackcurrants)
1 oz /25 g soured cream
1 tablespoon or less of sugar (or 1 tablespoon of blackcurrant juice and omit sugar)

Blanch the finely shredded white cabbage and refresh in cold water as directed for preparation of red cabbage (see below) Drain the cabbage well. Grate the raw beetroot and mix all the ingredients together.

Preparation of red cabbage for salad

Chop the cabbage very finely, removing coarse stalks. Pour boiling water over, cover with a lid and let it stand for 30 minutes. Drain, refresh in cold water and drain and squeeze it well. Dress with vinaigrette sauce and leave it for about half an hour before eating.

This cabbage may also be treated as described in method No. 1 for white cabbage until the juice begins to run. The cabbage will retain its bright red colour.

Red cabbage salad is nice with apple: for 1 lb /450 g of cabbage you need 2-3 apples. Eating apples are best.

Vegetable preparation

Onions: Pour vinegar over the finely sliced rings to soften the taste. Leave for a while, drain and dry. Always use a weak vinegar solution of 3% strength or cider vinegar or half wine vinegar and water. English vinegar is usually 6% strength.

Carrots: which have to be cooked for some salad recipes are best steamed in a savoury bouillon.

Vegetables to be cooked for salads should ideally be steamed and left with plenty of 'bite'.

Russian vegetable salad — vinegret iz ovoshchei

1 cooked beetroot, sliced or cubed
4 cooked potatoes, sliced or cubed
1 cooked carrot, sliced
1 fresh apple, cubed
2 gherkins or 1 fresh cucumber, sliced and drained
4 oz /100 g sauerkraut or marinated cabbage (see recipe p 190)
2 oz /50 g spring onions or ordinary onions sliced and blanched

Toss in a vinaigrette sauce made from 2 tablespoons each of oil and weak vinegar, a teaspoon of mustard seed crushed in a mortar and a pinch of sugar, salt and pepper, and herbs such as tarragon thyme, sage, chives and parsley for variation.

This basic salad may be varied with the additions of mushrooms, cooked beans, hard-boiled eggs. Sometimes olives are added, but by this time the salad will take on an international character!

Apple and vegetable salad

A favourite Russian combination.

1 crisp lettuce heart
2 raw grated or finely cut up carrots,
2 apples
2 tomatoes
3 - 4 tablespoons of soured cream or yoghurt
½ lemon
salt and sugar

Cut the vegetables finely, quarter the tomatoes, slice the apple and tear the lettuce into neat pieces. Mix the cream with the lemon and seasoning. Toss the salad in this and decorate with parsley or dill.

Vegetable and fruit salad (vinegret iz ovoshchei i fruktov)

1 each of apple, pear, mandarin or orange
3 -4 boiled potatoes
1 cooked sliced carrot
1 cucumber, sliced and drained
2 sticks of celery, sliced finely
½ cup (5 fl oz /150 ml) of cooked peas and some chopped parsley
lettuce for garnish

Cut the cooked vegetables finely and while still warm pour over an oil and vinegar dressing. - When cool, add the remaining vegetables and the fruit, except the lettuce. Sprinkle with salt and a little sugar and add 2 - 3 tablespoons of mayonnaise thinned with lemon juice. Surround the salad with lettuce and pieces of fruit as a garnish before serving. A really delicious and refreshing salad.

Radish salad with hard-boiled egg and soured-cream or yoghurt sauce

Salt and drain the finely cut radishes. Pound a hard-boiled egg with a few tablespoons of soured cream or yoghurt and a pinch of salt and fold the dressing into the radishes. Decorate with the finely chopped egg white and feathery fennel.

Beetroot and potato salad

The proportions of vegetables are five potatoes of medium size to one medium beetroot.

Wash and dry the beetroot. Bake in a moderate oven (180 C/Gas 4) until tender. Peel off the skin and cut up into small pieces.

Add the five boiled potatoes cut into rounds. Mix in two or three tablespoons of **smetana**, or yoghurt, and season with finely chopped tarragon leaves, salt and pepper and before serving sprinkle over finely chopped hard boiled egg yolks.

Variation: use grated horseradish mixed with mayonnaise or **smetana**.

Potato salad with wine

Take five potatoes and one carrot and cook them separately, or use a pressure cooker and separators. Don't overcook. If using a pressure cooker, leave the carrot whole and cut the potatoes in halves or quarters so that they are ready together. If using whole new potatoes leave the skins on. Add a very finely chopped onion or spring onions, salt, pepper and garlic, previously pounded in a mortar with a little salt.

Pour over three or four tablespoons of dry wine and leave the warm vegetables to soak up the wine for an hour before adding a vinaigrette sauce.

Carrot and Garlic - Morkov s chesnokom

4 oz /100 g carrot
1-2 cloves of garlic, pressed and mixed with a little salt
2 tablespoons of mayonnaise or soured cream or yoghurt or a mixture
salt to taste
parsley and or other herbs
squeeze of lemon juice

Clean the carrots and grate them. Sprinkle with lemon juice. Mix in the garlic and stir in the mayonnaise and seasoning. I like to add little black pepper.

Serve with the chopped herbs: tarragon or fennel go well with carrots.

Vegetable salad with horseradish

2 oz /50 g carrot
2 oz /50 g turnip
1 oz /30 g apple
1 teaspoon grated horseradish
1 teaspoon soured cream
salt/sugar to taste

Wash the root vegetables and grate them. Add the horseradish, salt, sugar, soured cream. Stir well and serve with herbs. A little melissa[1] or lemon mint and thyme, or fresh coriander leaves enhance this salad.

Bean salads in the southern style — Georgian, Moldovan and Armenian

These are distinguished by the wide range of herbs and spice seasonings used. The basic ingredients are the cooked drained beans — green flageolets are the nicest — and whilst still warm a vinaigrette sauce is added together with lightly cooked onion.

Additions:

1. Tomatoes, basil and parsley

2. Feta cheese or Caerphilly plus parsley, crumbled and mixed with paprika

3. Pounded walnuts and coriander, seasoned with cayenne. If you have fresh coriander this is all to the good. Cloves may be added. This is a fairly thick bean salad.

---

[1] Melissa: lemon balm.

GRAINS

KASHA: *"What is kasha - it is our Mother."*

Russian saying.

The nearest translation to **kasha** is porridge and next to **shchi,** it is most dear to Russian hearts.

Whole cereal grains **(krup)** of buckwheat, wheat, oats, rye and barley are used and are milled in varying degrees of coarseness, as well as millet, maize, rice and sago. The most favoured is buckwheat which has a light nutty flavour and is very nutritious, with a high vitamin content.

Kasha is served almost daily in some form or other, either sweet or savoury, and generally appears on special and festive occasions. It can make a light meal on its own or, like Italian pasta, be the basis for a main savoury dish.

It can take the place of potatoes and is delicious mixed with mushrooms or onions, **tvorog** *(curd cheese)* soured cream, or with nuts and herbs and fruit.

Kasha is used extensively in a multitude of stuffings and forcemeats for the various **pirozhki**[1] which accompany many Russian dishes. There seems to be almost as much discussion over ways of cooking buckwheat kasha as there is over rice.

Some recipes recommend lightly roasting the buckwheat grains in a dry frying pan for a few minutes until they start popping and become a light golden colour. They should on no account become dark brown. This process isn't strictly necessary and lowers the nutritional content somewhat.

A satisfactory way of cooking buckwheat kasha is to cook it initially in boiling water on the stove on a low heat until the surface water has gone. Then transfer it to an oven dish with as much butter as you wish and let it steam under foil in the oven.

Kasha is a candidate for hay-box cookery or the slow-cooker. An alterative is to use a simmer mat. Electric stoves are more easily regulated but even so care has to be taken to see that the buckwheat doesn't burn or stick.

The basic rule is not to overcook it and make it too soft. It should not become mushy.

---

[1] Pirozhki: baked or fried stuffed buns.

114

Buckwheat kasha

General proportions for this are **three** parts water to **one** of buckwheat.

Easy measurements for kasha with butter:

1 cup (10 fl oz /275 ml) buckwheat
3 cups(30 fl oz /850 ml) water
1 teaspoon salt
2 tablespoons butter

Method 1 — Boil the water and salt. Tip in the buckwheat, stirring until it comes back to the boil. Lower the heat and cook until it thickens - 15-20 minutes. Add the butter, cover and leave to stand in a warm place or put it in a low oven (140 C/Gas 1).

Some recipes recommend leaving it for a few hours to develop the flavour but I usually eat mine straight away. It is, however, very easily re-heated and even more tasty the next day so if you are as fond of buckwheat as I am it is worth doubling the recipe.

Method 2 – Put the groats in a dry pan over a low heat and stir them until the grains start popping. Then proceed as above.

Milk buckwheat porridge

18 fl oz /500 ml of milk
2½ oz /75 g buckwheat.

Boil the milk, add the buckwheat and a pinch salt. Cover and cook over a low heat *(use a simmer mat as it catches easily)* or bake in the oven 180 C /Gas 4 for about 40 minutes. You can also make this with buckwheat flour obtained by grinding the grains in a coffee grinder.

Savoury buckwheat kasha

Cook as for buckwheat kasha with butter and add crisply fried chopped bacon and fried onion to the basic recipe.

Buckwheat with liver

Fry a finely chopped onion
Mix with 5 oz /150 g cooked minced liver
1 tablespoon of butter.

Season and then mix with the hot cooked buckwheat kasha.

Buckwheat groats

5 oz /150 g buckwheat groats
1 raw egg
1 oz /30 g butter

Beat the egg lightly and fork it into the buckwheat and toast it lightly in a pan over moderate heat. Add the butter and a little salt and then pour on 11 fl oz /300 ml of boiling water. Simmer for 20 minutes. Watch it carefully as all the liquid will evaporate.

Smolensk kasha with parsnips

5 oz /140 g fine buckwheat (the grains can be crushed in a coffee mill)
35 fl oz /1 litre of water
2 medium size onions
2 parsnips, finely cut into julienne strips
2-3 tablespoons of freshly chopped parsley
1 teaspoon salt
½ teaspoon black pepper
2 tablespoons softened butter
4 tablespoons soured cream

Boil the salted water, put in the whole onions and the finely cut parsnips and cook for five minutes on medium heat. Then add the buckwheat in a fine stream and cook over a low heat, stirring until it thickens. Discard the onion, remove the pan from the heat and add the pepper, parsley, soured cream and butter. Add more salt to taste and stand the covered pan in a warm place for 15 minutes to steam. If convenient put it in a low oven (140 C/Gas 1).

Buckwheat cakes

7 oz /200 g buckwheat
13 fl oz /375 ml water
4 oz /100 g cottage cheese, strained and sieved
4 oz /100 g fresh breadcrumbs or sufficient dried breadcrumbs to coat the cakes
2 eggs
1 teaspoon sugar
½ teaspoon salt
2 tablespoons of softened butter

Cook the buckwheat as described on page 115. When the mixture is cooled and thick add the cheese, eggs and sugar and mix well. The mixture needs to be firm. Form into cakes, roll in the breadcrumbs and fry until golden. These may be served with **borshch** and **rassol'nik**, or as breakfast cakes with soured cream. A convenient alternative method is to smooth the mixture into a greased dish and bake with the crumbs and soured cream spread on top.

Barley flake cake

6 oz /175 g barley flakes
27 fl oz /775 ml water
6 oz /175 g cottage cheese, strained and sieved
1 dessertspoon of sugar
1 egg
6 tablespoons of fresh breadcrumbs
3-4 tablespoons of butter for frying

Boil the barley in salted water. When it starts to thicken, lower the heat and continue to cook it on a simmer mat or in a double saucepan for half an hour. Add the remaining ingredients and cook as described above. These are also nice with a fruit sauce.

Oat kasha

The Scots have always made their oat porridge with water and served the milk *(if used)* separately. This is the healthiest way of eating porridge; if it is cooked in milk valuable amino-acids combine with the milk sugar and prevent assimilation.

In old Rus[1] a wedding feast was called a **kasha** and was usually cooked at the bride's home. Then only wheat, barley, millet or rye grains were used for kasha and usually mixed with honey.

Rice kasha came later in the 17th century and was called 'saracen' rice from its eastern derivation. **Grechnaya kasha** (Greek buckwheat kasha) shows its Byzantine connection.

An old Russian book on home management and cooking called **Domostroi** tells that a peasant's diet in the 16th century consisted mainly of **kasha** and **shchi**. Sometimes poppy seed juice was added to a thick kasha of peas and cabbage. It was often mixed with oat flour and maybe salt herring.

Left-over **oat kasha** could also be turned into successful oat cakes with the addition of flour.

---

[1] Rus: A medieval state. Today, its territory is divided between Russia, Ukraine and Belarus.

Millet - Psheno/proso

One of Rimsky-Korsakov's interests was gathering Russian folk tales from the north. Millet figured so often in these tales and was for so long a basic agricultural staple that the composer incorporated the 'millet chorus' in his opera **Snegurochka** *(Snow Maiden)* — **"A my proso seyali, seyali"** — "and we sowed and we sowed millet", sung by the men, and the women feelingly reply "and we pound it and we pound it......."

I use millet flakes rather than the grains in cooking. I find these useful also as a substitute for breadcrumbs in frying. It is rich in B vitamins and has a delightful nutty texture and deserves to be used more often for puddings, cakes and in soups. Buy millet in small quantities. If it develops a bitter taste wash it in several changes of cold water.

20 fl oz /575 ml boiling water
11 oz /300 g millet flakes
salt to taste

Simmer together until the mixture thickens - about 15 minutes. It needs to be stirred fairly continuously or cooked in a double cooker.

An alternative recipe using millet grains:

Fill a saucepan two thirds full of boiling water, sprinkle in the grains and cook for 15 minutes. Then pour off the water, cover, and leave the millet kasha for three quarters of an hour. Then add butter or milk to taste.

Pshennik - millet pudding

3½ oz /100 g millet flakes
1 pint /575 ml milk
2 eggs
1 tablespoon of butter or soured cream
½ teaspoon salt

When the millet porridge has cooled slightly add any other given ingredients such as egg yolks, sugar, lemon rind, vanilla, sultanas or nuts, and finally fold in the beaten egg whites. Bake in a moderate oven 180 C /Gas 4.

Other recipes offer prunes with millet porridge

Use three times the volume of water to millet grains, cook as usual and add chopped cooked prunes and butter.

For curd cheese millet pudding:

> 3 oz /75 g millet grains
> 5 fl oz /150 ml water
> 2 oz /50 g curd cheese
> sugar and butter to taste

Partially cook the millet in salted water, add the other ingredients and cook until soft. Serve milk, yoghurt or kefir separately.

Plov - Rice (Pilau)

For those who find rice cookery tricky, use 'Uncle Ben's' rice or a similar converted product.

The Georgians, and Azerbaijanis soak their rice overnight, drain it and allow it to dry.

Alternatively, wash rice over and over again in a bowl of running water until it runs clear. Drain for half an hour.

To ensure separated grains, **either:** toss it lightly in some hot oil in a pan **or** add 1 teaspoon of oil to the cooking water.

Cook in boiling salted water, until grains are *al dente* – neither hard nor mushy.

There are many recipes for **Plov** or Pilau, the rice dish popular throughout the Middle East.

Any differences between Tatar, Arabian and Turkish rice dishes lie in the dryness or moistness of the rice and the size and amount of meat or fish included. Its popularity was spread by Turco-Tatar tribes, carried into Byzantium and the Greek peninsula, the Crimea, and South Russia.

Plov Ararat - a sweet rice dish

For this use either plain boiled rice with well separated grains *(cooked according to directions above)* or make a usual milk rice pudding with round grain rice:

**1 pint /575 ml milk
2 tablespoons of pudding rice, well washed alternately under hot and cold water,
1 tablespoon of sugar
a dash of vanilla.**

Boil the milk and pour it over the other ingredients, stir well and bake in a well buttered dish in the oven at 180 C/ Gas 4 until well thickened. Stir from time to time.

Peel 3 large cooking apples and 3 quinces *(if available - if not use more apple)*. Fry these in 2-3 tablespoons of butter with a handful of raisins, previously plumped up in hot water and drained. Turn out the heat and pour a tablespoon of brandy over the apples. Remove to a serving dish.

Fry any nuts or other fruit and fruit juices in the butter - add more as necessary. Pour this fruit and nut sauce over the rice, which should be mounded up, and arrange the brandied apples around the base of the 'mountain'. Choose fruit, herbs and spice flavourings from the following which are used freely in Caucasian style **plov.**

Fruit: approximately 4 oz /100 g of sharp plums, soaked cooked prunes and apricots, fresh melon, morello cherries

Nuts: cooked or raw chestnuts and chopped almonds, or walnuts with peppers and aubergines

Other ingredients for mixed sweet/savoury **plov** may be carrots, spring onions and spinach/sorrel **(sabza kourma plov).**

When using plain boiled rice add pomegranate juice and their seeds or lemon and grapefruit juice to fold into the rice. Herbs used for savoury and sweet **plov** in the Caucasus are mint, tarragon, thyme. Saffron is used to colour the rice - soak it in a little boiled water and use the liquid and the precious filaments.

For savoury **plov** from Azerbaijan use plain boiled saffron rice with cooked chicken, meat, fish or coddled eggs and omit the brandied apples.

PASTA

Noodles and dumplings, made from a flour and egg mixture were widely used in Russia before the advent of the potato and the many variations and refinements on this theme were largely spread by Tatar and Armenian traders who settled along the great rivers.

There-are many ways to make your own pasta, usually quite simple if you just need noodles (Ukrainian **lokshchina**) and **pel'meni** *(very similar to ravioli).* (p 124)

Ukraine has a large number of pasta and noodle dishes, Gogol's favourite food, and when abroad he was forever pestering his mother and sister to send him recipes of all kinds so that he could prepare them. He spent many years in Rome where he wrote most of the chapters of **Dead Souls**, often sitting in noisy cafes to do so. Italy was his favourite 'eating country' and on his return to Russia he liked to serve his guests various pasta dishes which he would personally supervise and often prepare himself.

Ukrainian galushki, vareniki, vatrushki, etc. are essentially noodle/dumpling mixtures of flour, egg and/or water, with soured cream and a little butter added for richer versions.

Unleavened dough is mainly used for making Russian **Pel'meni** and Ukrainian **vareniki**.

Yeast doughs are kept for **Olad'i**, some savoury **vatrushki**, all kinds of little pies and an assortment of fried pastries bearing delightful names such as **pyshki, ponchiki** and **ushki** *(little ears).*

There are other dumpling mixtures - **galushki, pampushki** and **kletski**.

Fillings for these noodle delights: see pages 127-128.

Pasta and Noodle Doughs

Ukrainian galushki

14 oz /400 g flour
4 fl oz /100 ml water mixed with a level teaspoon of salt
4 oz /700 g butter, softened
2 eggs, beaten
1 small carton of soured cream for serving

Sift the flour, make a well in the centre, pour in the water, add the eggs and butter mixed together. Make a fairly slack dough. Roll out ⅛ inch /3 mm thick or form into small balls. To cook the **galushki** drop them into gently boiling salted water and when they are ready they float to the surface. This takes about 10 minutes. Drain them and finish them off by tossing them in hot butter over a low heat to colour them slightly. Serve with soured cream. The Belarusian version often adds crisply fried bacon and onions.

Variations are achieved by the use of herbs and spices. A favourite combination is caraway seed with fried onion.

Vatrushki – pasta 'envelopes'

12 oz /350 g rye flour
5 fl oz /150 ml soured cream
1 large egg
½ teaspoon bicarbonate of soda
1 flat teaspoon of salt

Sift the flour with the bicarbonate of soda and the salt; beat the egg lightly and mix into the flour with the cream. The mixture should be firm enough to roll out. Cut into rounds and stuff with the following:

7 oz /200 g tvorog (curd cheese or sieved cottage cheese)
2 oz /50 g sugar
1 large egg for binding the stuffing
1 tablespoon of flour

To make the dough particularly light add two boiled, mashed potatoes which should be very dry. Mash them when they are hot to avoid lumps.

Dot with butter and bake at 190-200 C /Gas 5-6.

Potato vatrushki

5 oz /150 g potato
1 flat tablespoon flour
½ oz /15 g butter or 20 g smetana (approx 2 tablespoons)
1/2 egg

The potatoes are boiled in their jackets, dried, peeled and mashed and then the flour and **smetana** added together with a little egg to bind. Bake in a moderately hot oven until well browned (190-200 C /Gas 5- 6). Stuff them with the above filling or with a mushroom or carrot filling or any others selected from the list for pie fillings (pp 127-128).

Ukrainian vatrushki usually have a cottage cheese or sweet fruit filling.

Vatrushki made with yeast dough

11 oz /300 g flour
2 oz /50 g butter/margarine
1 oz /10 g yeast
1 tablespoon sugar (increase this amount if you want them as a sweet tea bun)
2 eggs
approx. 5 fl oz /150 ml water or milk
½ teaspoon salt

Make a yeast dough (p 182). Leave to rise, knead and form into a dozen rolls. Leave to rise again. Make an indentation in each and put in a curd cheese filling (p 128) or thick jam or fruit mixture. Push the sides over well to almost enclose the filling. Brush with beaten egg and bake for ten to fifteen minutes in a hot oven 220 C /Gas 7.

Vareniki from Ukraine

8 oz /225 g flour
6-7 tablespoons water
1 teaspoon salt
1 egg yolk
optional but recommended additions :
4 oz /100 g cold mashed potato
1 tablespoon fat

Sift the flour and salt, add the well dried potato, fat and egg yolk and water to make a fairly soft dough. Do not knead. Cover with cling foil and leave ten minutes.

Roll the dough very thinly and cut into rounds. Seal the **vareniki** well after filling. Keep them covered until ready for cooking in boiling salted water, dropping in a few at a time. They will puff up when they are ready. Drain and serve with melted butter.

Yaroslavl sochni with cottage cheese

Make a yeast dough (p 182), with the addition of 2 oz /50 g butter. Roll it out, cut into small squares and bake in a hot oven (220 C/Gas 7) until slightly coloured but not cooked. Take them out and spread half of them with well drained curd cheese and a teaspoonful of **smetana**. Clap them together in pairs, cover with butter and breadcrumbs and finish baking in a moderate oven 220 C /Gas 4.

Archangel sochni are identical but stuffed with a savoury meat filling of lamb, hard-boiled egg, fried onion, bacon and enough milk to make a juicy gravy. (**Sochni** *means juicy/ succulent, as its sound suggests.*)

Siberian pyshki — *yeast raised*

    8 oz /225 g flour
    ¾ oz /20 g yeast
    2 tablespoons sugar
    1 oz /25 g butter
    l egg
    salt
    3 fl oz /75 ml milk

These are little dough buns, baked and then spread with butter and soured cream and returned to the oven to brown; similar to **shanezhki** (p 182). Bake at 200 C /Gas 6.

Pel'meni

    12 oz /350 g flour
    1 egg
    7-8 tablespoons water or milk or a mixture
    salt

Make a fairly thick dough, mixing the liquid into the flour slowly then adding the egg and salt *(alternatively, use a blender to mix all ingredients in one go)*. Cover and put the batter aside for half an hour to rest. Roll out fairly thinly as if making pastry and cut into small circles about 2 inches /5 cm across.

See list of fillings for transforming **pel'meni** into:

- Azerbaijani **dyushpara**

- Turkmenian **manty**

- Russian **nalistniki.**

Oat flour kletski - dumplings

5 oz /140 g fine oat flour
4½ fl oz /130 ml water to make a porridge
1 egg
5 fl oz /125 ml milk
½ teaspoon salt

Cook the oats in the cold water and bring it up to the boil, stirring all the time. Add the lightly beaten egg and season. Form the dough into oval shaped quite small dumplings, and cook them in the hot milk for 8-10 minutes. These are served together with the milk in which they were boiled.

Potato kletski

3 potatoes
3-4 tablespoons flour
2 eggs (separated)

Wash and boil the potatoes in their jackets; peel and mash them. Add the flour, raw egg yolks and mix well. Beat the egg whites and fold in. Drop them into the hot bouillon and they will rise to the surface when ready.

Turkmenian manty — stuffed with fish — Balyk byorek

The dough - two versions: (note that second one makes twice as much)

Version 1:

> **5½ oz /160 g flour**
> **2-3 tablespoons water**

Version 2:

> **11 oz /300 g flour**
> **2 eggs**
> **4-5 fl oz /140 ml whey from cottage cheese drainings, yoghurt or kefir**
> **½ teaspoon salt**

In either case, make a firm dough, and roll out thinly.

The filling

> **1 lb /450 g raw fish cut into small pieces (or lightly steamed and flaked fish)**
> **1 egg yolk**
> **2 onions finely grated**
> **½ teaspoon black pepper**
> **pinch cayenne pepper**
> **a few crushed cardamom seeds**
> **2 tablespoons dill and parsley**
> **½ tablespoon of fennel and a pinch of saffron (optional)**

Mix the ingredients well and fill the thinly rolled out **manty** with teaspoonfuls of the mixture.

FILLINGS - for Vatrushki, pies, etc.

One — Rice/Sago/Buckwheat with egg

1 cup (10 fl oz /275 ml) of cooked rice, buckwheat or sago
3 hard-boiled eggs, mashed and mixed with 2 tablespoons of butter and flavoured with dill. Season to taste.

Additions may be 2-3 chopped spring onions and/or chopped mushrooms

Two — Cooked millet stuffing with raisins

1 cup(10 fl oz /275 ml) cooked millet
Sugar to taste
7 oz /200 g raisins plumped up in boiling water
1-2 tablespoons of butter

Mix all the ingredients smoothly together.

Three — Carrot filling

Cook 1 lb /450 g carrots, adding a little sugar and butter at the end of the cooking time. Mash and season them. Mash 3 hard-boiled eggs with 2 tablespoons butter and mix with the carrots.

Four —Turnip filling with soured cream

Cut up and blanch 1 lb /450 g of turnips for 5 minutes. Drain and then cook them in boiling water until tender. Drain again and dry them over a low heat or in a low oven (140 C/Gas 1). They will become dark and sweet. Mash or blend them and add a raw beaten egg, 1 tablespoon of butter, 1-2 tablespoons soured cream and salt to taste.

Five — Mushroom filling

1 lb /450 g mushrooms
1 tablespoon butter
1 medium onion, finely chopped
4 tablespoons smetana (soured cream)

Boil up the mushrooms briefly in a little water, Drain and fry them in the butter with the onion. Add the soured cream and salt. Cover and simmer 10 minutes and then add parsley and dill to taste. Cool before using.

Six — Curd/cottage cheese filling

1 lb /450 g cottage or curd cheese sieved or use a soft cheese to save time.
2-3 tablespoons sugar
1 tablespoon butter
1 egg
salt to taste

Mix all the ingredients together. Vanilla, raisins or grated lemon may be added for variation.

Seven — Buckwheat and kidney/and/or liver

½ lb /225 g kidney or liver
1 cup (10 fl oz /275 ml) of buckwheat porridge (cooked as per recipe p 115)
2 tablespoons butter
2 hard-boiled eggs, mashed
1 onion

Soak the kidneys or liver well *(overnight in salted water or milk is ideal to get rid of the bitter taste)*. Cook them gently in the butter, put through the mincer or blend in a blender with the butter and egg.

PASTRY & PIES

Kulebyaka – a classic Russian pie

This is Russia's classic pie (**pirog** – stemming from the old word **pir**, a feast) and is traditionally served for special occasions. In Chekhov's **Three Sisters** such a pie is baked for Irina's name day and exhibited to the assembled guests before the meal. I first encountered **kulebyaka** in 1949 aboard a Soviet ship bound for Leningrad[1]. It was my first taste of Russian cooking and a splendid introduction. It was made with traditional yeast dough but it can be made with ordinary short or flaky pastry. Its shape used to be narrow and high to accommodate the three or four varied layers of different stuffings, which can be rice/buckwheat, meat or fish, hard boiled eggs and mushrooms, and often combinations. Most cooks, however, find a roll shape easier to handle. The drier ingredients are at the bottom and sides.

Modern cookbooks give a few short cuts, and a very satisfactory pie can be made with frozen ready-made pastry. Put the rolled out pastry on a floured tea towel and layer up the fillings, starting with the driest ingredients.

The proper way to make **kulebyaka** is to line them with very thin cooked bliny (recipe p 141) to contain the juices and layers intact. Omitting the bliny lining saves time, but increases the risk of leakage.

The main points to bear in mind to produce an authentic Russian pie is that the dough should have some slight souring agent such as sour milk, buttermilk, **smetana** or beer. An old-style pie would have a bran sour-dough starter left to ferment overnight.

Ingredients for the pastry vary according to the stuffing and occasion. A pie for Lent would have had oil instead of butter. The fillings for **kulebyaka** are always cooked or partially cooked, except for fish which are just briefly coloured in a little hot butter.

Vyaziga - the dried spinal cord of fish such as the sturgeon is considered essential for a genuine kulebyaka, but is difficult to get here. Some cooks use sago and anchovy mixed as a substitute but I do without.

---

[1] now St. Petersburg.

Kulebyaka pastry - preparing and baking

Choice of pastry, depending on whether you like sugar added or otherwise:

Version 1:
- 21 oz /600 g strong plain flour
- 9 fl oz /250 ml warm boiled milk
- 7 oz /200 g butter
- 1 oz /25 g yeast
- 3 egg yolks
- 1 teaspoon salt

Version 2:
- 18 oz /500 g strong plain flour
- 7 fl oz /200 ml warm boiled milk
- 4-5 oz /125 g butter
- 1 oz /25 g yeast
- 2 egg yolks
- ½ teaspoon salt
- 1 tablespoon sugar

Making the yeast dough: follow the method for Siberian pie on page 132

Fillings: choose from those listed, pages 133 - 134.

After filling the pastry, seal the edges with cold water or egg white and turn it over, with the aid of a floured tea towel, onto a greased baking tray so that the seamed side is on the bottom.

I always place greased greaseproof paper on the baking tin.

Leave the pie to let the yeast dough rise again at this stage. Make a few vents in the top of the pie and brush it all over with the egg whites.

Decorate the pie with twisted strips of pastry cut into leaves etc. and according to your artistic abilities! Old style Russian decorations resembled wood-cuts.

Bake at 220 C /Gas 7 for 35-40 minutes. If it colours too quickly cover with a wet piece of greaseproof paper. Test with a clean skewer to make sure the bottom layer of dough is dry. If not, lower the heat to 150 C /Gas 1-2.

A yeast dough should not get hard, so on removing it from the oven, cover the pie with a tea towel.

Serve the pie with appropriate fish, chicken or meat bouillon.

Burkanu pardeveis or morkovnik - A Latvian vegetarian 'pizza'

Dough base

8 oz /225 g flour
6 tablespoons butter
3 tablespoons sugar
4-5 fl oz /125 ml smetana
½ oz /15 g yeast
1 egg

Filling

4 medium carrots, cooked and finely chopped
4 fl oz /125 ml soured cream (smetana) (warmed)
4 oz /100 g sugar
1 hard-boiled finely chopped egg
1 beaten raw egg for binding
3 tablespoons flour
3 tablespoons dried lemon and or zest of lemon

Mix the carrots, sugar, **smetana**, the hard-boiled egg and lemon peel. Leave for the flavours to absorb, before adding the raw egg.

Meanwhile, mix the yeast with the soured cream and the sugar. Let it froth. Rub the fat into the flour, pour in the yeast mixture and add the beaten egg.

The dough should not be too firm, so add a few tablespoons of warm milk if necessary. Leave to rise. Knock back and divide into small balls and roll out to the size of a saucer.

Cover with the carrot filling, brush with a little oil and keep them in a warm place to rise again.

Bake 15-20 minutes in a hot oven 200 C /Gas 6. This could be baked in one large pizza. Don't make the dough bases too thick.

For an Armenian vegetarian pizza recipe, see also page 27.

Siberian pie dough for Siberian Shangi

14 oz /400 g flour
7 fl oz /200 ml warm water or milk (boil and cool the milk)
1 tablespoon sugar
½ oz /15 g yeast
2-3 eggs, beaten
½ teaspoon salt
3 tablespoons softened butter

Making the dough

Sift the flour, make a well in it and crumble in the yeast with 5 fl oz /150 ml of the liquid. Leave to bubble for ten or fifteen minutes before adding the rest of the ingredients. Knead well.

To make the **Siberian fish pie**, divide the dough into two and leave to rise until doubled. Then roll out one half of the dough ½ inch /1 cm thick. Sprinkle lightly with flour and put it on a greased baking sheet. Layer up with the following fish and onion filling, seasoning well between layers.

1 lb /450 g raw white fish fillets (skinned and boned)
1 medium size finely sliced, lightly fried onion
salt and pepper
1-2 tablespoons butter
fennel (optional)

Dot the filling with the butter, roll out the second half of dough and cover the filling, sealing the edges well. Leave to rise for half an hour then bake in a hot to very hot oven 220-230 C /Gas 7-8 for 35-50 minutes.

I found this to be an excellent all round yeast dough which can be used for any number of savoury pies, using the fillings described pages 133 - 134. With the addition of more sugar and fat and a few raisins the dough can also be used for tea buns.

Savoury pie fillings

Meat filling
    1 lb /450 g meat
    2 tablespoons softened butter
    2 eggs, hard-boiled & sliced
    1 large onion, chopped
    dill or parsley
    1-2 tablespoons of well reduced jellied stock OR
    a few small chips of ice to provide moisture

Half cook the meat, chop finely and fry lightly with onion. Season and add grated nutmeg and hard boiled eggs. A few chopped pine nuts or crushed hazelnuts make an interesting variation, as well as different herbs according to the time of year.

Liver and buckwheat filling
    12 oz /350 g liver
    1 cup (10 fl oz /275 ml) of cooked buckwheat
    2-3 tablespoons butter
    3 eggs, hard-boiled
    2 large chopped onions

Soak the liver in salted or vinegar water and then in milk and leave overnight. Cut up, removing membranes and skin, fry in butter with onion. The Russians would normally put this through the mincer but it is not really necessary Season the liver. Mix with the cooked buckwheat (recipe p 115) and chopped hard-boiled eggs.

Chicken filling
Poach the chicken until partially cooked. Remove the breast and keep whole. Finish cooking the remainder until just tender and the flesh can be eased from the bone without difficulty. Cut this into small pieces. Make a well seasoned white sauce thinned with stock and add herbs of choice.

Cabbage filling

Three ways of preparing the cabbage:

One — Cut it finely, salt it and allow it to drain for an hour. Then press out the juice with a small plate, add the butter and finely chopped egg and a chopped fried onion and parsley

Two — Lightly steam shredded cabbage until just soft, drain and then stir-fry with the chopped onion and parsley. Add seasoning and chopped hard-boiled eggs.

Three— Blanch the chopped cabbage and refresh in cold water. Drain, and then proceed as above. A little sugar may be added with the seasoning. For 1 cabbage, take 3-4 hard-boiled eggs and 3 tablespoons of butter and 2 onions.

Mushroom filling

1 lb /450 g mushrooms
1 grated onion
2-3 tablespoons smetana (soured cream)

Cook the mushrooms lightly in salted water, then slice and fry them in butter with the onion. Add the soured cream. Season and simmer for ten minutes. Add fresh green herbs. Cool before using.

Carrot filling

1 lb /450 g finely cut carrots
3 hard-boiled eggs, finely chopped
2 tablespoons butter. Seasoning and a pinch of sugar.

Cook the carrots in very little water (about 5 fl oz /150 ml) and add a tablespoon of butter. Cover and simmer until soft. Mash and season them and add the sugar, remaining butter and finely chopped egg.

Pumpkin filling is done the same way

Turnip filling

1 turnip
1 egg (not hard boiled this time)
1 tablespoon softened butter
2 tablespoons soured cream
Seasoning

Slice the peeled turnip and cook in boiling water for 3-5 minutes. Strain off the water and finish cooking the turnip in freshly boiled water until soft. Drain, cover it and put in a warm airing cupboard for 4-5 hours. This darkens and sweetens it. Then mash or mince it, add the soured cream, egg and butter and seasoning. It is better to prepare this filling a day before.

Spinach filling

Make a fairly dry purée, add a tablespoon of butter, a chopped hardboiled egg and cream or cottage cheese and some grated onion and plenty of pepper and salt.

Soft pastry suitable for fruit pies

There are numerous Russian pastry recipes. The following are non-yeast based shortcrust suitable for most pies and open tarts.

Apple tart

14 oz /400 g self-raising flour
8 oz /225 g unsalted butter
5 oz /150 g caster sugar (3 oz /75 g for cooking apples and 2 oz /50 g for pastry)
1 egg yolk
2½ tablespoons milk
4 lb /1¾ kg tart Bramley apples, peeled & sliced
juice of half a lemon

Add the 3 oz /75 g caster sugar and the lemon juice. Cook until the apples become fairly soft. Cool completely in a colander and drain. Make your pastry in the usual way and divide into two.

Roll out and line a quiche dish *(well greased)* with one half of the pastry and bake blind in a very hot oven 230 C /Gas 8 for 5 minutes until just set. This minimises the chance of a soggy bottom to the tart.

Fill the shell with the cooled apples & cover with the other half of the pastry. Brush with a little milk or egg. Bake in hot oven (200 C/Gas 6) for 15 minutes. Reduce heat to 180 C /Gas 4 for another 15 minutes. Reduce again to 140 C /Gas 1 for the final 30 minutes.

This method of baking ensures a tender yet firm crust both top and bottom. A state greatly to be desired!

Fast apple pie - Tatar style

2 lb /1 kg apples
3-4 eggs
11 oz /300 g sugar
7 oz /200 g butter (softened)
2 tablespoons bread crumbs
11 - 12 oz /300 - 350 g flour
Pinch of salt
lemon juice (optional)

Peel and core the apples. Cut into four, then slice very finely and evenly. Put them straight into cold salted water while you make the pastry. Add a little lemon juice if convenient.

Beat the eggs, add the sugar, salt, butter and beat well. Sift in the flour and then fold in the drained apples, stirring well to distribute them. Grease a loose bottomed cake tin and cover with breadcrumbs.

Put in the mixture and then put the cake tin over a low heat on the stove for three to four minutes before putting the cake into a hot oven 220 C /Gas 7 to finish baking – approximately three quarters of an hour.

Lower the heat after 20 minutes (180 C /Gas 4).

Apple pie with a yeast dough

Make the dough as for 'Siberian shanezhki' (p 182)

For the filling you need:

2 large Bramley or cooking apples
2 oz /50 g sugar
5 fl. oz /150 g of soured cream
8 crushed biscuits (digestive are nice)

Roll out the dough to line a greased pie or quiche dish. Put in the apples cut as above. Cover with the sugar and soured cream and sprinkle over the biscuits. Leave to rise 20 minutes, then bake in a moderate oven 15-20 minutes, 180 C /Gas 4.

Quick 'flaky' pastry for pies

1 lb /450 g plain flour
10 oz /275 g butter or hard margarine
6 fl oz /175 ml boiling water

Cut the butter into small pieces. Put into a mixing bowl and pour over the boiling water. Stir well until the fat has dissolved. Add the flour and mix to a dough. This needs to be left overnight in a cold place, ideally the refrigerator. Bake at a high temperature 220 C /Gas 7.

Cream cheese pastry

This is a very rich pastry for special occasions.

12 oz /350 g softened butter/margarine
12 oz /350 g cream cheese
2 egg yolk
12 oz /350 g self-raising flour
½ teaspoon salt

Cream the butter and cheese and stir in the egg yolks. Add the flour and salt and mix to a smooth dough. Wrap in cling film and leave it to rest in the refrigerator for half an hour before using.

Bake at 200 C /Gas 6. Lower heat after 10 minutes to 180 C /Gas 4.

Crisp pastry for open tarts

8 oz /225 g flour
4 oz /100 g butter
1 egg
pinch of salt
sufficient water to make a firm dough

Leave it in the refrigerator for half an hour at least before using. I find it useful to roll out this pastry on a floured tea-towel as it can easily break.

Bake at 200 C /Gas 6. Lower heat after 10 minutes to 180 C /Gas 4.

> Russian cookbook tips are often marked **'Babushkiny sekrety'** (Grandmother's secrets).
> E.g.:   *"sprinkle salt on the bottom of the pie dish and the pastry won't burn".*

Rye flour pastry from Karelia

Two versions to choose from:

Version 1:	Version 2:
6 oz /175g rye flour	**4 oz /100 g rye flour**
1½ oz /40 g strong white flour	**1½ oz 40 g strong white flour**
4 fl oz /700 ml water	**2-4 tablespoons water**
3 tablespoons oil	**4 oz /100 g butter**
1 teaspoon salt	

Bake either of the above at 200 C /Gas 6. Lower heat after 10 minutes to 180 C /Gas 4.

Ukrainian pastry with vodka or rum

1 lb /450 g flour (can be self-raising or plain, depending on whether you like a soft or crisp pastry)
7 oz /200 g butter/margarine
1 tablespoon sugar (optional)
½ teaspoon salt
2 tablespoons of vodka/brandy/rum

Bake at 200 C /Gas 6. Lower heat after 10 minutes to 180 C /Gas 4.

Soured cream pastry

1 lb /450 g flour
9 fl oz /250 ml soured cream
3 tablespoons butter
2 eggs
1 tablespoon sugar
½ teaspoon salt

Bake at 200 C /Gas 6. Lower heat after 10 minutes to 180 C /Gas 4.

Pastry made with oil

A 'health' pastry and very easy to make. It also freezes well. It would be made without the milk for Lenten[1] dishes.

4 tablespoons sunflower or other oil
2-3 tablespoons cold top of the milk or water
6 oz /175 g flour
¾ teaspoon salt

Sift the flour and salt together. Pour in the liquids separately, then mix and form into a ball. Roll out between two sheets of waxed paper. A damp table will prevent it slipping as you roll.

Peel off the top paper and ease the pastry into the pie dish.

Bake in a hot oven 220 C /Gas 7 for only 10 minutes.

---

[1] Lenten dishes: Food prepared during Lent.

Simple yeast raised dough

For open fruit tarts where the fruit is previously cooked.

5 oz /150 g plain flour
½ oz /15 g yeast /2 level teaspoons dried yeast, dissolved in a little tepid water
2 oz /50 g softened butter
egg
salt

Mix the butter into the flour, add a pinch of salt, the whole egg and the yeast mixture. Thoroughly mix the ingredients and add a little milk if necessary.

Leave to rise in a warm place for 2 hours. Knock back, knead again and then press the dough into a greased 8 inch /20 cm pie or flan dish.

Filling

1½-2 lb /675-900 g fruit
6 oz /150 g sugar
1 tablespoon of water
butter (if using apples)
vanilla drops (optional)

If using apples, peel, core and slice them and cook them in butter, sugar and very little water. I also like to add a few drops of vanilla.

Fill the pastry with the fruit but not too much juice and put the flan on a baking sheet.

Bake in a moderate oven 180 C/Gas 4 for thirty-five to forty minutes.

BLINY - Pancakes

Russian literature is full of **bliny**[1] anecdotes. These yeast-raised pancakes were consumed in great numbers at Maslenitsa, the week before Lent. They are still eaten by the dozen and filled with savoury or sweet mixtures.

Bliny with soured cream or filled with caviar is one of my earliest Moscow memories, and the following are light, lacy pancakes with a nutty flavour suitable for most fillings.

Suggested fillings

Bliny fillings usually combine soured cream with a range of ingredients including smoked salmon, smoked cod's roe, crispy fried bacon and chopped spring onions.

Cream cheese with smoked salmon or cod's roe is another option, and also sliced hard-boiled eggs with butter.

Bliny can also be enjoyed with sweet fruit purées, like apricot with a squeeze of lemon juice or with various jams such as damson, plum or cherry.

1 level teaspoon dried yeast
4 oz /100 g strong white flour (warmed)
4 oz /100 g buckwheat flour (warmed)
1 teaspoon salt
11 fl oz /300 ml lukewarm milk
5 fl oz /150 ml soured cream[2] **(**at room temperature)
2 large eggs, separated (at room temperature)
Soured cream (to serve) and fillings of choice

Method 1

Add a little water to the dried yeast and allow to stand for 10 minutes before using.

Sift and then warm the flours in a low oven. Make sure the soured cream and eggs are at room temperature.

Mix the lukewarm milk with the yeast and then add the 2 egg yolks and soured cream. Pour this liquid mixture into the warmed, sifted four and salt, and mix together.

The batter should be thick. Leave in a warm place for at least an hour until it is bubbly. This batter can also be made and then left in a warm place overnight.

Shortly before making the pancakes, beat the egg whites until stiff and stir them into the batter.

─────────────────────────

[1] Correct transliteration of this word is **bliny** (accent on the y), but common usage seems to be **blini**. The singular is **blin**.
[2] Soured cream substitutes: 2 tablespoons softened butter OR yoghurt OR a mixture, as preferred!

Heat a little oil in a heavy-based frying pan over a medium heat. Pour off excess oil, leaving a thin film.

Pour a soup ladleful (about 2 fl oz /50 ml) of the batter into the pan and turn the bliny as soon as they become lacy and set.

Serve the bliny with soured cream and the variety of fillings suggested on page 141.

Method 2

For perfectionists, the classic recommended method for bliny is to make the first rising by using half the warm milk mixed with the yeast. When it froths pour it into half of the two flours. Leave to rise and bubble for an hour. Then add the other ingredients *(except the egg whites)* and proceed as above. Don't forget to re-warm the remaining milk and flours. Leave in a warm place overnight.

Ukrainian bliny

6 oz /175 g millet flour
6 oz /175 g buckwheat flour
2 tablespoons butter
1 egg
1 tablespoon sugar
3 tablespoons soured cream
4-5 fl oz /125 ml milk
¼ oz /10 g yeast

Sift the millet and mix with water to make a thick porridge; cool. Press this through a sieve. Boil half the milk and 1 tablespoon of butter together, then sprinkle in two thirds of the buckwheat to make a thick porridge. Cool to room temperature.

Mix the yeast with warm water and add to the buckwheat mix. Allow to rise, then add the sieved millet porridge and remaining buckwheat flour, the egg yolk mixed with the sugar, salt and remaining warm milk. Leave for a second rising, then add beaten egg white.

Olad'i

Olad'i are different from bliny in that they are thicker and more crumpet-like.

1 lb /450 g flour
18 fl oz /500 ml milk and water
1 oz /25 g yeast
2 eggs
1½ teaspoon sugar
½ teaspoon salt
3-4 tablespoons soured cream or softened butter

Mix yeast with warm liquid, sprinkle on the flour and stir. Put to rise in a warm place. Add the lightly-beaten eggs, sugar and salt and 1 tablespoon of the cream or softened butter.

Mix well and put to rise a second time; then without beating it again and using a wetted spoon,

Pour into a well greased frying pan and cook a -few minutes on each side. They will rise up and take a little longer to cook than **bliny**. Make sure there is enough but not too much fat in the pan.

The same mixture and method is used for making **apple olad'i** except that the sugar is increased to 1 tablespoon, the fat is melted and 3-4 finely sliced apples are added to the batter.

Potato Olad'i Minsk style

This dish is made without yeast and is similar to Swiss **rösti**.

Grate some raw potatoes, squeeze dry and add salt to taste. Shape into cakes and fry in 2 tablespoons of butter.

These **olad'i** are often stuffed; one side is fried with the stuffings on top, more raw grated potato added and then turned and fried on the other side.

2 tablespoons flour may be added to the potatoes to make it more of a cake.

Stuffings for these may be:
Minced meat, lightly fried mushrooms, fish and onion mixtures, mashed hard-boiled eggs and spring onions.

There are endless variations, as the potato is a great support dish in Belarusian cooking, often taking the place of pastry as a vehicle for stuffings and forcemeats.

Potato Olad'i using yeast

1 lb /500 g potatoes
2½ oz /75 g flour
1 egg (optional)
1 oz /25 g yeast
2 tablespoons butter

Quickly grate the potatoes, add the yeast mixed with 2-3 fl oz /70 ml warm water, add the salt, sift in the flour and add the lightly beaten egg.

Leave to rise in the usual way. Fry as described in the previous recipe.

Serve with melted butter or soured cream.

Kisel' - puréed fruit dessert

This is effectively a fruit soup thickened with arrowroot, potato flour or cornflour. Arrowroot makes the clearest and most delicate **kisel'**. Danish **rødgrød** is identical and so is German **Rote Grütze**. It is easy to make and my favourite dessert when made with a mixture of red and blackcurrants with whole strawberries and raspberries floating in it.

It is a very old recipe and mentioned in Russian folk and fairy tales of enchanted lands where rivers of milk flow between banks of **kisel'**. The word **kisel'** means sour and the thickening agent once used was obtained by a process of souring and pounding cereals. Oat **kisel'** is still popular in Belarus going under the name of **zhur**.

Any fruit may be used for kisel' - plums, gooseberries, apples and even honey and lemon. Rhubarb is another favourite. Use only young rhubarb and soak the stems in water beforehand to get rid of excess acidity.

Kisel' freezes well for a short period. For a long period freeze the mixture without the starch thickening agent and add the cornflour or arrowroot to half the defrosted liquid and boil up as set out below.

Kisel' – preparation

To make a clear glossy **kisel'** of medium consistency use:-

> **Arrowroot : 1 rounded tablespoon to 1 pint /575 ml of fruit juice and purée.**
> or
> **Cornflour: 1 rounded tablespoon to 17 fl oz /475 ml of liquid.**

Sweeten to taste. It should be on the sharp side.

If you end up with too thin a liquid, remedy it by mixing a little more starch in another saucepan with some cold water, add some of the **kisel'** and then boil it up before stirring it back slowly into the main body of the liquid. Bring the whole **kisel'** back to the boil. To thin over thick **kisel'** add a little cold water or extra juice and keep stirring over a low heat.

Red fruit kisel'

> **1 lb /450 g redcurrants**
> **½ lb /225 g each of raspberries, cherries[1] and blackcurrants[2]**
> **About 1½ pints /850 ml water**
> **3-4 tablespoons sugar**
> **2½ -3 tablespoons of cornflour**
> **lemon juice**

Cook the berries in the water in an enamel or stainless steel pan. *(Not aluminium)*. This takes a few minutes. Keep back half the berries for garnish. Put the cooked fruit through the blender

---

[1] Stone the cherries if you plan to purée the fruit in a blender.
[2] Any convenient soft fruits can be used.

with part of the juice and then through a nylon sieve to remove all pips. Dissolve the cornflour in a little cold water and mix with the juice and bring to the boil and cook for a few minutes. Then add the sieved purée, sugar and lemon juice and lastly stir in the whole berries. The heat of the **kisel'** will cook them without breaking them.

Fruit and milk kisel' pudding

A layered fruit and milk **kisel'** pudding may be made by making a thick fruit **kisel'**(double the amount of starch thickener) and putting it into a well rinsed jelly mould with cooled milk **kisel'**.

This is none other than our school friend blancmange, but should be made with arrowroot: take 4 heaped tablespoons to 1½ pints /850 ml of milk the zest of a lemon and sugar to taste. Steep the milk with the lemon. Mix the arrowroot with some of the cold milk, strain over the remaining milk and bring to the boil. Add the sugar. To make this more interesting add some nut liqueur or brandy or vanilla or almond essence. To layer up the pudding wet a mould, sprinkle with sugar and pour in the milk **kisel'**. Cool well before adding the fruit **kisel'** which should be not quite set. Chill and serve in slices.

Belarusian zhur - oatmeal based kisel'

4 cupfuls of water to 1 cupful of porridge oatmeal. Boil the water, stir in the oat flakes and add a piece of rye bread and put in a warm place to ferment and the flakes to swell. Drain the flakes and wash them in cold water. Cook them gently on the stove until the zhur thickens. In Belarus this is served with fried onions and potatoes.

This recipe is inserted more as a curiosity, and needs a good deal of flavouring, either with herbs or soft fruit, to make it interesting.

Belarusian kisel' thickened with rye flour - kulaga belorusskaya
   18 oz /500 g fruit
   16 fl oz /450 ml boiling water
   3-4 tablespoons rye flour[1]
   1-2 tablespoons of honey[1]
   6 oz /175 g sugar

Prepare and cook as described for 'Red fruit kisel' p 145.

---

[1] Or honey may be used as a sweetener, in which case increase the amount of flour to 5-6 tablespoons

Fruit soup of apricots and peaches

1 lb /450 g apricots or peaches fresh, dried or tinned fruit[1]
4 oz /100 g sugar
1 tablespoon of arrowroot or potato flour
4 oz /100 g cooked rice
4 tablespoons of soured cream or single cream

Cook the fresh fruit in enough water to cover. Use the soaking water for the dried fruit and chop them finely before cooking them to save time. Sieve the fruit or blend with their juice in the liquidiser. Add the sugar. Mix the arrowroot or potato flour with a little cold water, and stir it into the purée over a low heat, then boil up. When cold stir in the cooked rice and cream.

Latvian fruit soup

7 oz /200 g rye bread
1¾ pints /1 litre boiling water
2 tablespoons raisins
2 tablespoons sugar
2 medium apples, finely sliced
2 tablespoons of cranberries, blackberries or black currants, cooked and sieved
2 tablespoons thin cream
1 teaspoon sugar

Cut the bread into slices and grill or bake slowly in the oven until golden brown and crisp. Pour the boiling water over, cover and leave until it has swollen up. Then sieve it and add the raisins, sugar, apples and sieved berries and boil up together for 10 - 15 minutes. Cool the soup and serve with the cream mixed with the sugar.

Variation:
Cook extra apples separately with sugar and add these with lemon juice. The soup should be the consistency of thick cream.

---

[1] Tinned fruit: add the juice of a lemon, and omit sugar.

Sweet batter for apple fritters

3 tablespoons oil } - For frying
4 oz /100 g butter[1]
2 oz /50 g granulated sugar
1 tablespoon icing sugar
3 oz /75 g flour
½ teaspoon salt
4 eggs, separated
4 tablespoons milk
1½ lb /650 g Bramley cooking apples
vanilla flavouring

Peel, core and cut the apples into fairly thick rings, sprinkle them with the granulated sugar and leave them to soak up the sugar for half an hour. *(I often add a squeeze of lemon juice as I like the sharp taste).*

To make the batter, beat the egg yolks and add 1 tablespoon of cold milk. Sift in the flour, the icing sugar and salt. Slowly beat in the remaining milk. *(This batter can be made in one go in a blender if care is taken to scrape down the sides).*

Beat the egg whites and fold into the batter. Dip the apple rings in the batter, using a fork and fry over a fairly low heat until brown on each side. Finish them off in the oven and serve them with raspberry fruit syrup, apricot sauce (p 186) or with soured cream.

An alternative is to bake them in the oven with the batter poured over the fruit. This method is also good with plums.

BATTER for frying:

12 oz /350 g flour
5 fl oz /150 ml approx. of tepid water
3 tablespoons oil (olive or walnut preferably)
1 egg white or a dash of vinegar
salt

Pour the oil into the sieved flour, add the salt and the water and stir until it is creamy, or blend these ingredients together in the blender. Stand the batter for an hour or so and then stir in the beaten egg white or vinegar just before using.

---

[1] If using electric fryer, use all oil.

Yogurt making

Homemade yoghurt using a blender and electric yoghurt maker

Mix six cups of water with 1½ cups of powdered milk (not the instant variety) and 1 large can of evaporated whole milk. Bring this up to 40-48° C (104-118°F) temperature and add three tablespoons of natural yoghurt or yoghurt from the last batch. Pour this into jars and leave for about four hours until it is well set. Alternatively you can pour the mixture into jars and stand them in a large pan of warm water. The temperature needs to be kept warm at 40-48°C (104-118°F)

This yoghurt can be successfully frozen and it is thick so can be blended with fruit purées, and fruit juices to make sorbets. This is a foolproof recipe. Many fresh milk based recipes for yoghurt are not always successful and depend very much on the quality of the milk, the grazing and health of the herd and whether there are any traces of antibiotic in the milk.

Much fermented milk is drunk in the Russian Federation and throughout the Balkans in one form or another and go under a number of names - **prostokvasha, ryazhenka, varenets, kefir**. Various methods are employed. Kefir grains, for instance, must not be mixed with milk that has been boiled or is too warm. Kefir could be bought in bottles in most Russian foodstores; it came in different grades, depending on the fat content of the milk used. Some Soviet-era cookbooks held that one day old kefir is good for constipation while three day old is the reverse!

There are different varieties of **prostokvasha**, one of them called after the Russian biologist and Nobel prize winner of 1908, I. Mechnikov. If you can obtain kefir grains (I was fortunate to be given some by a friend), the grains multiply at a fast rate. I like it better than yoghurt and it can be very thick or can be taken as a drink. The whey part is like weak lemon juice and most pleasant and refreshing.

Tvorog – curd / cottage cheese

Italian **ricotta** is the closest equivalent. Curd cheese of different fat content and cottage cheese (which always has to be sieved) can all be easily obtained.

Many of the eastern recipes requiring tvorog can be made with drained yoghurt.

To make tvorog:
> **18 fl oz /500 ml milk**
> **1 tablespoon of ascorbic acid powder[1]**

Boil the milk, remove from the heat and add the ascorbic acid, stirring all the time. Cool and drain in muslin.

Tvorog can make a number of dishes. For a sweet pudding sieve the cheese and add sugar and cherry jam and then add hot milk. Leave in a cool place and serve chilled.

For 4 oz /100 g of cheese take 2-3 tablespoons of milk and a teaspoon each of sugar and jam.

---

[1] Ascorbic acid: 10% strength; obtainable from most chemists.

Tvorozhniki or syrniki - curd cheese fritters

I've put these with the puddings, although they are most often served for breakfast in Russia. They can be eaten any time of day.

1 lb /450 g curd or cottage cheese
3 oz /75 g flour
1-2 tablespoons caster sugar
pinch of salt
few drops of vanilla or better still vanilla sugar or vanilla stick cut up finely.
1 egg
1 small carton of soured cream or melted butter for serving

Sieve the cottage cheese to make it smooth; better still buy ricotta or smooth curd cheese to avoid this chore. Sift in half the flour, then the sugar, salt and vanilla. Add the raw egg and mix well. Form into a long roll and cut into about ten rounds. Dip each one into the remaining flour and fry them in butter. You will need a few tablespoons. They don't take long; remove them when they are golden on each side.

Serve hot, sprinkled with vanilla sugar and soured cream, or melted butter.

Fruit **kisel'** (p 145) is also delicious with syrniki.

Variations:
Add grated lemon zest to the basic mixture.

For savoury syrniki omit the vanilla, add fresh herbs and serve with melted butter.

Tvorozhniki with potato from Belarus

1 lb /450 g curd cottage cheese (Tvorog)
1½ lb /675 g cooked mashed potato
1 egg
5-6 oz /160 g flour
3 tablespoons sugar
½ teaspoon salt
3 tablespoons of butter
1 small carton of soured cream (smetana)

Mix the potato, sieved cheese and egg together. Add half the flour, the sugar and salt. Cook as above and serve with the **smetana**.

Paskha – festive cream cheese dish

Often eaten at Easter – the white cheese symbolising purity.

1 lb /450 g cream cheese[1]
½ lb /225 g unsalted butter
½ lb /225 g sugar
4 egg yolk
½ lb /225 g mixed sultanas and raisins, glacé cherries, angelica finely cut up pieces of vanilla stick.

Cream the butter, sugar and yolks. Add the vanilla and the cheese. Put into a cheese cloth to drain or into a sieve lined with muslin. Put a weight on top and leave in the refrigerator until firm.

When ready, mould by hand into a pyramid shape and decorate with angelica and cherries. Nuts may also be used in this recipe – preferably almonds.

Paskha using soured cream

1 lb /450 g cream cheese
½ lb /225 g unsalted butter (softened)
4 oz /100 g soured cream
2 tablespoons of thin cream
6 oz /175 g sugar
3-4 egg yolks
lemon rind and finely cut or grated vanilla stick to taste
½ lb /225 g mixed fruit - sultanas, raisins, glacé cherries, angelica
A pinch of salt

Cream the butter and sugar. Beat in the yolks. Add the soured cream and the thin cream and the remaining ingredients.

---

[1] Processed cream cheese will do very nicely - you don't need to sieve and beat the cheese so hard.

Baked cheese cake - Tvorozhnaya zapekanka

   1 lb /450 g curd or cottage cheese[1]
   3 tablespoons melted butter
   1 egg
   3 tablespoons caster sugar
   2 tablespoons semolina
   ½ teaspoon salt
   2 tablespoons bread crumbs
   4 oz /100 g raisins, plumped up in boiling water and drained vanilla essence to taste or lemon zest
   3-4 tablespoons soured cream or yoghurt or a mixture

Sieve and well drain the cheese. Add two tablespoons of the melted butter, the sugar mixed with the beaten egg, the semolina, salt and flavourings. Fold in the raisins. Grease a shallow dish, such as a 'Swiss roll' tin, strew in the breadcrumbs and smooth in the mixture. Spread the soured cream and remaining melted butter on top. Bake in a hot oven 200 C /Gas 6, for about half an hour.

A richer offering is:

Tvorog pudding with orange and lemon peel

   1 lb /450 g curd cheese
   4 eggs - separated
   4 oz /100 g sugar
   2 tablespoons semolina
   4 oz /100 g grated dried peel from oranges or lemons or use freshly grated zest if the other is not convenient
   2 oz /50 g raisins previously plumped up in boiling water
   3 tablespoons butter
   ¼ teaspoon salt

Drain and sieve the cheese, add the egg yolks, sugar, salt and semolina and pour in the melted butter. Beat well before adding the raisins and finely grated peel or zest. Fold in the stiffly beaten egg whites. This pudding can be steamed in a greased basin for 3-4 hours or baked as above in a shallow dish strewn with breadcrumbs, Serve this with additional fruit **kisel'** compôte or thin strawberry **varen'ye** *(jam)*.

---

[1] A smooth cream cheese will save time - no need to sieve or beat.

Apple pelt'ya from Moldova

4 lb /1¾ kg of washed apples cut in quarters
3 pints /1¾ litres of water
1 lb or 1 kg of sugar for each pint /litre of juice extracted.

Cook the fruit in a covered pan over a low heat. After 15 minutes drain off the liquid into a separate pan and leave the apple pulp in a sieve to drain for half an hour. Do not squeeze or mash. Return the liquid only to the pan. Add the sugar and dissolve it well before bringing it to the boil and cook over a low heat until the jelly thickens. Use the cold saucer test. This may be served as a sweetmeat and cut into cubes as above or poured into jars to use on bread, biscuits and sponges.

Variation:
 Use half quinces and half apples and adding the juice and finely grated zest of a lemon.

Guy'evskaya kasha - classic Russian semolina pudding

Semolina pudding incorporating nuts and fruit and is regarded as one of the classic Russian puddings.

8 oz /225 g of semolina
4 oz /100 g sugar
2 eggs, beaten
18 fl oz /500 ml milk
2 tablespoons butter
2 oz /50 g almonds, skinned and chopped
Small tin of mixed fruit, or fruit soft fruits
Vanilla flavouring and 3 tablespoons of breadcrumbs

Boil the milk with a vanilla stick or add vanilla flavouring and the sugar and pour in the semolina very slowly in a fine stream, constantly stirring and cook for ten minutes. Continue stirring. Add the butter and beaten eggs. Put the mixture into a greased casserole sprinkled with the breadcrumbs, top with a little brown sugar before baking in a moderately hot oven (190 C/Gas 5) until golden and slightly puffed up. Serve with chopped fresh fruit and grated lemon.

There are more elaborate versions of this dish involving slow baking of the milk in the oven, removing the skins which form at intervals, and layering them up with the cooked pudding and fruits.

Note: Semolina dishes are only successful when the cereal is fresh and bought from a reliable source. Stale semolina easily goes into lumps when cooked.

Apple pastila

This is a pleasant confection popular in Ukraine and sometimes handed out at the end of a meal. I used to eat a lot of this in Moscow in the 1950's, but did not see it in the shops in later years.

Sharp apples are the best. Wash and cut them in half crossways and bake them in an enamel or ceramic covered bowl in a moderate oven (180 C/Gas 4). They may also be steamed in a double steamer or in a basin in a pressure cooker.

The idea is to keep them as dry as possible. Sieve them and beat the purée in an electric mixer.

To each cupful (10 fl oz /275 g) of purée add a beaten egg white and flavour it with a little vanilla sugar. Smooth the mixture out in a well greased baking tin and cook in a very low oven (110-120 C/Gas ¼-½).

Cool and cut into lozenges. Or line a tin with greased baking parchment or foil and drop spoonfuls onto the tray.

Additional flavourings: lemon juice, orange flower water, almond essence, pinch of cinnamon.

I prefer a simpler version without egg white where the sweetened apple purée is slowly baked in the oven until set and the jellied slices rolled in a little icing sugar before eating.

These are **Kisel'** based cakes. Quinces mixed with the apples help the setting. Liquid pectin added to the apple would also speed up the setting time.

NOTE:

A good **cream substitute** for use in puddings or ice-cream can be obtained by using unsweetened evaporated tinned milk (14 fl oz /400 g).

Place the **unopened** tin in cold water, bring slowly to the boil and boil ten minutes. Remove the tin and cool. Do not open the tin while it is hot. Chill the tin overnight in the refrigerator. Keep there until required. Beat well before using in any recipe.

To make **caramelised milk** for puddings in a pressure cooker, prepare it the day before required. Place an **unopened** 14 fl oz /400 g tin of sweetened condensed milk and pressure cook for an hour, using 1½ pints /850 ml of water for the cooking period[1].

Reduce pressure slowly. Remember that tin is still under pressure, so allow cooker to cool to room temperature before removing tin. Cool and use next day.

---

[1] Timed from when cooker reaches full pressure.

BISCUITS

Pryaniki – spiced biscuits

Jam filled pryaniki

    7 oz /200 g 80% wholemeal self-raising flour
    2 tablespoons each of rye and plain white flour
    ½ teaspoon of baking powder
    3 tablespoons of buckwheat honey or other clear honey
    2 oz /50 g butter
    1 egg

Spices

    ¼ teaspoon of freshly grated nutmeg
    ¼ teaspoon grated ginger root
    ¼ teaspoon grated cinnamon bark (this is hard to do and a coffee mill would help,
    otherwise use ready powdered cinnamon)
    ¾ teaspoon allspice
    1 tablespoon of ground almonds

Filling

    Thick jam for sandwiching biscuits together.
    Alternatively, you could try using cooked dried fruit, well drained.

Cream the butter and warmed honey. Add the egg, together with a little flour to prevent curdling. Stir in the dry ingredients to make a soft dough. If time allows, chill for an hour.

Roll out thinly. Cut into rounds or diamonds and spread jam over half the number. Cover with the remainder and press down well and crimp edges with the back of a knife.

Put on a greased baking tin and bake for the first ten minutes at 180 C /Gas 4, then lower heat to 160 C /Gas 3 for the last ten minutes.

A thin lemon icing glaze is sometimes added, using 2 tablespoons of lemon juice to about 4 tablespoons of icing sugar.

Pryaniki iz rzhanoi muki - Lithuanian rye biscuits

    20 oz /575 g rye flour
    7 oz /200 g sugar
    5 eggs, separated
    ½ pint /275 ml soured cream or yoghurt
    ¼ pint /150 ml softened butter
    8 tablespoons honey
    4 tablespoons syrup
    1 teaspoon bicarbonate of soda
    1 teaspoon cream of tartar
    1 teaspoon spices - cinnamon, cloves, cardamom, ginger, caraway
    salt to taste

Warm the honey and treacle. Mix the yolks and sugar and beat until white, adding the honey, butter, spices and soured cream or yoghurt. Sift in the flour, cream of tartar and bicarbonate of soda. Fold in the whipped egg whites. Mix well together and spread out on a greased baking tin - a swiss roll tin would be the right size. It should not be more than ¾ inch /2 cm thick.

Bake in a moderate oven 180 C /Gas 4 for 45 minutes or until firm to the touch. When cool, cut into slices.

Kovrizhka derevenskaya- Country style honey spice cake

    10 oz /275 g plain flour
    3 eggs, separated
    ½ pint /275 ml soured cream and the same amount of sugar and honey
    1 tablespoon of breadcrumbs
    1 tablespoon of softened butter
    1 teaspoon of mixed spice-cinnamon, cloves, plus crushed cardamom and a few grated nuts
    ½ teaspoon of baking soda
    ½ teaspoon of bicarbonate of soda
    salt to taste

Cream the egg yolks and sugar, add the soured cream, warmed honey and spices. Mix the flour and baking soda and gradually add half of this. Beat the egg whites and sprinkle over the remaining flour, then mix all together carefully. Bake in a greased loaf tin for 30 minutes at moderate temperature, 180 C /Gas 4.

Korzhiki

These 'biscuits' remind me somewhat of my mother's Cornish heavy cake – a cross between a scone and a cake.

10 oz /275 g flour (plain or wholemeal or a mixture)
2 tablespoons softened butter
8 tablespoons soured cream

OR

4 oz /100 g butter plus 1 tablespoon each of top of the milk and lemon juice
1 egg
3 tablespoons sugar
½ teaspoon bicarbonate of soda

Sift the flour into a bowl, make a well in the centre and pour in the cream, egg and other ingredients and work into a dough. Roll out ¼ inch/ 6 mm thick. Cut into rounds.

Prick each cake, paint with a little milk and bake them on a greased baking sheet in a hot oven 220 C /Gas 7 for 10-15 minutes. Split them open and serve with jam and cream.

Lepeshki - Russian almond biscuits

These are a rather rich shortbread type of biscuit.

8 oz /225 g plain flour
8 oz /225 g butter
3-4 tablespoons sugar
½ teaspoon each of vanilla and almond essence
2-3 oz /50-75g split almonds, to decorate

Cream the butter and sugar, add the remaining ingredients. Chill.

Roll into balls, flatten slightly and place an almond on top.

Bake in a low oven 150 C /Gas 2 for 18-20 minutes. The yield is about two dozen biscuits.

Estonian Rye Biscuits

   5 oz /150 g rye flour
   1½ tablespoons sugar
   1 egg
   1 tablespoon smetana (soured cream)
   2½ oz /70 g butter
   ¼ teaspoon bicarbonate of soda

Sift flour. Mix egg and sugar together and gradually add the softened butter and then the cold **smetana**. Mix the soda with half the flour, sift it into the mixture and fold in remaining flour.

 Flour a board and roll out dough very thinly. Brush tops with egg yolk mixed with a little sugar and make zigzag patterns. This can be done before cutting the biscuits into rounds.

Sandwich rounds together with a stiff jam, such as plum cheese or thick apricot or even a stiff fruit purée.

Bake on greased trays at 200 C /Gas 6. These can also be baked without the jam if preferred.

160

BREAD

"The Ukraine is the Kingdom of Grain"
Honoré de Balzac.

"And some had faces like badly baked loaves of bread"
- Nikolai Gogol.

The kind of good bread one has eaten lingers in the memory longer than the remembrance of other foods : the poppy-strewn **bulochki** and the black bread of Moscow, the sesame rings of Greece, the crackling baguettes of France and the hearty greys and browns of tasty German breads.

The Russian term **est' khleb** (to eat bread) was once synonymous with 'to eat a meal', and in the 19th century the Russian peasant consumed on average three pounds of bread a day and at harvest time as much as five. Bread was literally the staff of life and Chagall the painter, who experienced much hardship and privation in childhood, was said to carry a piece of bread in his pocket in later life, just for reassurance.

In old Russia bread was nearly always broken rather than cut. Grain was venerated, and at the turn of the 19th century when there was an apocalyptical feeling of doom and change in the air it was envisaged that when Christ came again on earth he would arise from among the corn-sheaves in the fields.

Russian bread is good, but on visits to Russia in the 1970's and 80's the bread supplied in hotels was less good than I remembered and I had to keep asking for the dark black Moscow bread which is my favourite, and in the end had to buy my own. I noticed many bakeries stocked more white loaves than in previous years and magazine articles and radio programmes urged the eating of more **zhitnyi** bread - satisfying bread made of wholemeal rye and wheat flours. The proportions given are:

100 "parts" rye flour to 4 "parts" of yeast.

Additions to the loaf are salt and treacle/molasses, plus dried milk whey.

The magazine article underlined the point by quoting the folk saying: "Wheat nourishes some but 'mother-rye' satisfies everyone." Somehow or other, rye bread had slipped into second category and the aim was to put this right in accordance with good rye harvests. Rye also requires less attention than wheat.

By studying old recipes and reducing their proportions I have evolved my own satisfying Moscow bread with the addition of a little oil added to it to improve its keeping qualities.

The flour has to be of good quality and coarsely ground. A little internet research usually reveals a suitable supplier, if none is available locally.

161

Bread is bread, and no matter how many recipes there are, the basic proportions of yeast and liquid must always be related to the kind of flour used and its power of absorption. Coarsely ground rye flour needs more liquid and slightly more yeast than the average loaf. **Borodinskii** bread, flavoured with coriander, and Minsk and Riga breads, flavoured with caraway, are made with a mixture of rye and wheatmeal flours with the addition of red malt, treacle or molasses, and other additions, which some Russian cookbooks only mysteriously allude to.

Moscow bakeries offer dozens of different breads of varying degrees of darkness, sourness and coarseness, plus their companion rolls and plaits, as well as trays of semi-sweet buns, rusks and pretzels. Balzac noted at least seventy different varieties of bread when he lived in Ukraine after his marriage to Madame Hanska, a wealthy Polish landowner. The Hanska estate[1] was in Poland (then part of Imperial Russia). The family owned 40,000 'souls', but as Balzac noted it would have needed at least 400,000 'souls' to cultivate all the rich farmland owned by the family. Balzac enthused over the land itself: 'It is a black earth, rich with humus, going down fifty feet deep'; but poetic licence, plus some changes in topsoil over the years, probably must be allowed for as most geography books say the true humus is three to five feet deep.

Ukraine and Moldova excel in the different shapes of enriched breads used on festive occasions. At Christmas the sweet **kalach** loaf is formed into a round as a reminder of the sun and warmer seasons, and may be plaited from four to eight dough strands. Chaliapin, the great Russian singer, remembered **kalachi** baked in the shape of a padlock - a handle baked on for the gilders' workers so that they should not touch the bread with acid smelling hands.

In northern Moldova they bake **kolindets,** round bracelets of twisted bread (called **kol'endari** in Bulgaria, and **Kollaitos** in Greece). These are given to children on Christmas Eve, and seem to be connected with the winter solstice and are to be found in agricultural communities in Europe, the Caucasus and Near East. In the Bukhovina, in addition to making sun and moon shapes they twist their bread into figures of eight. The writer Isaac Babel, a native of Odessa and inhabitant of the warm south, once remarked that no-one had described the sun in Russian literature. He put right that omission and the sun as well as the moon and evening star appear symbolically in many of his short stories, and much of the action takes place in the burning heat of day or at fiery sunset.

Moldova has kept many customs relating to harvest. At Christmas and New Year straw and a sprinkling of flour are placed under the tablecloth — this is also a Polish and Ukrainian custom, once pagan, but now kept in remembrance of Christ's nativity, though Russian ethnologists stressed the folklorist aspect of this custom.

In his Memoirs Dobuzhinsky the painter recalls the Polish habit of his uncle and aunt in Vilnius of putting hay under the tablecloth at Christmas; there would be a serving of twelve different savoury 'fasting' dishes, one for each of the Apostles. These would be mostly of fish, mushrooms or marinated vegetables. The sweet pudding would be **kut'ya,** a rice dish also made in Ukraine. The accompanying sweet bread **kalachi,** St. Petersburg favourites, were supposed to be made only from water taken from the Moskva river and which was brought up to St. Petersburg regularly.

---

[1] Now an agricultural institute.

Bread-making, once acquired as a habit, is relatively simple. Moreover homemade yeast-raised bread is healthier than factory produce. In Russia they use the verb **'tvorit'** *(to create)* dough, but this is the last word one could use in connection with many commercial breads. Phytic acid, present in wholemeals, is neutralised by the working of the yeast when the dough is raised slowly, unlike the fast system used in modern bakeries.

There are two basic preliminary processes in starting the working of the yeast. The yeast is mixed with warmed water or milk. (*Milk should previously be boiled to kill the enzymes*). Use a cupful from the given amount of liquid and leave this in a warm place for ten minutes. A very simple method my mother always used and one I note is often used in Greek and Middle Eastern recipes or anywhere where dishes and utensils are few, is to make a well in the bowl of flour, crumble in the yeast and pour in a cupful of warm liquid and lightly sprinkle some flour from the sides over the top of the yeast. This is fine if you know your yeast is fresh. If not it is better to mix it separately to test it, and also of course if you are using dried yeast.

Bread making - White / Wholemeal

Basic proportions for a white loaf are:

10 fl oz /275 ml liquid to 18 oz /500 g of flour
½ oz /15 g fresh yeast,
½ - ¾ oz /15-20 g salt
This makes a 2 lb /900 g loaf.

Wholemeal needs more liquid and the proportions are:

12 - 15 fl oz /350 - 450 g liquid to 20 oz /575 g flour
½ oz /15 g fresh yeast OR ¼ oz /7 g dried yeast (1 flat teaspoon)
½ - ¾ oz /15-20 g salt, or to taste

Extra salt means allowing extra raising time.

A general rule in bread making is: the less yeast used the tastier and better keeping the loaf, though it may take longer to rise. When doubling or increasing flour quantities for a recipe don't double the amount of yeast.

Overnight raising of dough, or two or three risings of the dough to suit yourself, also means you need far less yeast. Generally speaking if you are going to bake a number of loaves 1 oz /25 g of fresh yeast is enough for 4½ lb /2 kg of flour for two risings. I notice that the bread recipes given in my Tatar cookbook use very small amounts of yeast in recipes. Another point to bear in mind is that richer cake-breads can take more yeast because of their higher fat content.

* * *

Many Soviet-era cookbooks still recommended a preliminary sponging method, using about a third to half of the flour and about ¾ of the water and setting it aside for an hour or so. This is not really necessary with fresh yeast and just as good results can be obtained by normal mixing, plus two risings.

My method then is:

1. Warm the flour briefly in the oven (don't make it too hot)

2. Mix yeast in a cup of warm water and allow to stand ten minutes

3. Pour this into the flour *(alternatively crumble yeast into a well in the flour and pour in a little water and stir with a finger and sift over a little flour from the sides of the bowl as suggested earlier).* Leave in a warm place until it starts bubbling and working.

4. Add other ingredients which should be at room temperature. If using butter it should be softened. Mix and knead well. Cover in oiled paper or polythene.

5. Leave in a warm place 1½ - 2 hours or until doubled.

6. Knock back and allow to rise again.

7. Knock back and put into tins and allow to rise to the top.

Note: Do not allow rye dough to rise too high once it is in the tin as this could result in a flattened loaf.

Some special breads are baked for Russian Orthodox communities and handed out in church.

The bakers for this bread in pre-revolutionary Moscow and St. Petersburg and some other big cities had to be a cut above the ordinary, and traditionally priests' widows were called on for this task. The playwright A.N.Ostrovsky's[1] grandmother was one of these **'prosvirni'**. Alexander Pushkin, with a poet's keen ear, noted their pure and correct language.

The recipe for white 'Church bread' given on p 165, which is slightly enriched, was for the usual kind served in monasteries on special occasions or name days.

Such a loaf preserves the life of the Prioress in E. Zamyatin's story, known usually under the title of **The Protectress of Sinners**[2] - a tale set during the Revolution. The three pound communion loaf saves her and prevents the Convent from falling into the hands of the Bolsheviks.

Théophile Gautier in his **Travels in Russia** in the 1850's also notes the excellent convent bread at St. Sergius convent at Zagorsk. The loaves were baked in moulds with scenes of the Old and New testament stamped on them.

It was in this monastery where Tolstoy and his family picnicked in the chapel on mushrooms and pancakes and also where the famous quarrel took place in Dostoevsky's

---

[1] A. N. Ostrovsky wrote many plays, of which the most famous is **The Thunderstorm**, written in 1859.
[2] Spodruchnitsa greshnykh - written in 1918.

Brothers Karamazov. Because of this, the exquisite meal laid and ready was never eaten. Dostoevsky rarely refers to food, but in the **House of the Dead** the prison bread is considered by the whole town to be of a very high standard.

At Christmas time the priest would come to bless the food sent to the 'unfortunates' by the townspeople - the **kalachi, vatrushki, pryazhniki, shangi, bliny** and various enriched biscuits and pastries.

On Christmas Day each convict would received a pound of meat, plenty of millet **kasha** with lots of butter. One convict had even got hold of a sucking pig and a goose. A custom in the prison at Christmas was to strew the floors with hay.

Church Bread

This dough is made the night before baking

> **18 oz /500 g sieved strong flour**
> **9 oz /250 g butter**
> **1/3 oz /10 g yeast**
> **9-10 fl oz /250 ml approx. of boiled milk, cooled to lukewarm**
> **pinch of salt**

Mix part of the flour with the yeast and some of the milk. Cover *(an oiled polythene bag prevents a dry crust forming)* and leave overnight in a cool place.

Next day mix in the remaining ingredients and allow to rise in the usual way before forming into small narrow loaves.

Cocoa tins with their base removed are good. Reverse the lidless tins and slip the base inside where it will be held in place. Grease the tins very well.

Bake in a hot oven 200 C /Gas 6 until well risen and lightly coloured - about thirty minutes depending on size.

This is a very fine white bread and very similar to Jewish **challah** or Ukrainian **kalach.**

Baltic Ryes

One cannot discount the long German influence here and in some other European parts of Russia.

Pushkin notes the 'Exact German baker' in his **Evgenii Onegin**[1] :

> '..Petersburg awakes... the girl hurries along with her milk jug.. the snow crunching underfoot, while the precise German baker **(khlebnik, nemets akkuratnyi)** in his high cook's hat pushes up his trapdoor once again'.

The trapdoor is amusingly called a **'vasisdas'** *(German 'was ist das'- what is that?)* in answer to a customer's knock and presumably because the German did not always understand his clients' requests. That this expression was already current vocabulary in Pushkin's day is some indication of how long the German bakers had dominated the scene, at least in St. Petersburg, and accounts for many similarities between German and Russian breads, pretzels etc.

The following six recipes are from the Baltic states but almost identical ones are to be found in Germany and the Scandinavian countries. They make ideal open sandwiches and 'supports' for tasty **zakuski.**

Aniseed and cardamom flavoured bread from the Baltic states

    20 oz /575 g white flour
    10 – 11 oz /300 g rye flour
    1 teaspoon salt
    14 fl oz 400 ml water
    3 oz /75 g yeast
    1 teaspoon sugar
    1 teaspoon ground star anise
    1 teaspoon crushed cardamom
    4 tablespoons black or ordinary treacle

Make a very sticky dough. You will need to wet your hands to handle it. Allow to rise. Knead it with a little flour. Put it into greased loaf tins and allow to rise again. Bake at 200 C /Gas 6 for 50 to 60 minutes.

---

[1] Chapter 1, Verse XXV

Aniseed and fennel bread.

20 oz /575 g white flour
9 oz /250 g rye flour
1 teaspoon salt
18 fl oz /500 ml water
2 oz /50 g yeast
1 teaspoon each of sugar and golden syrup
1 teaspoon each of star anise and fennel seeds

Make as described above but bake in a moderately hot oven 190 C/Gas 5 for 50 to 60 minutes.

Sweet pumpernickel – salt free

1 lb /450 g white flour
1 lb /450 g rye flour
18 fl oz /500 ml water (warm)
3 oz /75 g fresh yeast
7 oz /200 g dark brown molasses sugar (or less according to taste)
2 eggs, beaten

Dissolve the yeast in a little water. Stand for ten minutes and then mix all the ingredients together to make an elastic dough. Leave in a warm place to double. Knead again. Form into a loaf and allow to rise once more. Bake at 190 C/Gas 5 for 50 - 60 minutes.

Sweet pumpernickel – with fennel

18 oz /500 g white flour
11 oz /300 g dark rye flour
1 teaspoon salt
21 fl oz /600 ml milk
3 oz /75 g yeast
2 tablespoons treacle or molasses
1 tablespoon of fennel seeds
1 tablespoon star anise crushed

Make a fairly stiff dough. Give it one rising. Spread dough in a shallow greased baking tray. Allow to rise. Bake in a hot to very hot oven 220-230 C /Gas 7-8.

Estonian rye and wholemeal sourdough loaf

This recipe requires coarse dark rye flour. If you can't get it double the amount of light rye flour and add some bran and rye flakes,-adjusting the quantity accordingly.

7 oz /200 g strong white unbleached flour
7 oz /200 g coarse dark rye flour
9 oz /250 g light rye flour
1/3 to ½ oz /10 - 15 g salt (2 teaspoons or according to taste)
13 fl oz /375 ml yoghurt, kefir, buttermilk or cottage cheese drainings or soured cream thinned with milk
1½ oz /40 g yeast (fresh)
9 oz /250 g sourdough (p 180)
1 tablespoon of vegetable oil
1 teaspoon sugar
½ teaspoon each of grated nutmeg and crushed star anise
3 teaspoons of crushed coriander

Put the yeast in a little warm water or buttermilk to froth. Warm the flours in the oven and then follow the general bread making instructions.

Make a fairly firm dough. Leave in a warm place to double. Knock back and knead well and form into a loaf. Put onto a greased baking tray and leave to rise. Bake at 200-220 C /Gas 6 - 7 for 1 hour or more.

Before baking make three deep slashes in the top and prick deeply all over. Sometimes the loaf is glazed and made shiny with a painting of sweetened black coffee.

An alternative glaze is 1 tablespoon of rice flour or potato flour mixed with half a pint /225 ml of boiling water. Brush the loaves with this just before putting them in the oven and towards the end of baking.

Estonian barley or wheat flour and barley bread - Sepik baked on cabbage leaves

28-30 oz /800-850 g of 85% wheatmeal OR
a mixture of flours - a third of barley flour to two thirds wheatmeal
18 fl oz /500 ml milk or milk and water or buttermilk and water
1 oz /25 g yeast
1 teaspoon salt
4 tablespoons melted butter.
Cabbage leaves

Warm the flour. Mix the yeast with some of the warm water in the usual way, then add the flour, salt and fat. Make a firm dough and knead well. Leave to rise for an hour in a warm place. Knock back and leave to rise again.

Put into greased tins or a greased baking tray lined with cabbage leaves and leave to rise again.

Brush with milk and bake at 220 C /Gas 7 for the first 15 minutes, then reduce to 190 C/Gas 5 for a further 20 minutes to half an hour, then lower the oven again to 180 C/Gas 4 for a further 15 minutes, depending on how your oven cooks.

The loaf is ready when tapped on the bottom and gives out a hollow sound. Baking the barley loaf in a loaf tin helps to keep a moister loaf, as do the cabbage leaves.

Rye loaf

   3½ teaspoons dried yeast
   11 fl oz /300 ml buttermilk (or natural yoghurt thinned with milk)
   14 oz /400 g rye flour
   ½ teaspoon salt
   2-3 tablespoons water
   2 teaspoons vodka (optional)

In this recipe, a little vodka can be added which helps to keep the bread fresh.
All ingredients should be at room temperature.

Heat the buttermilk to lukewarm. Stir in the yeast, then gradually add flour and salt to make a dough. Rye flour needs more liquid than other flours, so add the water, and more if necessary, until the mixture becomes a ball of dough.

Knead the dough until smooth, about 10 minutes.
Place in a bowl and cover with oiled cling film or a damp tea towel and leave to rise in a warm place for 2 hours.

When risen, add the vodka and knead lightly, about 5 minutes.

Put the dough into a 1 lb /450 g loaf tin and leave to rise again for 1 hour, covering again with oiled cling film or a damp tea towel. It is important to keep the rye dough moist as it easily cracks and dries out.

Before putting in the oven, brush with water then bake at 200 C/Gas 6 for 1¼ hours, brushing with water every 15-20 minutes during baking.

Caraway bread

2 oz /50 g yeast
3-5 tablespoons water
½ pint /275 ml buttermilk or mixture as above
14 oz /400 g rye flour mixed with a little bran
1½ -2 teaspoons salt
2-3 tablespoons of caraway seeds

Crumble the yeast and stir into the lukewarm water and buttermilk. Add remaining ingredients, knead until smooth. Cover with a damp cloth and leave to rise in a warm place for about an hour. Knead again and form into a loaf. Put into a greased 1 lb baking tin or on a baking tray. Cover and leave to rise in a warm place for about an hour. Make deep slashes on the top of the loaf and brush with egg white mixed with a little water and sprinkle over the caraway seeds.

Borodinskii bread flavoured with coriander

After much experimentation, I feel I have achieved the equivalent of this dark moist loaf in my own kitchen.

The darkness is achieved without resorting to curious ingredients suggested by some recipes and which I'm sure the Russians would not have used in the 1980s, such as expensive squares of chocolate or coffee (which would surely have put up the price of the state subsidised bread – the Borodinskii is the most expensive of the rye loaves).

I returned home from Moscow with such a loaf and thus was able to compare the real thing with my own creation and declare that I've got the authentic taste and texture and very nearly the dark colour by baking my loaf for a fairly long time in a wet Römertopf — a Roman clay pot type dish with a high lid which encourages the crumb to expand sufficiently before the hard crust forms.

I baked it a long time — 2 hours with the lid, and then a further 15 minutes with the lid off. This gives a very hard crust which may not suit everyone and this last stage can be omitted.

For baking without a Römertopf the loaf takes about 1¼ hours.

Dry ingredients sieved and mixed together.

> 18 oz /500 g rye flour (dark)
> 6 oz /175 g wheatmeal
> 1 tablespoon each of crushed coriander[1] and bran
> 1½ -2 teaspoons salt
> 1 oz 25 g fresh yeast

Liquid

> 15 fl oz /425 ml of liquid comprising: 1 tub of yoghurt and buttermilk or water
> 1 cup(10 fl oz /275 ml) of sourdough liquid (see recipe 'Sour rye starter' p 175)
> 1 tablespoon oil
> 1 tablespoon molasses
> 1 tablespoon malt

Use a little white strong flour for mixing if the dough is too sticky. The ingredients should be at room temperature. Heat the buttermilk until lukewarm and mix with the yeast. Let it froth. Add the rest of the liquid (warmed) together with the molasses and malt. Pour into a well in the flour mixture.

Knead well by electric mixer, or by hand if you have the strength! Cover with a damp cloth.

You'll need to wet your hands while handling and smoothing the dough as rye flour makes a sticky dough.

Let it rise in a warm place – it will take some time and you could leave it overnight.

Knock back and smooth with wetted hands. Line the Römertopf with a large piece of well oiled foil, big enough to be 'tented' over the dough.

Place the dough in it and leave it to rise again and then prick it really deeply all over to prevent the loaf cracking. Fold over the foil, put the Römertopf lid on.

I put my Römertopf into a low heated oven and raise the temperature to 230 C /Gas 8 gradually as I feared that it might crack under too sudden and high a heat. Bake at this temperature for 15 minutes then at 190-200 C /Gas 5-6 for 2 hours.

To bake the loaf without a Römertopf bake it first at the high temperature as above for 15 minutes then at the lower temperature for approximately an hour.

---

[1] For Minsk bread, substitute caraway in place of coriander.

Barley bread from the North

9 oz /250 g white unblenched flour
7 oz /200 g barley flour
5 oz /150 g rice flour
9 fl oz /250 ml water
2 eggs
1 teaspoon salt
1¾ oz /40 g yeast
½ teaspoon crushed star anise seeds
½ teaspoon fennel seeds
1 teaspoon of caraway seeds

The dough should not be too sticky and depends on the absorbency of the flour; not all the liquid given in the recipe may be required so add it carefully and gradually. Give it one rising. Form into a loaf and put into a greased bread tin and allow to rise until double its bulk. Bake at 200 C /Gas 5-6.

Flatbread with barley meal and mashed potato

11 oz /300 g wheatmeal
7 oz /200 g barley meal
9 oz /250 g cooked, mashed potato
17 fl oz /475 ml water
1 teaspoon salt
1¾ oz /40 g yeast
1 teaspoon sugar

Make the dough in the usual way. It should not be too sticky. Give it one rising. Spread the mixture with wetted hands into a shallow greased baking tin. Allow it to rise. Make holes in the dough, pricking right through to the bottom. This prevents cracking. Bake in a moderately hot oven 190-200 C /Gas 5-6.

Buckwheat bread made with baking powder

14 oz /400 g buckwheat flour
9 fl oz /250 ml buttermilk
1 teaspoon baking powder
4 tablespoons brown sugar

Mix the buttermilk in carefully so as to make a fairly firm dough. Not all the given quantity may be required. Bake in a hot to very hot oven 220-230 C /Gas 7-8 for 40 to 50 minutes.

Grechaniki - buckwheat yeast rolls

15 oz /425 g buckwheat flour
1 oz /25 g yeast
1 egg
2 tablespoons of vegetable oil for brushing over the tops before baking
5 fl oz /150 ml milk
2 teaspoons of sugar
½ teaspoon salt
5 fl oz 150 ml soured cream (smetana) for serving (optional).

Heat the milk to lukewarm, mix in the yeast, salt and sugar. Beat the egg and sift in the buckwheat flour and mix to a dough.

Allow to rise 1½ to 2 hours for the first rising. Knock back and allow to rise again, knead and form into small oval rolls. Brush with a little extra melted butter. Allow to double in bulk.

Slash their tops diagonally and brush them with the oil. Bake in a hot oven, 200 C /Gas 6 for 15 to 20 minutes. Serve while still warm with **smetana**.

Polish buckwheat flatbread

18 oz /500 g buckwheat flour
5 oz /150 g plain flour
1 oz /25 g yeast / 1/2 tablespoons dried, dissolved in some of the tepid water.
9 oz /250 g melted fat
1 teaspoon salt
17 fl oz /475 ml tepid water

Put buckwheat flour in bowl, add fat and mix. Add other flour, and ingredients and remaining lukewarm water. Allow to rise for one hour.

Put in shallow 10 inch/25 cm tins and allow to rise again for 30 minutes. Bake for one hour at 180 C /Gas 4.

In hard times the Russian peasant would bake bread with different flours — eking out the precious wheat or rye flour with buckwheat, oat or barley flours.

In potato growing areas of Belarus for instance, a few floury mashed potatoes would be added to make a delicious loaf. Potato bread is also popular in Poland and is called **kaszubski.**

Potato bread with caraway seeds

The Caraway seeds are optional.

> **1 lb /450 g white unbleached flour**
> **2 potatoes, steamed in their jackets, peeled and mashed. They should be dry, and you should get about 4 oz /100 g**
> **½ oz /15 g fresh yeast**
> **8 fl oz /225 ml of warm water or milk and water, approximately**
> **1 teaspoon of salt**
> **½ teaspoon of caraway seeds, crushed**
> **1 dessertspoon of oil**

Mix yeast with a cup of warm water as usual. Mix the flour and potatoes well. Add the rest of the dry ingredient to the flour and potatoes. Dribble in the oil slowly to distribute it. Add the yeast mixture and remaining fluid. You should have a soft dough, so add more water if you feel it is necessary.

Knead well, cover with a damp cloth and leave to rise until double or you can leave it in a cool place overnight if convenient. The next day knock back the dough, knead again, put into a greased tin and allow to rise thirty minutes, previously slashing the tops deeply and adding more caraway seeds **(This is a fast rising dough).** Bake at 190 C /Gas 5 for about 1 hour.

Buckwheat rolls - using Polish sourdough

> **This recipe calls for a lot of yeast.**
> **18 oz /500 g of cooked potatoes, well mashed**
> **1 generous pint /600 ml lukewarm water**
> **3 oz /75 g yeast (dissolved in some of the water)**
> **2-3 tablespoons of treacle or malt or half and half**
> **9 oz /250 g sourdough (see below)**
> **14 oz /400 g white flour**
> **22 oz /650 g rye flour**
> **1 flat teaspoon of salt**

Mix the potatoes with the warm water and syrup. Add the sourdough, yeast, flour and salt. This makes a very sticky dough. Leave in a warm place to double, then knead it well with extra flour and with well floured hands. Form into a loaf and put into a greased tin. Make some deep incisions and brush with a little sugar water. Let it rise again, then bake at 190-200 C /Gas 5-6 (moderately hot oven) for an hour and ten minutes.

Sour rye starter

11 oz /300 g rye or white flour or a mixture of both.
(You can also add a tablespoon of granary flour for interest.)
1 oz /25 g yeast
7 fl oz /200 ml warm water (Potato water makes a good starter)

Stir all together, cover and allow to stand 5-6 days at room temperature. Stir well from time to time. Replace the amount used each time by mixing in equal quantities of flour and water. Occasionally add a pinch of yeast to live it up. Keep refrigerated when not in use.

The artist Chagall in his memoirs remembers oatmeal bread with bran in it. This would be a 'hard times' loaf, but now thought of as something healthy and desirable. When it is made with only a small quantity of oats in relation to the wheat flour it is most acceptable and delicious.

Brown oatmeal bread

1 lb /450 g strong white flour, preferably unbleached or 8% wholemeal
4 oz /100 g medium stoneground oatmeal (not quick cooking oats)
½ oz /15 g yeast
½ oz 15 g salt or a little more according to whether you like your bread salty
2 tablespoons soured cream (warmed) or yoghurt or drainings from cottage cheese or buttermilk. (Failing this the top of the milk or cream with a little lemon juice mixed in)
11 fl oz /300 ml warm water

Sift the flours and salt together. Mix yeast with half a cup of the warmed water and pour it into a well in the flour and leave to bubble for 10 minutes.

Add the rest of the liquid ingredients. The dough should be fairly slack and moist, and a little more water may be needed if using wholemeal flour. Knead in the usual way.

Give it two risings — the first takes a few hours and the second about an hour. I bake mine in a loaf tin but traditionally this bread is baked on a greased baking sheet.

Make deep diamond cross cuts into the bread. Leave to rise again before baking in a hot to very hot oven 220-230 C /Gas 7-8.

Flat Armenian bread - Lavash

1½ lb /675 g flour (can be half wholemeal or part granary and part white)
16-18 fl oz /450-500 ml warm water
1/3 oz /10 g yeast (fresh)
1 teaspoon sugar
2 teaspoons salt

Make a bread dough in the usual way and as described below for 'Tatar bread rolls'. The above recipe is almost identical except that it uses water alone for mixing.

Divide the dough into about 14 or 15 rolls and roll them out thinly about 10 inch /25 cm in diameter. Prick them with a fork and bake in a hot oven 200 C /Gas 6 for about 10 minutes.

Tatar bread rolls

1½ lb /650-700 g flour – a mixture of wholemeal and strong white unbleached (a little granary flour mixed in makes this into a very good loaf or rolls)
1 oz /25 g sugar
1½ oz /40 g margarine
1/3 oz /10 g yeast
1 teaspoon salt
11 fl oz /300 ml tepid milk
7 fl oz /200 ml /9 tablespoons tepid water

Mix the water, milk and melted margarine, add the sugar, salt and yeast altogether until it is smooth. Sift in the flour and mix well. This can all be done in a blender, using half the amount of flour and adding the rest by hand.

Put in a warm place to prove. When the dough is well risen shape into rolls and allow to rise (takes 10-15 minutes).

Bake in a moderately hot oven 190 C /Gas 5.

Buttermilk loaf flavoured with aniseed

7 oz /200 g wholemeal flour
14 oz /400 g white flour
Pinch of aniseed (star anise crushed in a coffee grinder or pestle)
18 fl oz /500 ml yoghurt, buttermilk or kefir (or half yoghurt and water)
3 tablespoons oil
1½ oz /40 g fresh yeast, dissolved in a little tepid water
1 teaspoon sugar

Mix the flour and add the aniseed. Warm the liquids. Add the yeast mixture and sugar.

Allow to stand in a warm place for 10 minutes before sifting in the flour. Knead well. The dough should be fairly slack and sticky. Allow to double in volume in the usual way.

Knock back and knead well. Form into a loaf or loaves and allow to rise again.

Bake in a hot oven between 200-220 C /Gas 6-7 for 40-50 minutes.

Kalach, Kolindets - Plaited loaf from Ukraine and Moldova

Russians enjoy enriched white breads and rolls. There are many recipes for these, varying in degrees of complication, sweetness and richness.

Kalach is really delicious served Russian or Ukrainian style with cherry jam and soured cream, or as an English teatime treat with damson jam and clotted cream.

This recipe calls for two risings and works really well either as a loaf or as rolls. The limited amount of yeast and a good measure of salt help this bread to keep well..

1 lb /450 g strong flour
2 level teaspoons dried yeast
1 large egg, plus 1 yolk (for dough)
8 fl oz /225 ml lukewarm water
2 level teaspoons salt
3 teaspoons caster sugar
2 tablespoons oil
1 egg yolk (for glazing)
Sesame seeds or poppy seeds to decorate (optional)

Take 6-8 tablespoons of flour, and the yeast and sugar, then mix all together with the lukewarm water. Leave to work for 15-20 minutes, then add the remaining flour, the 'egg plus one yolk', oil and salt.

Knead well for about 10 minutes, either by hand or using an electric mixer.

The dough should be fairly soft. Shape into a ball and leave to rise and double in bulk. Leave in a cool kitchen overnight.

The next day, knead the dough again and allow to come to room temperature.

To make the six plait ring
Divide the dough into 6 rounds. Roll them between your hands into long strands, each about 18 inches /45 cm in length.

Take 2 dough strands and starting at the centre, twist them together going from left to right. Turn the strands around and repeat, always remembering to work from the centre. Repeat this for the remaining strands.

You will now have 3 twisted strands. Put these side by side and start making a plait, again working from the centre. Turn it around and plait from the other end. Bring the ends together to make your kalach into a ring, (or you can leave it to bake as a long twisted loaf).

Leave the plait or ring to rise well on an oiled baking tray for about half an hour, then glaze with the extra egg yolk.

Decorate by scattering sesame or poppy seeds over the loaf (optional).

Bake in a hot oven at 220 C/Gas 7 for 15 minutes, then at 190 C/Gas 5 for a further 15–20 minutes. Be careful not to overcook it!

Cake

Kulich

This traditional yeast cake, shaped into a high cylinder, is eaten at Easter with **Paskha**. I bake mine in a large cocoa tin without a lid. Remove the base of the tin with a tin opener, turn the tin upside down and slip the loose base inside where it is held in place. This loose base facilitates removal of the cake which is not always easy. Grease the tin well and line it with baking parchment. Use the same dough recipe and method as for poppy seed roll (p 181) adding the following ingredients:

4 oz /100 g raisins, previously plumped up in boiling water and dried.
1 oz /25 g each of candied peel, chopped angelica and finely chopped almonds
3-4 crushed cardamom seeds

Bake in a moderately hot oven 190-200 C /Gas 5-6 for the first 15 minutes, then turn the oven down to 180 C /Gas 4 covering the top with slightly damp greaseproof paper.

Test the cake for readiness. You could do this 'Russian style', with a matchstick! I usually use a warm skewer, which should come out cleanly.

The cake may be glazed with a brushing of warm milk and sugar or iced in the traditional Russian way. Mix lemon juice into the icing to offset the sweetness. Decorate the top with glacé cherries, angelica, nuts or crystallised fruit.

To serve, cut off the top of the kulich and slice portions across, replacing the decorative top after serving to keep the cake fresh as long as possible. The above recipe will produce two loaves or rounds.

The **Kulich** is also baked for Remembrance Monday, the equivalent of our All Souls Day, and was brought to the church to be blessed along with round krendels and other cakes and biscuits, pies, eggs, honey etc.

The historian Kohl records that on each loaf there would be a small book of remembrance and the priest would look into it and include the name on his prayer list. The food was eaten at the graves which were covered with table cloths and laid out for the meal. The priest would take a snack at each grave and would also receive drinks of vodka from carriages drawn up nearby. Beggars would also receive their share of whatever was going.

A certain amount of graveside 'festivity' still continued in the Soviet Union, especially in country areas, but cookbooks of that era described the Kulich as a rich yeast dough baked in olden times to celebrate spring festivals.

Kulich made with raisins, vanilla and syrup

This recipe dates from the 1950's.

1 lb /450 g flour
1 oz /25 g yeast
4 oz /100 g sugar
5 oz /150 g butter or margarine
5-6 eggs, beaten
4 fl oz /100 ml milk
3 oz /75 g raisins
Vanilla stick cut up very finely or 1 teaspoon vanilla essence
1 flat teaspoon salt

Syrup for pouring over the finished cake
2 oz /50 g sugar
1 fl oz /25 ml red wine
2 fl oz /50 ml water
flavouring essence

Dissolve the sugar in the water, add the wine and the flavouring essence of vanilla, almond or mint.

Take 1/3 of the flour and mix with an equal quantity of water. Mix the yeast separately in a little warm water, then add it to the flour mixture and set aside for 1½ hours. Knead.

Mix the softened butter, sugar, salt, beaten eggs and washed plumped up raisins and add these to the dough with the remaining flour. Put into greased tins. Allow to rise to twice or two and a half times its volume.

If you like a closer texture fill the tins two thirds full and allow the dough only just to reach the top. For a more open texture half fill the tins and wait until the dough reaches the top.

Bake in a moderately hot oven 190 C /Gas 5 for 50 minutes, depending on the size of the tins used. Cover with oiled greaseproof paper if tops are baking too quickly.

The syrup may be poured over the cake after it has cooled but while still slightly warm. A well flavoured icing may also be added when the cake is cold.

Keks Leningradskii

This is a useful standby fruit cake. It has quite a lot of fat in it and keeps very well, although the first time I encountered it in Leningrad[1], hungry friends and I devoured it straight away while still warm from the bakery.

8 oz /225 g self raising flour
5 oz /150 g sugar
7 oz /200 g butter or margarine, softened
2 eggs, separated
Grated lemon and its juice
¼ teaspoon salt
¼ teaspoon baking powder
about 2 tablespoons of water, depending of the absorbency of the flour
4 oz /100 g raisins, plumped up in hot water and dried, and a little citrus peel, the fruit may be omitted and vanilla essence substituted for variety.

Take part of the sugar and the egg yolks and beat together. Add the softened fat, the remaining sugar and the baking powder dissolved in a little water.

Beat well until white, then sift in the flour and the remaining ingredients, finally folding in the well beaten egg whites.

The mixture should not be too dry, but not as loose as for a sponge. Turn into a greased lined 1 lb /450 g loaf tin.

Bake in a hot oven at 200-210 C /Gas 6-6½ for about 40 minutes. If it browns too quickly put a double thickness of greaseproof paper over it for the last quarter of an hour.

Test with a warm skewer.

---

[1] Leningrad is now St. Petersburg, but the cake retains its Soviet name!

Poppy seed roll made with yeast

This is a very hard to resist cake with a delightfully moist light texture and delicious and unusual filling.

The filling can be varied and Russian cookbooks give a number of permutations. I have chosen the less sweet ones. Poppy seeds can be expensive, so ground almonds nuts and finely chopped raisins may be added to make an adequate filling.

The Dough

1 lb /450 g flour
13 fl oz /375 ml milk
3 egg yolks
4 oz /100 g sugar
5 oz /150 g butter or margarine
½ teaspoon salt
1 oz /25 g yeast
Vanilla or grated lemon (optional)

Filling One - preparation

8 oz /225 g poppy seeds and 2 oz /50 g ground almonds
1½ tablespoons honey
4 oz /100 g sugar

Mince the seeds (see note p 182) and add the remaining ingredients.

OR

Filling Two - preparation

4 oz /100 g poppy seeds
1 oz /25 g butter or margarine
2 oz /50 g caster sugar
2 level tablespoons syrup
½ teaspoon vanilla or lemon and or cinnamon
2 oz /50 g walnuts chopped
2 oz /50 g muscatel raisins, chopped
4 fl oz /100 ml milk

Mince the seeds (see note p 182). Add the remaining ingredients except the vanilla or lemon rind and cook until thick - about five minutes.

Add the vanilla or lemon when the filling is cold.

Mix the dough, add the filling of your choice, bake

Mix the yeast in the warm milk, sift in half the flour and leave to rise. When doubled, add salt and egg yolks beaten with the sugar, then add the remaining flour and beat again. Add the melted butter or margarine. Mix until the dough leaves the sides of the bowl. Sift a little flour over, cover and put in a warm place to rise.

When it has doubled roll it out to about ½ inch /1 cm thick and strew with the prepared seeds. Roll up, put on a greased tray to rise. Then glaze with egg and bake in a hot oven (200 C/Gas 6) for 20-30 minutes.

Before serving cover in icing sugar.

Note:

> **Poppy seeds** are very hard and need washing and then boiling up twice before crushing them. Some recipes recommend soaking the seeds overnight. The seeds are crushed in a mortar until they give off a white juice. This can be rather hard going.
>
> A mincing machine would reduce the work, but mincing the seed 2 or 3 times is recommended in many recipes.

Siberian shanezhki

These are little yeast buns with a topping of soured cream, butter, flour and sugar.

Yeast dough

> **18 oz /500 g flour (plain or half wholemeal) warmed**
> **4 oz /100 g sugar**
> **4 oz /100 g butter**
> **¾ oz /25 g yeast**
> **6 fl oz /150 ml milk (approx, depending on how large the eggs are)**
> **3 eggs: (2 yolk plus 1 whole egg, mixed)**

Topping

> **3 tablespoons smetana (soured cream)**
> **2 oz /50 g butter**
> **1 tablespoon flour and sugar**

Boil the milk, cool to lukewarm and mix with the yeast and half the warmed flour. Put in a warm place to rise for an hour. Mix the egg, softened butter and sugar together and add it to the yeast mixture with the remaining flour. Knead well and leave to rise for 1½-2 hours.

Form into little buns the size of an egg; put them on a greased tin to rise for another 30 minutes. Mix the topping and spread over the tops of the buns. Bake 15-20 minutes in a hot oven — 220 C /Gas 7.

Drachena - a Belarusian speciality

These are nice eaten with soured cream and jam. They are an interesting cross between a scone and a cake and as they are not very sweet are a useful standby.

5 oz /150 g rye flour
3 oz /75 g buckwheat flour
3 egg yolk
1 egg white, beaten
4-5 fl oz /100-150 ml buttermilk or use a mixture of drainings from cottage cheese, milk and soured cream)
7 fl oz /200 ml milk
3 oz /75 g butter or margarine (softened)
½ tablespoon of icing sugar (or more, to taste)

Mix the rye flour with the water and buttermilk. Leave for 3-4 hours in a warm place. Add the buckwheat flour and beat well. In a separate bowl cream the softened butter, egg yolks and icing sugar. Put the two mixtures together, making sure they are well blended. Pour in the milk slowly, stirring all the time and then fold in the egg white. Bake in a greased loaf tin for half an hour at 200 C /Gas 6.

Icing sugar could be omitted, replacing it with a little salt.

Sauces and Marinades

Nineteenth century travellers to Georgia noted the fine walnut trees, often bowed down to the ground with their burden of nuts. Today these trees are highly prized for their walnut oil, which is delicious in salads. It's more expensive than olive oil, but available in most supermarkets in small quantities.

The following nut sauce recipes can be used with meat, chicken and fish dishes and I have served them to vegetarian guests as a pâté. They are good with lightly cooked spinach and onion, sweet peppers, hot beetroot and onion mixtures. Buy the nuts in their shells to make sure of freshness.

Walnut sauce

3 oz /75 g shelled walnuts
2 cloves of garlic
papika, salt and pepper to taste
1 teaspoon ground cinnamon
1 tablespoon vinegar/lemon juice/grapefruit juice or pomegranate juice
3-4 small chopped onions
½ teaspoon each of parsley and dill

Pound the walnuts together with the next four ingredients. Add sufficient cooking liquid from the main dish to make a thick pouring cream. Pour into a pan, add the chopped onions and simmer for ten minutes. Add seasonings and fruit juice or vinegar.

This sauce is usually served hot as I had it in the Caucasus. It is equally good cold, providing the main dish is oil based.

Walnut sauce made with bread

3 oz /75 g chopped walnuts
2 cloves of garlic, peeled, chopped with the green centres removed
2 slice of white bread soaked in water
some weak vinegar, vegetable oil and salt

Crush the garlic in a little salt. Pound all the ingredients to a paste in a mortar and pestle or blend in a blender.

Georgian Garo sauce (walnut and garlic)

8 oz /225 g walnuts
2 tablespoons fresh coriander or use fresh dill or parsley to provide the green colour
coriander seeds, crushed to provide the flavour
melissa, a few leaves of (optional)
2 tablespoons wine or cider vinegar and 2 tablespoons water mixed
15 fl oz /425 ml chicken stock
2 egg yolks
2 small onions, grated
2 cloves of garlic or more according to taste
salt to taste

Pound the walnuts, chopped coriander/dill/parsley/melissa leaves and crushed coriander with the salt, mix in the vinegar and water mixture and chicken stock - a blender is useful. Add finely grated onion and cook the sauce for ten minutes. Cool and then pour a little warm stock over the egg yolks before mixing this into the sauce. Reheat sufficiently, stirring all the time as if making a custard. It should not be too hot or it may curdle.

This sauce may be used by vegetarians if they "replace" the chicken stock with a little well flavoured celery or mushroom based vegetable stock, or water thickened with a little crumbled wholemeal bread.

Satsivi[1] sauce – (walnut sauce served cold)

Georgians serve this thick sauce cold, to accompany fish or meat.

8 oz /225 g finely chopped or pounded walnuts
4 onions, finely chopped
1 tablespoon maize flour and enough fat or oil to make a roux
2 crushed garlic cloves
½ teaspoon each crushed coriander and cayenne pepper, suneli (p 207) and fresh
thyme, mint, melissa, powdered cloves
a light seasoning of black pepper and salt
1 teaspoon wine vinegar or grapefruit juice
a pinch of saffron or a little turmeric
1 cup (10 fl oz /275 ml) of chicken or vegetable stock
chicken fat or sunflower oil for frying

Fry the onion lightly, blend in the roux, pour over the stock, stirring all the time. Add the rest of the ingredients, except the fresh herbs which are added just before serving, and cook very gently for 15 minutes.

A quicker method is to put all the ingredients into a blender and bring up to the boil. In some parts of Georgia they add two egg yolks. This helps to thicken the sauce, but makes it rather rich.

---

[1] 'tsivi' means 'cold.'

Nut and garlic sauce (skordolya) from Moldova

4 oz /100 g walnuts
2 oz /50 g white bread, soaked in water and squeezed out
2 tablespoons sunflower oil
1 teaspoon wine vinegar and water/or lemon juice
3 cloves garlic (or more!)

Crush the nuts in a mortar or in a blender, add the garlic and soaked bread. Slowly pour over the oil in a steady stream and beat until the mixture thickens.

Finally mix in the vinegar or lemon. Any meat gravy from the accompanying dish may be added to the basic sauce which is suitable for meat, poultry fish, vegetables or for a salad.

Apricot/cherry or prune/plum sauce with wine

Mix two teaspoons of flour or cornflour with a few tablespoons of wine or water and lemon juice. Add more water if it is too thick. Cook until smooth - it should be on the thin side.

Add the sieved apricots/prunes/stoned cherries plus some of their juice, a bay leaf and some crushed garlic and herbs of your choice. Boil for a few minutes to amalgamate flavours. This is a most versatile sauce and can be used for hot and cold dishes. Without the garlic of course and with a pinch of sugar it makes a suitable sauce for fruit tarts.

The old word for 'sous' (sauce) was **podlivka** from the verb to 'pour over' and an even earlier word was **vzvar** meaning to boil up. Sauces were indispensable to eke out vegetarian dishes or to make meat and fish go further.

The oldest **podlivki** were onion, mushroom and berry based. Today tomato paste or purée is a constant ingredient in meat, fish and vegetarian dishes. Some sauces are thinned **kvas**[1], which gives a lightly piquant flavour to brown sauce.

There are numerous sauces to go with fish as this was eaten more than meat. Capers are grown all over the Caucasus, in the Crimea and in Central Asia and horseradish also grows freely. Enthusiasm for these sauces remains undiminished, and prepared the Russian way one can see why.

'Southern sauce' used in recipes is a ready-made commercial concoction of crushed rye crumbs, apple and tomato purée, oil, salt, sugar, garlic, grated onion, pepper, ginger, cloves, coriander and wine. This is recommended to be mixed with mayonnaise and other sauces to add piquancy.

---

[1] Or you can use light beer.

Celery sauce to go with Cauliflower

1 stick of celery, finely chopped
4 tablespoons of hot milk, plus vegetable water to make a thin cream consistency
1 tablespoon of flour
2 tablespoons of butter or margarine

Melt the fat, and fry the celery for a few minutes. Add the flour, mix well before gradually adding the hot milk and some of the vegetable water. Add seasoning and a sprinkling of fresh herbs. Cook for a few minutes before pouring over the cauliflower. An additional touch is to scatter over some fresh breadcrumbs, dot with butter and bake until the top is crisp and golden.

Onion vzvar (Honey sweetened onion sauce)

5-6 onions
2 tablespoons white wine or cider vinegar
1 tablespoon butter or oil
1 tablespoon of honey
pepper to taste

Cut the onions into rings and soak them in the vinegar for 10 minutes. Drain and then cook them in the oil or butter until soft. Sweeten with honey and add pepper.

Variations:
I.   Mix 1 tablespoon flour with 11 fl oz /300 ml beef or vegetable stock until it thickens slightly, then stir it into the onion mixture. Finally, add 1 teaspoon of caraway seeds (or fennel seeds).

II. Onion vzvar can also be puréed and a little mustard added.

Russian mustard

2 oz /50 g mustard powder or crushed mustard seeds
1 tablespoon sugar
½ teaspoon salt
2 tablespoons weak vinegar (use cider vinegar or 1 tablespoon of wine vinegar mixed with water)
2 tablespoons oil
1 tablespoon of spiced marinade (nastoi), made from cloves, grated nutmeg, black pepper and cardamom. Crush a few of these and pour over a little hot water and leave to stand for a few hours.

Mix the mustard with 4 tablespoons of boiling water to make a thick paste, then add another six tablespoons of boiling water sufficient to cover. Leave to stand for about six hours or overnight. Then pour off excess water, add the sugar and salt and stir in the vinegar, oil and spiced marinade **'nastoi'**. Put into a clean jar and leave for two or three days to develop the flavour.

Egg and dill sauce

No Russian cookbook would be complete without a dill sauce, though I must confess I prefer the more delicate flavour of fennel.

Wild Caucasian dill is very strong tasting and I was served it in such quantities in restaurants every day when I spent a month there, that I am somewhat prejudiced.

For table use, only young shoots should be served. The mature shoots are more suitable for pickling. Dill is rich in vitamin C. The British variety is milder and the following sauce, sharpened with sorrel goes well with boiled beef and is a useful sauce for other hors d'oeuvres and salads.

To make a small quantity, hard boil one egg. Use the yolk for making a smooth mayonnaise with a little sunflower or grapeseed oil. Chop young sorrel leaves, chives, and dill very finely. Add these and a little stock, milk or water according to what you have on hand to make a thin pouring sauce. Cut the egg white up finely and scatter it over the sauce before serving. Season to taste. Herbs may be varied.

Purslane sauce

A thick green sauce to go with fish and meat.

8 oz /250 g purslane
1 tablespoon weak vinegar (cider vinegar or vinegar and water mixed with lemon juice)
1 clove garlic, crushed
salt, a little black pepper and milled parsley.

Steam the purslane until the stalks are tender. Blend it with the weak vinegar, garlic and seasonings.

Beetroot and Horseradish relish

10 medium beetroot
½ cup of grated horseradish
2 cups wine vinegar diluted with 2 cups water
½ cup sugar
2 teaspoons salt
1 tablespoon mixed spices

Wash the beetroot, leaving most of the root and stalks on. Cook until tender. When cool, slip them out of their skins and grate them. Mix with the horseradish. Boil up the vinegar, sugar, spices and salt. Pour over the beetroot mixture. Pack into sterilised jars, cover with pergamon paper and stand for a day or so before using.

Beetroot and cabbage relish

1 lb /450 g cooked peeled beetroot
1 lb /450 g raw white cabbage
2 tablespoons dried grated horseradish (can be bought ready-grated)
8 oz /225 g sugar
20 fl oz /575 ml vinegar
1 tablespoon dry mustard
Pinch of black pepper.

Shred cabbage, cut out thick stems. Chop the beetroot. Put this with all the remaining ingredients into a pan and stir to dissolve the sugar. Simmer for 30 minutes; put into warm jars and cover. Keep for several weeks before using.

Marinated vegetables - the Azerbaijan way

The vegetables should be fresh and young for this recipe.

½ medium size cabbage
2 each of aubergines, sweet peppers, green tomatoes, carrots
1 each of beetroot, fresh cucumber, onion

Fresh herbs
2 branch of tarragon
2 head of garlic
2 tablespoons each of coriander and dill
1 tablespoon each of mint and parsley

Liquid for marinade

18 fl oz /500 ml water and 1 tablespoon salt
2 fl oz /75 ml cider or wine vinegar plus a tablespoon of vinegar and water

To make the **rassol'** marinade:

Boil the water with the salt, add the wine vinegar, bring up to the boil and put in the herbs. Allow to cool.

Prepare the vegetables by cutting the aubergines in large slices, blanch them in salted water for 1 minute and drain. Blanch the whole carrots and well scrubbed beetroot in unsalted water for 2-3 minutes. Then peel the beetroot and cut it and the carrot into large pieces. Slice the onion into rings and divide the garlic into cloves. Pour over the prepared marinade and keep for about ten days before using.

Marinated cabbage

This is not fully fermented like sauerkraut and is easily prepared. You will need a two pint /1¼ litre jar for this recipe.

> **2 lb /900 g of cabbage (approx.) - preferably a close white one**
> **1 tablespoon of salt.**
> **Other additions may be: a carrot, eating apple, or a few berry fruits**
> **Herbs: Choose from coriander, star anise and or bay leaf**
> **Spices: 6 Jamaican spice berries**
> **6 black peppercorns**
> **¼ teaspoon each of caraway and dill seed**
> **salt for sprinkling**

Shred the cabbage very finely and grate the carrot and apple. Sprinkle the salt over and leave it for an hour and then squeeze out the mixture. Keep this juice on one side. Layer up the cabbage mixture, sprinkling salt and herbs between each. Pour over the reserved juice which should just cover the vegetables. Cover with muslin and stand at room temperature for four days.

Serve the cabbage with oil and vinegar dressing, chives or spring onions.

Marinated grapes I

> **2 lb /900 g grapes**
> **1 pint /575 ml water**
> **9 fl oz /250 ml 3% wine vinegar or half vinegar and half water (not malt or white vinegar)**
> **5 oz /150 g sugar**
> **1 teaspoon crushed coriander**
> **4 Jamaican pepper corns and 4 cloves**
> **½ teaspoon of crushed star anise**

Boil the water with the sugar, pour in the vinegar. Pour the hot marinade over the spices and allow to stand 2-3 hours. Wash the grapes and dry them. Pour over the marinade and keep for three to four days in a cool place before using. These marinated grapes improve with keeping.

Marinated grapes or plums II

18 fl oz /500 ml of wine vinegar
35 fl oz /1 litre of water
1 teaspoon salt
7 oz /200 g sugar
2 lb /1 kg of grapes or plums

Boil up the water, vinegar, sugar and salt for ten minutes. When it is cool pour it over the washed and drained fruit. Pack into glass jars and cover with a thin film of oil before closing down with pergamon parchment.

192

PRESERVES

Jams and jellies

'Arkady...felt it his duty to try out the four different kinds of freshly made varen'ye...Then came tea, cream and sweet dough buns.' **Fathers and Sons,** Ivan Turgenev.

Russians aim to keep the fruit whole when making **varen'ye,** the fruit preserve most liked for serving on a saucer to go with tea.[1] Jellies - **peltya** are much as we know them. A thick variety can be baked slowly to form delicious sweetmeats. **Povidlo** and **dzhem** are thicker than **varen'ye. Povidlo** is a useful fruit cheese of puréed fruit and can be made from any fruit flesh left after making jelly.

For each cup of purée add ¾ cup of sugar and cook over a low heat, stirring continuously. It makes a solid conserve, ideal for filling pies and biscuits.

Preparation of fruit for varen'ye

A syrup is made of at least equal quantities of fruit and sugar (sometimes the sweetening agent can be a mixture of honey and treacle). Approximately 18 fl oz /500 ml of water is needed but slightly less for very juicy fruit such as strawberries and raspberries.

These are sprinkled with some of the sugar and left a number of hours or overnight in a cool place to draw out the juice. Gooseberries are sprinkled with cold water and left for a few hours. When the syrup has been boiled, put in any juice and the soft fruit and cook in the usual way.

I must confess that I prefer our English style of jam. It may not look so beautiful but it is less cloying than the whole fruit suspended in syrup. Most Russian recipes call for 1 kg of fruit to 1½ kg of sugar, which I would find too sweet.

One exception I came across is the following:

Apple jam/jelly
35 oz /1 kg of sharp fruit
14 oz /400 g of sugar
22 fl oz /625 ml water

Core the washed apples, cut in eighths, and cook gently in the water in a closed casserole for 20-30 minutes. Drain off the juice, mix with the sugar and cook over a low heat. Test in the usual way. The apple flesh can be sieved and then used for making **povidlo** *(fruit cheese)* or used in pies. A useful and easy recipe.

---

[1] Russians like to eat a small teaspoonful of jam, followed by a sip of tea. In the 19th century, it was common practice to sip tea through a sugar cube held between the teeth!

Plum and apple 'cheese'

35 fl oz /1 kg of apple, plums and sugar
9 fl oz /250 ml water

Core the apples and stone the plums and cook as indicated above. Sieve the purée, add the sugar and stir over a low heat until ready - approximately 1½ hours. This is tedious, and a simmer mat or cooking in a moderate oven (180 C/Gas 4).with the fruit covered would avoid this.

APPLES

One of the most popular and widely used apples is the Antonovka which keeps well until March. From Kazakhstan come Aport apples and Sinap apples from the Crimea. Once apples would travel thousand of miles from the Black Sea to Petersburg, via Stettin[1], and became known as Stettin apples. The historian Kohl and other travellers also noted the curious 'glass' translucent apples from Siberia. Once there used to be hundreds of varieties but now only the best and most commercially viable are grown.

In Chekhov's story **'The Black Monk'** there is a description of a 90 acre estate with an orchard full of fancifully shaped trees - pear trees in the shape of pyramids, umbrella shaped apple trees, plum trees trained into arches and candelabra. The work in the garden took teams of labouring peasants and a day and night watch of relays of gardeners to look out for the first frost. They would sleep underneath the trees in the icy cold. The ground temperature, of course, was much lower than the air above where the smoke and bonfires protected the precious trees, but not the poor gardeners.

---

[1] Now Szczecin, in Poland

BEVERAGES

Tea

The samovar became something of a status symbol to the peasants in the late 19th century. Tea was the most popular non-alcoholic drink, as it still is.

Chekhov, as usual, tells us in his indirect way more about the social habits of the time than bookfuls of statistics which are soon forgotten. In his story **'Peasants'** the samovar smelt of fish and lay neglected on the floor in a corner of the family hut. There is even talk of it being claimed in lieu of taxes - a real indication of peasant poverty, which was widespread in the late 1890s. In Chekhov's **'The Student'**, a priest's son has just visited his parents and is depressed because his old mother has not even polished the samovar, symbol of hospitality, for the coming Easter.

Tea was also drunk copiously in bourgeois families; in Chekhov's **'The Bride'** the poor consumptive student Sasha almost lived on tea and would drink cup after cup, as many as twenty a day, until he perspired.

Kandinsky, writing of northern Vologda in this same period, describes the yellow colour of the peasants' faces from drinking carrot tea. In the windows of their houses is the melancholy sight of unused samovars.

Visitors to the home of Alexandre Benois (1870-1960) recall 'cosy' evenings assembled round the samovar, where his old nanny dispensed tea to the lively 'World of Art' group who would meet weekly to formulate their ideas. Old nannies hovering over samovars seem indispensable in Russian literature — there she is again in Chekhov's **Uncle Vanya** and **The Three Sisters** doling out comfort to her erstwhile charges. Perhaps it was the 'song' of the samovar which brought the feeling of comfort, unlike the eerie sounds of the Russian stove in **The Three Sisters**, bringing melancholy thoughts.

Tea in Russia can be drunk with honey, jam, sugar and lemon or wine. In summer it can be drunk cold with orange, lemon or cherry juice added. Wine added to a weak brew and served with lumps of ice is regarded as a treat. For colds, herb mixtures of dried raspberry, crushed star anise and lime leaves are sometimes used.

Old Tatar recipes give teas made from beetroot and carrots. More attractive sounding ones were prepared from black currant leaves, willow-herb and meadow sweet.

One well known Tatar tea has often been commented on by travellers – usually adversely. It consisted of pressed 'brick[1] tea' and hot milk boiled together for 5-8 minutes, stirred constantly. Salt and possibly pepper are added; then served with butter. I haven't tried it!

---

[1] Tea bricks: blocks of whole or finely ground black or green tea, or post-fermented tea leaves.

Coffee

Coffee was definitely upper class and slightly 'foreign' in the 19th century. Madame Ranevkaya on her return from Paris to the family estate in **The Cherry Orchard** *(Chekhov)* has her servant Firs scurrying about preparing her coffee late at night. Coffee with lemon is one way the Russians drink it.

During my visits, lemons were so expensive, that even in the Caucasus where they grow I was looked at pityingly in restaurants if I asked for either tea or coffee with lemon. I have drunk coffee with lemon and can say it is very nice and worth trying. Condensed and powdered milk was generally offered with beverages. It was better to drink your tea or coffee without.

Globalisation has fuelled a growing coffee culture in today's Russia; 21st century consumers expect similar standards and choice as in the rest of the developed world.

DRINKS

Vodka

The way to drink this national drink is to serve it ice cold in small liqueur glasses. I keep my bottle in the freezer so that it emerges 'steaming' when poured out. In Russian restaurants you order your vodka by the gramme—**sto gramme** (100 g) is the usual measure to go with your **zakuski** — that is if you are a westerner.

A variation is to slip thin slivers of lemon or orange peel into the required amount of vodka a few hours before drinking. Remove the peel from any left over vodka to stop it turning bitter. Use a lemon zester for the job to avoid getting any white pith into the drink.

Siberskaya 45%AbV, is considered one of the best Russian vodkas, distilled from **pshenichnaya**[1]. This is the most expensive kind. A good vodka more easily obtained in the UK is **Stolichnaya**.

Vodka is usually colourless, but Nikolai Gogol describes a provincial party in **Dead Souls** where a dark green olive-coloured one is served, the colour of which is 'only to be seen in certain kinds of Siberian stones'[2]

It could possibly be a herb or mushroom vodka or even the recipe given to the old wife Pul'kheria Ivanovna in **Old World Landowners** by a passing Turkish lady and brewed with cloves and walnuts.

The old woman explains to her guest the different qualities of the vodka she has brewed and their medicinal properties: One vodka infused with sage is good for shoulder and back pains;

---

[1] Pshenichnaya: a grade of wheat provided for distilling during the Soviet era. Prohibitive cost means it is rarely used for distillery purposes today.

[2] Gogol had a painterly eye for exact shades, shape and texture. This can be seen in many of his stories, especially the ones describing the Dnieper and Ukraine. One of his close friends was A. A. Ivanov (1806-58) whose famous painting 'Christ appearing before the people' hangs in the Tretyakov Gallery in Moscow, and always draws a large crowd.

another made from centaury is good for ringing in the ears or for shingles. Yet another made from apricot kernels is for bumps and bruises. She might be on the right track with apricot kernels for bruises, with their vitamin C content, though I don't know how much would survive the alcoholic infusion!

You can buy various flavoured vodkas in Russia, but many are sweetened. A peppery one the Russians use for colds (**pertsovka**) you can make yourself from ordinary vodka, adding about 25 each of black and white peppercorns to 1 pint /575 ml of vodka.

Russian cookbooks generally remain silent on the question of vodka — but I have come across references to the relative merits of different cognacs.

Cognac

The strongest is 'Erivan' with a high 57% AbV[1]. Below are some of the cognacs given in Cyrillic initials for recognition by would-be buyers:

KV: **kon'yak vyderzhanyi**, kept for 6-7 years. 42% AbV.

KWK: cognac of the highest quality 8-10 years old, 45% AbV.

KC: at least ten years old, 43% AbV.

OC: more than 10 years old.

Wine

Wine is produced in Moldova, the Caucasus and the Crimea. The Don is also proud of some of its wines and local ones are **Sibirkovyi, Puchlyakovskii, Dolgii** among others. The best known Caucasian wine is **tsinandali.**

In Tbilisi many houses have their own vines against their walls or in the courtyards. At the Chavchavadse Museum we tasted grapes from a vine planted by Chavchavadse himself[2].

Just outside Tbilisi, the well known Bagration[3] family had their large estates which became a collective vineyard during the Soviet era.

---

[1] AbV : Alcohol by Volume
[2] Chavchavadse, Ilya (1837-1907), a liberal writer who was murdered for his beliefs and nationalist outlook.
[3] Prince Bagration of **War and Peace** fame was in charge of the 2nd Army in the war of 1812.

Kvas

This is a favourite Russian drink and a very old one. Modern cookbooks maintain that the lactic acid in it is good for the kidneys. Kvas based on rye bread or rye and other flours comes in various degrees of sourness and sweetness, and can be flavoured with caraway or mint, or, as in the north, with blackcurrant leaves and in Ukraine with cinnamon. The Polish version is with lemon juice and the Lithuanians add raisins as well as the lemon.

Basic rye bread based kvas

1 lb /450 g rye bread
8 pints /4½ litres water
4 oz /100 g sugar
1/3 oz /10 g yeast
2 tablespoons of rye or buckwheat flour or a mixture

Cut the bread into small pieces and dry off in a low oven (140 C/Gas 1). until slightly coloured. Put them into a large enamelled or plastic bucket and pour over the boiling water, cover and leave for 3-4 hours. An hour before this time is up mix the yeast in a bowl with a cup of warm water and the flours. Leave for an hour. Drain off and keep the liquid from the bread. This is the **kvas basis.** Add the yeast mixture and the sugar to the liquid and keep in a warm place for 4-5 hours and then cool off before bottling. Keep in a cold place. Serve chilled.

Kvas made with malt and buckwheat and other flours

5½ oz /160 g of malt extract
18 oz /500 g rye flour
4 oz /100 g each of buckwheat and wheat flour sifted together
½ oz /15 g fresh yeast
5 pints /2¾ litres hot water

For a mint flavouring either add ½ teaspoon of mint essence or make your own by pouring boiling water to cover, over a large handful of freshly chopped mint with a teaspoon of sugar added and leaving it to draw before use- Alternatively add 1½ tablespoons of dried mint.

Dissolve-the yeast in half a cup of warm water and mix with a tablespoon of flour and allow to froth. Pour a little warm water over the malt. Sift the flours into the malt, stirring to avoid lumps and adding half the water from the recipe as you go. Leave for 5 hours. Add the remaining hot water, (it will need re-heating), the yeast mixture and the mint. Leave for 12 hours in a warm place and pour into bottles. Do not put the corks in too tightly.

Kvas recipe for smaller quantities

2½ oz /75 g malt extract
½ oz /15 g yeast (fresh)
7 oz /200 g rye flour
2 oz /50 g each of buckwheat and wheat flours
2 pints /1¼ litres of water

Mint or other flavouring (if using blackcurrant leaves, chop them and. bring them to the boil in a little water, then cool and use the liquid).

Tatar Kvas

This is a simple recipe made in a small quantity.

7 oz /200 g of stale rye bread crusts (create rusks by drying bread in the oven).
1½ pints /850 ml of warm boiled water.

Put the crusts in a bag and crush them, or else put them in a blender. Place them in an enamel bowl and pour over the warm boiled water, cover the bowl tightly and stand for 7-8 days in a warm place. This can be used for soups or in recipes requiring weak vinegar.

Recipes suitable for young children

Why give your children expensive cereals from packets or tins of food when you can make delicious and nourishing **kasha** and soups at half the price and without the addition of doubtful 'improvers'?

Try the recipes listed below, reducing quantities to suit your purpose.

Meal	Recipe	Page
Breakfast	Millet **kasha** (porridge)	118
Breakfast	**Buckwheat kasha** (porridge) This can be sieved for very small children	115
Main course	**Kotletki** Meat cutlets	76
Main course	Fish **tefteli** (fish patties)	64
Main or Pudding	**Tvorozhniki (syrniki)** - curd cheese fritters	150

A 'nursery' meatball or beef burger

8 oz /225 g minced meat
5 oz /150 g white bread, soaked in milk and squeezed out
2 tablespoons on oil/butter

Stuffing
8 tablespoons of prepared buckwheat porridge (p 115) or boiled rice
1 onion sliced and fried
1 hard-boiled egg
1 tablespoon flour
1 tablespoon flour and 2 tablespoons of soured cream and stock to make a sauce

Mix together the meat and soaked bread. Form into flattish rounds and fill with the stuffing.

Turn up the edges and seal well and fry in oil or butter.

Remove them to a plate to keep warm while you make the sauce by mixing the flour into the pan juices with the soured cream, gradually adding a little stock or water.

Cabbage olad'i

This is one way of encouraging your child to eat cabbage! —

7 oz /120 g cabbage, finely chopped
¼ cup (2-3 fl oz /60 ml) milk
½ egg
1 teaspoon breadcrumbs
2 teaspoons butter for frying
1 tablespoon smetana (soured cream)

Gently cook the cabbage in milk until tender. Sieve or blend the cooked cabbage and milk, add a small pinch of salt, mix with the raw egg and breadcrumbs and form the mixture into little patties with the aid of a tablespoon. Fry in butter until golden and serve with the soured cream.

Carrot bake

1 carrot very lightly cooked and chopped
4 tablespoons of breadcrumbs
1 egg
1 teaspoon sugar
1 teaspoon butter (half for the carrot mixture, half for the crumb mixture).

Cook the carrot in a very little water. It helps if it is cut into julienne strips before cooking. Drain and chop it and add the sugar and half the butter. Pour a little hot water over the breadcrumbs to moisten them and add the egg and remaining butter. Put half the crumb mixture into a greased Pyrex dish, then the carrot, and cover with the remaining crumb mixture and bake in a moderate oven ((180 C/Gas 4).until lightly golden and crisp.

Carrot and apple kotlety (semolina)

1 carrot and 1 apple peeled and coarsely grated
1 teaspoon of semolina
½ teaspoon sugar
2 teaspoons butter
Breadcrumbs
2-3 fl oz /60 ml water

Pour the water over the carrot and steam until partially cooked. Then add the apple and cook both together until soft. Sprinkle in the semolina, add a pinch of salt and the sugar and cook together for 5 minutes, stirring all the time. Cool the mixture and divide into little patties, roll them in breadcrumbs and fry in the butter on both sides until golden.

Semolina pudding with apple

5 teaspoons of semolina
7 fl oz /200 ml milk
1 egg, separated
1 teaspoon sugar
1 cooked apple
2 teaspoons butter
breadcrumbs

Boil the milk, sprinkle in the semolina slowly, add a tiny pinch of salt and cook in the usual way, stirring continuously. Add the sugar, (this is always best added after the semolina has cooked as there is less danger burning it.

Add the butter, egg yolk and mix well. When it had cooled add the well beaten egg white. You may not need all of this if the egg is large.

Grease a Pyrex dish and strew with breadcrumbs and put in a layer of semolina and apple, finishing with a layer of semolina. Dot with butter and more breadcrumbs and bake in a moderate oven (180 C/Gas 4) until brown.

Restorative and easily digested recipes

A number of these are generally included in Russian cookbooks, perhaps to offset days of feasting and immoderation. Larger old-fashioned volumes usually devote a chapter or two to dishes for specific illnesses.

Oatmeal vegetable soup

1 oz /25 g fine oatmeal or ordinary porridge oats
1 pint /575 ml water
5 fl oz /150 ml milk
4 oz /100 g puréed vegetables
1 tablespoon butter
½ an egg

Sprinkle the oats into the boiling water and cook gently as for making porridge, stirring continuously. It should be on the thin side. Add the puréed vegetables, bring to the boil. In a separate pan warm the milk and add the egg, butter and salt and whisk lightly until well heated through, but don't allow to boil. Pour this into the oat mixture.

Barley soup with meat purée

1 oz /25 g barley flour or flakes
1 pint /575 ml water
2 oz /60 g cooked minced meat keep the juice)
1 tablespoon butter
5 fl oz /150 g milk or 2 fl oz /50 ml cream
salt

If you can't obtain barley flour, grind barley flakes in a coffee grinder. Cover the barley with boiling water and bring up to the boil. Put the barley mixture and the meat and any meat juice or gravy into the blender and blend for one minute. Thicken the soup with the butter and milk mixture as above.

Beef Stroganoff with boiled beef

Braise or steam the meat. Do not overcook. Alternatively slice frozen raw beef in wafer thin slices, briefly fry it and serve it in a white sauce with two tablespoons of **smetana** and 1 tablespoon of tomato purée added. **Smetana** (soured cream) is more digestible than fresh cream.

Carrot and cottage cheese soufflé for one person

4 oz /100 g carrots, sliced
2 oz /50 g cottage cheese, sieved
2 oz /50 g milk
1 tablespoon sugar
½ an egg
2 teaspoons of semolina

Cook the carrots in the milk over a low heat. Watch that it doesn't burn.

Sieve or blend the mixture, add the cheese, sugar, egg yolk and sprinkle in the semolina.

Beat the egg white stiffly and fold into the mixture.

Grease a soufflé dish and steam or bake the soufflé for 15-20 minutes in a very hot oven 230 C /Gas 8 or until just lightly golden. Do not overcook; go partly by the smell, as ovens vary so much.

Buckwheat and cottage cheese soufflé

2 oz /50 g buckwheat
2 tablespoons milk
2 oz /50 g cottage cheese, sieved
1 egg
1 teaspoon sugar
knob of butter

Make a thick buckwheat porridge (p 115). Or use up left-over buckwheat porridge. Mix the sugar, cheese and egg yolk together and then the milk. Stir into the buckwheat. Beat the egg white stiffly. Put into a greased soufflé dish and cook as directed above. Serve with **smetana** and melted butter.

Vegetarian borshch

(Cook together)
5 oz /150 g beetroot
1 carrot, sliced into julienne strips
4-5 parsley stalks (keep the tops for
serving)
1 medium onion, sliced
1½ tablespoons sunflower oil
2 tablespoons tomato purée
2 dessertspoons vinegar
pinch sugar

(Cook separately, then add)
4 oz /100 g cabbage, finely sliced
4 oz /100 g potatoes finely sliced

salt and seasoning (before final boil)

((To serve with borshch)
4 tablespoons smetana
dill

Put everything in the left column of ingredients in a pan, pour in sufficient water, stir well, cover and simmer gently for 40 minutes.

Cook the cabbage and potatoes separately and then add them to the other vegetables. Season and bring the soup to the boil before serving with the **smetana** and dill.

This soup can be adapted, using any other vegetables in season. It is made very quickly in a pressure cooker, using the separator baskets.

It is also nice puréed. Quantities can be doubled or tripled for general family use.

Cold borshch (svekol'nik)

5 oz /150 g beetroot
5 oz /150 g fresh cucumber, peeled and thinly sliced
1 medium potato, finely cut
A few spring onions, plus their tops, finely sliced
dill
pinch of salt, sugar
smetana and lemon juice mixed
½ a hard-boiled egg

Put aside 1 raw beetroot for grating to improve the colour of the soup. Add this ten minutes before the end of cooking. Cook and finely slice the rest.

I find that pressure cooking the beetroots whole in a little vinegar keeps the colour beautifully and I don't usually need to resort to last minute grating. I also use the beetroot juice which is usually a deep ruby colour).

Cook the potato in 1½ pints /850 ml of water, allow to cool in the water and then add in the remaining ingredients. Serve with the soured cream and dill, garnished with the egg.

COOKING INGREDIENTS, HERBS AND SPICES

Smetana - soured cream is used freely in Russian cooking. It tastes slightly acid, with a fresh tang. Most supermarkets stock it.

It keeps better and longer than ordinary cream and if flour is mixed with it doesn't separate out in cooking. Thickened yoghurt is a useful substitute.

You can make your own soured cream with double cream and buttermilk. 1 tablespoon of cottage/curd cheese drainings mixed in with 10 fl oz /275 ml of double cream, left for 24 hours in a warm place, will produce soured cream.

A substitute **smetana** can be made by stirring a teaspoon of lemon juice into cream and leaving it for a few hours.

Tvorog - curd / cottage cheese - See page 149.

Radishes: sometimes a recipe calls for a black radish. These large ones come from Spain and are rarely found in the shops here. *(Cooking radishes rids them of their hotness).*

Horseradish (khren) is also mild when served hot. It is said to be richer in vitamin C than oranges and lemons. It was once wild all over England, but now you would need to search.

HERBS

Russian favourites are the flat bladed **Hamburg parsley** and **dill**. Parsley stalks are a good substitute when a recipe calls for parsley roots. Few people would interfere with a well established bed of parsley to dig up the precious roots.

Dill is used in so many Russian dishes and can be overdone. I prefer fennel which is easier to come by and to grow. Fennel and dill are not good bed fellows for some reason, fennel tending to take over.

Well known herbs used freely in Russian dishes are **tarragon** and **thyme** (good with fish and chicken) and delicate **chervil**, which once well established in the garden grows vigorously. It can also be easily vanquished by a careless gardener. It grows wild in south east Russia.

Most dried herbs such as **mint, savory, lovage, basil, coriander, fenugreek** can be obtained fairly easily in most towns. **Fenugreek** is said to have a high protein content, but one is unlikely to eat enough to feel the benefit.

Purslane: Recommend for making a thick green sauce to go with fish and meat. (p 188)

Two herbs mentioned occasionally in Russian literary works:

Goosefoot: a kind of wild spinach. The seeds are also used for culinary purposes in Siberia.

Goosegrass: sometimes used as a tea substitute in Siberia. It has a carroty taste.

SPICES

Supermarkets stock a wide range; **cardamom** is a lovely one to have and delicious in cakes. Crush the tiny seeds, which are inside a capsule, with a kitchen hammer or in a mortar and pestle and enjoy their refreshing lemony flavour. I often chew them and also star anise when I'm busy cooking.

Some coffee purists like a few crushed star anise seeds in their coffee, which they then stir with a vanilla stick. A lovely change!

Saffron is very expensive; I generally use it for my mother's Cornish saffron cake recipe at Christmas. She always soaked the saffron overnight and used the liquid and the threads. Poppy seeds may be eked out in recipes with minced raisins or ground almonds

Angelica is used in cakes and especially in Easter **paskha**. Chekhov noted the huge angelica growing on Sakhalin Island when he travelled there in 1890. Apparently the bears loved to eat the gigantic stalks. Another northern country which uses angelica in baking is Norway, where they sometimes use the roots in bread making. The stalk can also be boiled and used in place of celery.

Caucasian spices

Adzhiki is hot and made up of cayenne and chilli powder, salt and pepper and crushed bay leaves.

Khmeli suneli: (In the Caucasus many families have their own special and secret recipes). Take more or less equal quantities of the following: crushed bay leaf, coriander, celery and dill seed, and fenugreek and mix them with fresh or dried parsley, thyme, mint and basil.

REGIONS AND NATIONALITIES
WHERE THEY ARE, WHAT THEY GROW, WHAT THEY EAT

In writing about such a vast territory it helps to have a minimal outline of a few geographical/historical features to hand concerning shifting populations and topography in order to relate place names and regional dishes. The maps will, I hope, make this even clearer. A bibliography follows for those who want more background information.

In the notes on food preparation in the individual countries my main task has been to show original regional tendencies so that a fair idea can be obtained of what embellishments might have been added at later stages by travellers, inventive cooks and fancy restaurateurs.

Agriculture, climate, and food

It is not always fully appreciated how difficult it is for the Russian Federation, the world's largest country, to supply enough of its own food. For instance in many parts around the Novgorod[1] and St. Petersburg area the working season is as low as four months for the farmer. Moreover geographic and climatic features are such that rain falls where it is least needed and at times least appropriate so that there is always the possibility of drought or floods somewhere.

Many important growing areas, even where the land is rich, are plagued by strong winds which can blow for days on end with few mountain ranges to stop them. It is not for nothing that the wind in Russian literature, poetry and folklore seems to assume a personality of its own.

In one of Chekhov's stories a character called Gusev firmly believed that winds were chained up at one side of the world and unleashed at intervals to chastise mankind. Chekhov, with his scientific and medical background had a thorough understanding of figure types and their metabolism and how they were affected by their environment. He also had a prophetic understanding of what man was capable of doing to it. In **Uncle Vanya** he described the careless cutting down of trees with the ensuing drying up of streams and alteration of flora and fauna.

In **Steppe** he observed 'rational agronomy' in the dry south steppeland which was based on endless killing of animals and insects. "They kill swallows, sparrows, bumblebees, ravens and magpies so that the fruit blossom should not be damaged and they fell trees so that they should not impoverish the soil".

Conditions vary across the country, but distribution of food is a big problem because of the immense distances and the bad state of the roads for much of the year, particularly in winter months when blizzards can arise within minutes and blot out a landscape, as Pushkin describes in his poem '**Devils**' and also in his delightful novel '**The Captain's Daughter**'.

During the Soviet era, pickling, bottling, salting and marinating were a necessity, but continue to be a favourite way of preparing food and suit the national taste for 'something sour'.

---

[1] Novgorod Oblast: Federal area SE of St. Petersburg.

The great rivers of Central European Russia play an important part in transporting food. The interlinking of the Western Dvina, Dnieper and the Volga, which in turn link the Baltic coast to the Black and Caspian Seas, have not only contributed to Russia's historical and economic development but spread cultural and culinary ideas.

However, they mainly flow north to south so the much longer distances going from east to west have to be served by rail and road. The difficulty here is that fuel can freeze in locomotives and the very loads solidify. Rail track too also has to be constantly re-laid after frost distortion.

Nationalities: A few facts

Within the area covered by this book live over eight hundred ethnic denominations and one hundred and twenty-two different nationalities which account for the immense variety of regional dishes.

Seventy per cent of the population is Slav, made up of Russians, Ukrainians and Belarusians. Then come some twenty nationalities of the Turkic group, followed by the peoples of the Caucasus - the Christian Georgians and Armenians sandwiched in between Moslem Azerbaijanis, Chechens and many other ethnic groups. In this region alone thirty or more different languages are spoken.

In some inaccessible valleys and mountain areas there still live members of once large tribes who keep up old traditional style of dress. For a description of the Chechens, Inguishi and Kabardinians you can do no better than read Lermontov's **A Hero of our Time**. Other important ethnic groups in the region are the Finnic Ugrians and the Baltic peoples.

RUSSIAN FEDERATION

The Russian Federation is about 1.7 times larger than the USA. But size alone is not the most important thing — the Russian Federation has only 2¼ times as many people as the United Kingdom, but is over seventy times larger.

The 'Russian Federation' is made up of 85 governing regions with varying degrees of autonomy. They are grouped into 7 'Federal Districts' e.g. 'Urals, Siberian, Volga Region'.

22 regions are classed as 'Republics' with greater autonomy and the right to use their own language.

Chekhov's journey from Moscow to Sakhalin Island took 11 weeks covering over 5000 miles by rail, steamboat and long distances across Siberia by cart. Much of the way he followed the 'Tea Road' - Russian 'Caravan Tea' deriving its name from 'camel caravans' which transported tea from China to Europe along this route.

A glance at the map will show the enormous area covered here, so cooking varies widely between north, south, east and west and is naturally influenced by what can be grown.

Some points have already been made about the general Russian approach to food preparation which is based on a liking for 'something sour'. Chekhov often expressed this national desire after an excess of foreign food, however delicious, or when people around him were too cloying and obsequious!

Russian food

Russian cooking is distinguished by the variety of its **zakuski** *(hors d'oeuvres)*, breads, pancakes raised yeast pies, grain porridges, thick soups both hot and cold, fish and mushroom dishes. It also makes wide use of preserved salted and fermented vegetables, especially beetroot and souring agents. The many church fasts and festivals account for the proliferation of ingenious vegetarian dishes as well as the variety of cake-breads and rich doughs.

The fast table and its rules were kept strictly well into the 19th century and up to the time of the Revolution. For this reason many foods were served separately so that forbidden ingredients were not slipped in. Many dishes were based on oil — hemp, nut, poppy or olive, and later on sunflower — the advantage is that they can be eaten either hot or cold as the Greeks do. The main flavourings are onion, garlic, horseradish and dill and parsley. In the 10th to 11th centuries dishes containing parsley, star anise, coriander, bay leaf, black pepper and cloves are mentioned. The 15th to 16th centuries saw the addition of ginger, cardamom and cinnamon.

An important feature of Russian cooking is their thick soups which can be almost stew-like in consistency. Other soups containing noodles and noodle doughs such as **lapsha, pel'meni** were added in the 17th century due to Tatar influences after the annexation by Russia of Astrakhan, Kazan, Bashkiria and Siberia. Sweet dishes from the east were introduced and there were some curious mixtures of carrots with honey and ginger and radishes in treacle.

Food continued to be served *à la russe* - that is everything put on the table together: also the idea of cooking and serving the whole thing, a whole pig, a whole fish, lasted up to the 18th century.

"Give me the whole pig, the whole fish..." declares the stolid land owner Sobakevich in **Dead Souls**, thereby declaring himself a traditionalist. Pies used to be stuffed and filled with the whole bird and fish together with all their anatomical bits of liver, lights etc. One stuffing went inside another like the traditional wooden Russian doll.

In the 19th century under the influence of western cooks such as Antoine Carême and others food was cut up to go into pies and there was a turn to pâtés and the pounding of meat as well as a different presentation of the dish.

A peculiarity of Russian cooking is the adding of salt towards the end of cooking. No doubt this was an economic measure as salt was once a State monopoly and in the difficult years following emancipation an impoverished peasantry could not always buy this precious commodity — which together with bread has always been a symbol of hospitality. In Nekrasov's poem 'Who can be happy in Russia?' a crying, hungry child is only induced to eat its dry tasteless crust of bread when it finally becomes saturated with salt from his own tears.

FOOD AND AGRICULTURE

UKRAINE

Ukraine[1] is of comparable size to France and traditionally regarded as the bread basket of the region, supplying more than one fifth of its agricultural produce.

Good soil and climate, high density of population and the people's long experience in horticulture and agriculture, together with a good transport and geographical position make it attractive for food production.

The famous **chernozem** (black earth belt), a dramatic sight seen from the air, runs through it south of Kiev, the capital, and through wooded steppeland and steppe to beyond the Urals and Siberia.

When you first see its glossy blackness you can understand how its promise of fruitfulness attracted myriads of settlers down the ages.

Ukraine has seven distinct geographical areas quite unlike each other, ranging from the wooded steppeland to the marshy lands of the Poles'ye and taking in the Carpathian foothills, part of the Black Sea coastline and the Sea of Azov.

The Dnieper is its most important river, whose calm smooth flow Gogol has described many times in his writings, as well as the luscious fish caught from it and the pies made with them!

As a frontier state Ukraine has had to endure many invasions and been subject to the influences of Lithuania, Hungary, Poland and Romania and this can be seen in a similarity of some dishes and their preparation. Turkish and Tatar influences are stronger in the south.

Ukrainian food

A distinct national style emerged in the 18th century, largely freed from Polish and other influences.

Today's regional dishes reflect the historically mixed population of Russians, Belarusians, Tatars, Nogai, Hungarians, Germans, Moldovans, Turks and Greeks who have lived within its borders as well as economic and geographic circumstances.

Particularly striking is the influence of the Turks in the Bukovina region.

---

[1] *"… hard to envisage the Soviet Union without the Ukraine"* wrote the author in the first edition. Ukraine declared independence in 1991, but political tensions remain.
Crimea was annexed by the Russian Federation in 2014.

UKRAINE

Some general features of Ukrainian cooking

Meat is pre-prepared and softened before cooking; generally vegetables are puréed to thicken soup and borshch, which is not done so much in Russian cooking.

Vegetables are often stewed *à la Grecque*, with a little oil, and like the Greeks, Ukrainians don't mind eating them half warm or cold. Vegetables are seen as dishes in their own right: prime favourite is the beetroot and each region has its own particular borshch recipes (see soup section).

Ukrainian bread has endless variety. Balzac, who spent some time on the Ukrainian estate of Madame Hanska, whom he later married, was ecstatic about the great prairies of corn and the rich black earth; he declared that he had counted more than a hundred different varieties of breads and loaves. If only one could track down these recipes! In the south and west white wheat bread is mainly eaten and in the mountainous regions a certain amount of oat bread is favoured. Ukrainians also have hundreds of rich bread doughs which are formed and plaited and decorated for different festivals.

Mrs. Beeton would not have been shocked by Ukrainian recipes which even today can start with "take ten eggs".

Nikolai Gogol, whose homeland was Ukraine, described many of its classic dishes. He was a great gourmet and fond of wandering into people's kitchens and tasting the contents of bubbling pans. Mountains of food have been lovingly described by him both in its raw and cooked state.

In letters home he referred to restaurants as temples and waiters as priests and speaks of the delicious smell and taste of the sacrificial victims. He declared that his stomach was the most noble part of himself! In writing of people, figure types he likens to certain vegetables or sees their faces as rather badly baked loaves of bread.

During a pious period of his life he referred to the Bible as a kind of superior cookbook and recommended young women to read it to prepare for the future as they would prepare a fine dish. This holy 'cookbook' was to be read after tea or coffee so that they would not be distracted by appetite.

Sadly, he developed an aversion to food at the end of his life and died mainly as a result of malnutrition. It is ironic that in his last hours hot white loaves of bread were placed around his body in an endeavour to warm him. A comic touch greater even than that which befell Chekhov's body which was returned to Russia in a wagon marked "Oysters"!

BELARUS

Belarus is a predominantly agricultural region bordered in the west by Poland, in the south by Ukraine and in the north by the Baltic states and Russian Federation. It is a territory more marched over than most by invading armies.

Early on in its history it was associated with Lithuania and Poland and had the beginnings of its own literature. In the past religion has played no small part in its history and cuisine as they have been subject to the Orthodox, Catholic and Uniate church feasts, fasts and rites of their neighbours.

There are over nine million Belarusians, an eastern Slav people who live in an enormous area of over 80,000 square miles, mostly of flat land of endless horizons and much boggy terrain in the north and south, which has been the downfall of more than one invader.

During world War II, it lost much of its orchards and woodlands and its capital Minsk had to be largely rebuilt.

Many rivers and their tributaries flow through it. — the Dnieper, West Dvina, the Neman and the Berezina of Napoleonic and **War and Peace** fame.

Improved drainage schemes in the marshy areas and lands subject to constant flooding have improved the agricultural picture.

BELARUS

FINLAND

Baltic

Sea

Gulf of Finland

St. Petersburg

ESTONIA

RUSSIAN FEDERATION

LATVIA

LITHUANIA

Polotsk

Vitebsk

R. Dnieper

KALININGRAD
Oblast (Russian)

MINSK

BELARUS

Warsaw

Gomel

Brest

Pripyat
Marshes

POLAND

UKRAINE

0   Miles (approx)   500

217

Belarusian food

Their cooking is a mixture of plain peasant dishes of ancient tradition and more refined ones from Poland and their richer neighbour Ukraine.

The potato is the number one commodity which came earlier to Belarus than to other parts of Russia, and dozens of their recipes are extraordinarily inventive. Hand in hand with potato growing goes hog raising as the animals can be fed on surplus potatoes. Grain has to be imported because of the poor soil and climate. The northern damp areas produce flax and hemp and many old recipes and some new ones call for these ingredients.

In their method of food preparation they have a liking for the whole thing (old style) or else they mince meat after the Polish influence. Their general cooking technique is to cook things slowly. Boiling is favoured in old recipes and everything put in one casserole and slowly simmered – sometimes for several days. The Russian stove was a help in this regard and no doubt the style suited the housewife who would be away all day in the fields and often a long distance from home. Seasonings are mainly onions, garlic, dill, caraway, peppers, bay leaf, coriander seeds.

Food is served sizzling hot, which is reassuring to hear, and many of the national dishes have a thick stew-like consistency. Soups are also thick and hearty and an interesting turnip borshch is highly regarded.

The flour mostly used is rye, and much use is made too of oats, barley, buckwheat and pea flour. Good rye and oat bread are specialities and Minsk bread is very popular with Moscovites. Not a lot of yeast is used but a ferment is made by mixing flour and water together and allowing it to stand. In bad times when harvests were poor, thick pancakes called drachoni were used as a substitute bread.

Vegetables are mainly steamed or boiled, not fried or marinated. Sunflower oil is being used today, but pork fat has traditionally been favoured and various cracklings are included in many recipes to go with potatoes.

MOLDOVA

(See map p 215)

Border lands which have changed hands many times usually have a mixed cuisine as well as a painful and complicated history, although it can be said that certain indigenous dishes in outlying regions are often clung to all the more fiercely and jealously because of this. Present day Moldova consists of the central part of Bessarabia, quarrelled over by Russia, Turkey and Romania for hundreds of years, and the northern Bukovina — the handsome wooded area of beeches which Romania lost during the course of the last war. It lies south-west of Ukraine between the rivers Prut and Dniester with Romania on the west.

The population today is sixty per cent Moldovan who speak a Romanian dialect, though they use the Cyrillic alphabet. Other ethnic groups are Bulgars, Romanis, Greeks and Armenians. It is a warm region and vines and fruit grow well in the sheltered Dniester valley. Other crops are wheat, barley, corn, sunflowers, sugar beet and flowers such as roses, irises and geraniums are grown for the perfume industry. There is an abundance of vegetables, especially celery which is added to the local borshch and is also fermented like cabbage.

Some southern parts are dry and treeless and depend on irrigation for growing vegetables. Over-usage of land here as elsewhere has led to the formation of deep gullies, which may partly explain why in Russian literature someone is always galloping into a ravine or being pulled up short by one.

Moldovan food

Many Moldovan recipes have a remarkable similarity to Greek ones — perhaps because Moldova once traded with Greek Black Sea settlements and Byzantium. Dishes they have in common with the Balkan countries are **givech** (a delicious vegetable ragout), moussaka made with a salty goat cheese and stuffed fila pastries.

They also prepare the usual typical Russian and Ukrainian dishes and like them, enjoy fermented and salted food. Their food preparation is Mediterranean in style and they have the necessary ingredients to hand such as olives and dry wine and fresh vegetables.

Moldovan cookery is a vegetarian's delight and a great variety of sauces are added to vegetables to create a main dish. These ragouts of vegetables are cooked slowly in the oven, while meat dishes are often cooked on top of the stove.

Maize is grown and **mamaliga** made from maize flour is the basis for many savoury and sweet dishes as it is in Romania. Maize production in Russia and its areas of influence increased massively post-war. Consequently, the ways and means of cooking with maize flour have also multiplied.

The Moldovans have a penchant for purées of all kinds — especially those made from beans and lentils which are often served with garlic sauce **(mujdei)** (p 84). Like the Russians and Ukrainians, they often marinade vegetables and use soured cream lavishly.

Favourite herbs are coriander and tarragon, and tomato juice and wine vinegar are used liberally to achieve the desired sour taste. Being a wine-growing area, wine-vinegar is plentiful[1].

Desserts are usually fruit based. Moldovans often make apple and quince pastila (p 154) — a really good way of using up a glut of apples or windfalls, and better than any sweet I know of. **Pelt'ya** (p 153) is a variation.

Kisel', a thickened sweet soup made from wine and/or fruit is as popular here as in Ukraine and most of eastern Europe.

As in many agricultural communities, Moldova keeps up a number of old customs based on pagan and religious beliefs.

At New Year the festive table is piled with plaited **kalachi** (a rich bread) and decorated with a domed basilica. A separate one is placed in the middle with the **Kutya**, (a rice and raisin pudding) for the priest to bless to ensure a good harvest.

TRANSCAUCASIA

---

[1] During the Soviet era, many parts of the USSR had to make do with acid spirit (wood vinegar).

Transcaucasia is a warm and southerly region bordered by the Black and Caspian seas with nearby Turkey and Iran in the south.

The scenery ranges from sub-tropical forests to dry desert steppeland, high mountains to low humid coastline where palms, oranges and tea are grown:

Coastal Batumi[1] can be very humid and gets a hundred inches of rain a year.

The greatest concentration of people live in West Georgia and Kakhetia and along the Black Sea littoral where three minorities - the Adzhars, Abkhaz and Ossetians live.

The Abkhazians attribute their longevity to a diet of trout, onions, garlic and parsley and to the avoidance of pork, salt and water; they claim to drink only wine!

Transcaucasia gradually came under Russian rule over a period of sixty-odd years from 1801 onwards ending with the defeat of the intrepid Moslem leader Sharnil in 1859; he seemed to have led a charmed life and narrowly escaped capture many times by retreating further and further into the inaccessible fastnesses[2] of Dagestan.

His followers were no less hardy than he and tales are told of their abstemious eating habits and wasp-like waists. Often they fought on nothing more than a simple millet cake and a few rhododendron leaves so it is said. Any information on the nutritional/medicinal properties of the latter would be gratefully received.

The Caucasus has been the source of inspiration for many Russian poets, writers and painters. Lermontov describes the wild fast flowing river Terek[3] and the more placid Aragva in his poem **Demon**.

The 19th century painter Vrubel took up this demonic theme in many of his paintings, setting his own 'demon' against the plunging 'romantic' scenery of waterfalls and gorges.

Pushkin and Tolstoy were no less inspired by the awesome grandeur of the mountains and of Mount Elbruz, where legend has it that Prometheus was chained. of the Kasbek,

---

[1] Batumi in 1975: the 1st edition remarks "A place to be avoided!" There was fine scenery and good restaurants, but the beaches were very heavily guarded at night. This postscript was recorded in her husband's journal: "Search lights sweep the beach with gigantic beams… armed soldiers every 100 yards… patrol boats offshore." The entry continues "No wonder the atmosphere on the promenade is not exactly a heady one. 'They' are determined that no one shall escape to Turkey. The daytime hours are a façade – the night is real."
Batumi has changed out of all recognition since then, particularly after spending £350 million redeveloping the city and restoring the old town district.

[2] Fastness: 'a secure place protected by natural features'. Dagestan (north of Azerbaijan) 'translates as 'the land of mountains'.

[3] River Terek flows to the east of mount Kasbek and surges through the Darial gorge.

GEORGIA

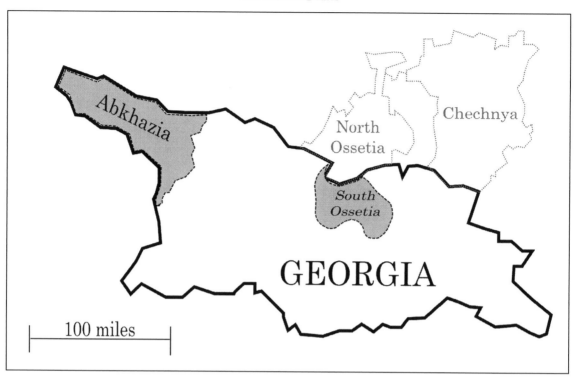

Georgia is on the eastern end of the Black Sea with the main Caucasian range to its north, Armenia to its south and Azerbaijan on the east. Over half the country is mountainous and the climate varies from humid sub-tropical on the Black Sea to the drier warm Mediterranean type inland.

Over the centuries and despite incursions of successive waves of Persians, Turks and mountain tribesmen, the two ancient Christian nations in the Caucasus, the Georgians and Armenians, have kept a strong sense of national identity, mainly by clinging tenaciously to their language, religion and customs.

Tbilisi (once Tiflis) the capital, is an old city founded on the historical caravan route linking Europe to India. The famous bazaar where traders once converged from a dozen countries is now no more and has been replaced by the more modern and hygienic market. When I visited, prices for fruit here were surprisingly high — lemons costing the equivalent of more than a £1[1]. I enjoyed shopping more in the little dark basement shops in Tbilisi, tended by lively moustachioed shop-keepers, where there was generally a good supply of vegetables and fruit at more reasonable prices and where animated debate with customers seemed part of the service. A wide variety of citrus fruits as well as apricots, peaches, plums, mulberries, figs and walnuts are grown. Walnuts especially grow so profusely that many a traveller has exclaimed at the heartily burdened trees.

---

[1] Equivalent to about £4 in 2015.

The Georgians are a vivacious and entrepreneurial people so it was disappointing to find the usual 'Soviet' standardisation[1] of food in many restaurants, the same inadequate serving of fruit and vegetables when so much grows round about.

Food and drink distribution could be curious in most places in the Soviet Union - sometimes you could only get champagne to drink and at others it couldn't be found at all, or only the restaurants had it and not the shops. Twenty varieties of ice-cream may be written up on the menu board but chocolate ice-cream is unceremoniously dumped down before all customers — a consignment of chocolate ice-cream had arrived....!

The best food I had in Georgia was in a little mountain village on our way to Mtskheta, the ancient capital, where we waited for our individual orders of **shaslyk** (kebabs) which were grilled over charcoal on long skewers and arrived sizzling and freely sprinkled with herbs and pomegranate juice. This was washed down with the excellent local Tzinandali wine.

Georgian food

There are specific differences between east and west. The western side eats less meat and prefers poultry and they like their dishes to be spicier and sharper. Not much fish is eaten and they usually steam the carp and trout and serve it with much the same sauces used for meat.

Georgian dishes for church fast days were based on the local fruit and vegetables mixed together and made piquant by the many wild herbs and greens, nettles, mallow leaves and so on which give some of their soups a glutinous texture. It reminds me very much of Greek **hortopita** which is made in the spring from wild greens growing by waysides, and these are often stuffed into pastries.

Vegetable dishes are usually cooked rather than made into salads. **Lobio** is a famous Georgian bean soup. (see recipe p 51).

Nuts, especially walnuts, form the basis of many sauces, which turn an ordinary dish into something special (p 184). Different breads are eaten in different areas: in the west maize bread is eaten while in the east they prefer wheaten bread. In Abkhazia and Mingrelia they bake millet bread. Some other regional differences are the preference for noodles (**pel'meni**) in the north east part.

Sauces are important in a Georgian kitchen. They are usually thick and based on natural fruit juices or on nuts and can be regarded as a dish in their own right and are useful served as dips. Herbs and spices are freely used in all areas and favourite sauces are **tkemali**, a sharp sauce made from wild plums with red pepper herbs, and **adzhiki** which is especially popular in west Georgia and is a mixture of red pepper, herbs, garlic, coriander, dill, salt and wine vinegar. Like the Armenians they reduce minced meats to a smooth mass. Cheese pies, like the Greek **melitera**, are a main dish and there are many regional variations.

---

[1] Present day visitors will notice big improvements in both food quality and choice compared to the Soviet era.

ARMENIA

Armenia (map p 220) is on a high upland plateau with a dry climate which can become very hot in summer. The population is mainly Armenian, sizeable numbers of whom also settled in nearby Georgia, Azerbaijan and the northern Caucasus. Significant numbers also live in Moldova and the Russian Federation.

The ancient capital Yerevan is an attractive rose-coloured city surrounded by orchards and trees. From it you can get a view across the border of twin-headed Ararat where the biblical ark is said to have come to rest. There is an elaborate Azerbaijan recipe for rice pilaf (**plov**) where the rice is piled up to resemble Ararat and its 'slopes' suitably decorated with coloured sauces.

The Armenians have an ancient culture and many Byzantine emperors were Armenian. A long unbroken religious cohesion and a strong national consciousness over the centuries, despite decimation and dispersion of their numbers over the globe, has kept their culture intact. Because of this they have tended to influence rather than be influenced in their manner of cooking. They travelled around the Caucasus more than the other nationalities and were the main commercial traders. Their customers probably assimilated more of their habits through trading with them than through a dozen conquerors. Their wine and brandy was considered first class and Dumas père observes that "more of these commodities were consumed in the Caucasus per head of population than in almost any other country in the world!"

Armenian food

The Armenian way of cooking is the oldest in the Caucasus, and many ancient dishes have been retained, some of Byzantine origin. Their refined and sophisticated cuisine evoked high praise from that enterprising and critical traveller Alexandre Dumas père as well as by other journeying writers and poets. A peculiarity of Armenian cooking is that dishes are called after the various types of utensils they are cooked in rather than after the ingredients. In reading the recipes, however, one gets the impression that there must be a horde of unseen hands ready to pound and grind to produce many of the smooth inventive dishes. Their special bread is **lavash**, a flat but leavened bread cooked swiftly on the side of a red hot *tonir*, a round cast iron stove. See bread section for more details.

Like the Georgians they make use of the hundreds of wild herbs at their disposal. Besides **shaslyk** and the many minced meat dishes they like to cook several kinds of meats in one dish such as the ancient recipe **Arganak**. Salted cheeses, often served as a first course, **tvorog**, yoghurt, as well as many kinds of porridges made from roasted wheat berries and a mixture of cereals are their specialities. They also like to mix their flours with others — potato and maize - which makes for variety in their cooking and illustrates the inventiveness of their cuisine.

Some soups, like many Middle Eastern and Balkan ones are yoghurt-egg based. The fats used in cooking are mainly butter, and vegetable oils are used for fish and in dishes which can be eaten cold as well as hot. Sunflower oil has been used more since it began to be intensively cultivated. Trout is the main fish dish and is prepared carefully to keep its softness and juiciness, and this is the prime aim of Armenian cooking — to make everything soft and tender and melt-in-the-mouth.

AZERBAIJAN

Azerbaijan (map p 220) is on the eastern side of Transcaucasia on the Caspian Sea. The central steppeland can be very hot and dry but on the slopes of the Greater Caucasus there is a certain amount of fruit growing and the humid lowland area produces rice, tea and citrus fruits.

Fish comes from the Caspian Sea but in recent years there has been some pollution from the nearby oil workings at Baku, its capital, and supplies of the once prolific sturgeon have diminished and with it the precious caviar.

There are about five million Azerbaijanis, a Turkic people, who have been greatly under the influence of Persia[1].

Azerbaijani food

Many dishes are similar to Armenian but have Turkish names. Fish is their speciality and is often grilled on skewers or baked and served with fruit and nuts, or just gently steamed. They like their food well flavoured and sharp, using a sour sauce for marinating meat called **sumac** made from berberis which may be difficult to obtain; the nearest substitute is lemon juice.

Vegetables, fruit and greens and fresh herbs and nuts are used abundantly; salads are preferred to cooked vegetables. Spring onions and wild garlic are freely used in their salads as well as cress and herbs such as parsley, tarragon, mint and apple mint, melissa, coriander and basil, and to a lesser degree thyme. Fruit and chestnuts are often cooked in butter, and rose petal syrups and jams are prepared which indicates an abundance of roses somewhere. A popular dish is poultry stuffed with nuts, thick sharp jam and onions, and then roasted on a spit. They are famous for their **plov** coloured with the locally grown saffron, which is costly everywhere, and substitutes of **imerety** saffron made from golden headed thistles or turmeric are often used. A north-west speciality is noodles stuffed with meat, onion and cheese. Their cakes, biscuits and sweetmeats are, generally speaking, too sweet for European tastes but I have cut down amounts of sugar in many recipes. Clapping biscuits together with a sharp fruit filling overcomes the excessive sweetness. They also have a delightful way of stuffing plain bread or pastry dough with crushed nuts, cinnamon and cardamom which make most acceptable deserts.

---

[1] Iran: During WWII, Churchill requested the name 'Persia' be used, to avoid confusion with 'Iraq'. Today, 'Iran' is generally used in a political context and 'Persia' for historical references.

CENTRAL ASIA

Kazakhstan, Kyrgyzstan, Tajikistan, Turkmenistan and Uzbekistan were part of the Soviet Union, but are now independent states.

Kazakhstan is the largest economy in Central Asia, with vast oil reserves.

Turkmenistan and Uzbekistan were major cotton producers at independence, but wheat is becoming a much more significant crop.

Uzbekistan continued Soviet style cotton farming in the 1990's. Massively inefficient irrigation has caused the Aral sea to shrink drastically to 15% of its former size, destroying its fishing industry. Kazakhstan completed a dam in 2008, which is helping to replenish the North Aral.

Kyrgyzstan and Tajikistan are more mountainous, with large agrarian populations. Cotton and wheat are again prime crops.

THE VOLGA REGION

The Volga is the most important waterway of the Russian Federation and geographically and economically it is usually divided into three regions: the Upper forested section, the Middle wooded steppe area and the lower reaches which are mostly open steppeland.

The broad river can be as much as twenty-five miles wide in parts with numerous islands, inlets and sandbanks. Its many tributaries link it to St. Petersburg, Moscow and Perm in the Urals and it is possible to travel along it from the Baltic and Arctic Seas to the Caspian in the south.

Over this vast stretch of territory, climate and growing conditions vary considerably and with it the style of cooking. In the forested upper region, much bee-keeping is carried on by the Mari people (Finnish-Ugric race).

After the 17th century Russian colonization displaced many Volga dwellers - the Mordvinians, Chuvash, and Tatars and put them into separate ethnic groupings.

Parts of the Volga go through the Black Earth Belt in the Tatarstan Republic in the middle region (capital Kazan) where farming conditions are good. Only half the population here is Tatar, the rest are Russian, Chuvash, Mordvinians, Udmart and Mari.

The Lower Volga is warmer and favourable to fruit growing as well as the usual crops. Here the population is mainly Russian.

Before the last war, three quarters were German and Kalmuk who were dispersed and re-settled following their alleged collaboration with the Germans during the war. They were then replaced by Ukrainians in the north and some Tatar, Mordvinian and Chuvash minorities.

In the Astrakhan region, which is often associated with fur, the Kalmuks carried on nomadic sheep raising, but now irrigation has changed all that and melons, fruit and vines are grown as well as wheat and sunflowers and so on.

The Volga region is densely populated and cooking very varied; Tatar and Russian cuisines are the chief influences.

TATARSTAN REPUBLIC[1]

The Tatars descend from a Turkic speaking people who settled in the Central Volga and Lower Prikam'ya long before the main Mongol invasion. Their Central Asian neighbours - Uzbeks, Tajiks as well as Russians have influenced their way of cooking. Today, the population is half Tatar.

Tatars were also indigenous in the Crimean peninsula before the Russian conquest in 1783 and even attempted to form an independent Crimean nation after the Revolution. In 1944 after the German invasion the Tatars were accused of treason and Stalin had a quarter of a million deported to arid regions in Central Asia. Almost half of them died, but in 1967 they were reinstated although not allowed to return to the Crimea.

During the Soviet era there was no reference to them in the press and censorship extended to cutting out all mention of them in editions of Chekhov's letters.

The food

A few notes have already been made in the introduction on their style of cooking but more needs to be said about their general way of preparing food, as traces of their influence can be seen in so many of the dishes found all over the Russian Federation.

Many of the ingredients used can be found wherever there is woodland - mushrooms, honey, wild berries and greens of all kinds such as wild spinach and sorrel.

Milk is usually taken in the form of yoghurt and cream cheeses or in milky soups with the addition of noodles which come in various shapes and sizes. Their speciality is bread making based on sour dough, though in more recent years bread is mass produced too, with both rye and wheat bread being eaten.

Meat is generally boiled or steamed and cut into small flat pieces and sometimes lightly fried afterwards. Poultry raising is increasing and a speciality is steamed chicken stuffed between the skin and breast with a scrambled egg and cream mixture.

As elsewhere, all kinds of **kasha** are eaten and different flours are used for making an infinite variety of sweet and semi-sweet biscuits and pastries with all sorts of stuffings.

Alexandre Dumas père visited the region in 1858 and his comments on Tatar kitchens are worth repeating:

"Food undergoes such transformations in a Tatar kitchen that if a man is hungry he had better eat what is set before him without enquiring too closely what it is".

He notes too such items as cutlets with honey and the general love of cinnamon and rose-leaf preserves.

---

[1] Part of the Russian Federation. On the Volga situated east of Ural mountains.

THE BALTIC STATES

Situated to the west of the Russian Federation, the generally damp and humid climate is good for growing rye, oats and barley. Crops grown are similar to those grown in Belarus and much use is made of potatoes and pork. There are a few differences between the three countries as far as cooking is concerned.

ESTONIA

Estonian dishes have some Finnish and Swedish overtones.

From the 17th to 18th century Estonia belonged to Sweden; later it formed part of the Russian Empire, and after the Revolution until 1940 it was an independent state. The people are successful, experienced farmers and make good use of available products.

Meat and vegetables are generally boiled either in water, beer or milk or a mixture of these. Some specialities are their black and grey bread of rye, oats and potatoes. Honey and malt are often added and the sweet-sour rye bread, Baltic pumpernickel, is popular, so is rye-potato roll served with a milk sauce.

Soups, whether meat, fish or vegetable are mainly based on fresh milk[1], and flavoured by the addition of smoked bacon or pork fat. Pies are made from rye flour which makes them distinctive if somewhat heavy unless skilfully leavened. Fish is often smoked and dried and they have many recipes.

Toasted rye berries mixed with oats and barley or peas and black beans make interesting and tasty **kashas** (porridges).

Herbs used in the three states are the usual ones of dill, marjoram, parsley etc. but their use is strictly adhered to for specific dishes, i.e. dill with salad and so forth.

LATVIA

Latvian cooking mainly reflects the influence of the other two Baltic states. Their speciality is an ancient dish with the unpromising name of **'putry'**, and is a vegetable-grain porridge with suet and pork fat, plus smoked meat or mushrooms. Sour milk products are added and the dish is set to ferment for a few hours and it is then beaten smooth.

Latvians grow caraway; its availability is reflected in many local dishes and drinks.

---

[1] Dairy faming is extensive in Estonia.

LITHUANIA

Lithuanian cooking is an interesting mixture of the other Baltic states, but with stronger Polish and German overtones, and in the eastern part there are Tatar influences.

In the 14th to the 15th century Lithuania had a well-developed governmental and administrative system and close trade links with the eastern khanates of the Crimea and the Golden Horde (the early invading armies of the Mongol-Tatar state, set up by Batu Khan, grandson of Genghis Khan) and the Turkish Ottoman Empire.

These eastern influences are seen in the way stuffed vegetables are prepared and in the use of pomegranate juice in old recipes.

Some old fish recipes may include sour cabbage or horseradish. Wild game and fowl flourished in the wooded and boggy terrain and many old recipes give details of the smoking and preserving process and these products were in great demand in Germany and Western Europe.

The meats and fish were smoked slowly for several days over oak, ash, elm, hornbeam, hazel and juniper wood, all to be found in the nearby forests.

Today, old-fashioned smoking is done on a limited scale and factory produced goods are the norm.

These same woods once yielded up high quality honey and there are many honey based dishes. This individual style of cooking declined at the end of the 18th century when Lithuania and Poland lost their independent status.

MEASUREMENT & CONVERSION TABLES

UK ounces / fluid ounces	gram / millilitre to the nearest unit	gram / millilitre to the nearest unit of 25
1	28	25
2	57	50
3	85	75
4	113	100
5	142	150
6	170	175
7	198	200
8	226	225
9	255	250
10	283	275
11	311	300
12	340	350
13	368	375
14	396	400
15	428	425
16	456	450
17	486	475
18	512	500
19	541	550
20	569	575
21	595	600
22	624	625
23	652	650
24	680	675
25	709	700
26	739	750
27	767	775
28	794	800
29	824	825
30	850	850
32	907	900
34	964	975
35	992	1000

Ratio of ingredients is often more important for recipes than exact weight. Such proportions are best maintained by keeping entirely to *either* imperial *or* metric measures.

LIQUID MEASURES

British		UK Fl oz	American		US Fl oz
1 pint =		= 20	1 pint		16
½ pint = 1 UK cup		= 10	½ pint	1 US cup	8
¼ pint = 8 UK tablespoons		= 5	¼ pint	8 US tablespoons	4
5 UK teaspoons		1		6 US teaspoons	1

Approximate equivalents used for recipes

British units	Metric	American units
1 pint	575 ml	1¼ pints
½ pint (1 UK cup)	275 ml	10 fl oz (1¼ US cups)
1 fl oz		1 fl oz
1 tablespoon	18 ml	1.2 US tablespoons
1 dessertspoon	12 ml	1.2 US dessertspoons
1 teaspoon	6 ml	1.2 US teaspoons

Metric units (ml)	British Fl oz	American Fl oz
1000 (1 litre)	35	33½
500	17½	17
250 (1 Metric cup)	9	8½
100	3½	3½
.25	1	1
28.4 ml	1.00 UK Fl oz	0.96 US Fl oz

Cup & Spoon measures	Metric size (ml)	UK size (ml)	US size (ml)
1 Cup	250	284	240
1 Tablespoon	15	18	15
1 Dessertspoon	10	12	10
1 Teaspoon	5	6	5

SOLID MEASURES

Approximate equivalents used for recipes

British	to	Metric (Approx)	Metric	to	British (Approx)
2 lb (32 oz)		900 g	1000 g (1 kg)		2 lb 3 oz
1 lb (16 oz)		450 g	500 g		1 lb 2 oz
½ lb (8 oz)		225 g	250 g		9 oz
4 oz		100 g	100 g		4 oz
1 oz		25 g	25 g		1 oz

HANDY MEASURES (approx.)

		Tablespoons (level)
Almonds, ground	1 oz =	3¾
Breadcrumbs, fresh	1 oz =	7
Breadcrumbs, dried	1 oz =	3¼
Butter, Margarine etc.	1 oz =	2
Cheese, cheddar type grated	1 oz =	3
Chocolate, grated	1 oz =	3¼
Cocoa	1 oz =	2¾
Coconut, desiccated	1 oz =	5
Coffee, instant	1 oz =	6½
Cornflour or custard powder	1 oz =	2½
Flour	1 oz =	3
Gelatine	1 oz =	2½
Rice	1 oz =	1½
Sugar	1 oz =	2
Sugar, icing	1 oz =	2½
Yeast dried	1 oz =	1½

LIQUID MEASURES

Syrup	1 oz = approximately	1	level tablespoon
Corn oil, milk, water	1¼ fl oz =	2	tablespoons
	2½ fl oz =	4	tablespoons
	5 fl oz	9	tablespoons

OVEN TEMPERATURES

OVEN	°F	°C	Gas mark
Very cool / very low	225-265	110-130	¼ - ½
Cool / Low	275-300	140-150	1-2
Warm	325	160	3
Moderate	350	180	4
Moderately hot	375-400	190-200	5-6
Hot	425	220	7
Very hot	450-475	230-240	8-9

QUICK CHECK GLOSSARY

Some commonly used Russian words and other culinary terms.

Term	Meaning
bliny	pancakes
bouillon	thin broth, gruel or stock made from water used to cook meat
bulochki	rolls
fumet	a fish or vegetable flavoured broth
golubtsy	stuffed cabbage leaves
ikra	caviar
julienne strips	fine long strips of vegetables – carrots are often done this way
kalach	round shaped enriched bread
kefir	type of yoghurt
kisel'	fruit soup, usually thickened with arrowroot or cornflour
kulebyaka	a pie for special occasions
kvas	a kind of light beer
nastoi	liquid from marinated vegetables or herb flavoured vinegars
olad'i	a thick crumpet-like bliny
pilaff, pilau, plov	the same - they are all steamed rice
pirog	a pie
pryazhnik	biscuit - usually spiced and somewhat like gingerbread
rassol'	marinade made from beetroot and cucumber
roux	flour and butter mixed together before adding liquid to make a sauce
shchi	cabbage soup
shaslyk	skewered, grilled meat or fish
smetana	soured cream
sol'yanka	a sharp flavoured soup or stew of vegetables, or meat or poultry
suneli	spice
tefteli	fish or meat balls or patties
ushki	stuffed noodles - means 'little ears'. Similar to **ponchiki** and **pel'meni** (see index of recipes)
vzvar'	stew
zapekanka	a bake

SOURCES AND BIBLIOGRAPHY

A note on Sources

The bulk of the recipes in this book come from the few Russian pre-revolutionary cookery books available and from standard pre-World War II manuals, which give all the recipes of typical classic Russian fare and which seem to remain unchanging when one looks at different editions.

Other recipes I came across were found pinned on notice boards in obscure canteens and eating places; where these originated I cannot say. I only know that what turned out to be delicious recipes when tried out at home did not appear on the menus of these establishments!

In the Caucasus I sampled chicken **tabaka**, aubergine **'ikra'** (caviar) and **bliny** filled with curd cheese and cherry purée, prepared by a sweet old Ukrainian babushka, who happily combined Georgian flair and ingredients with her own traditional dishes. When pressed for the recipes she screwed up her eyes tightly and rattled off the ingredients, assuming I would know all methods.

Measurements are nearly always given in glasses[1] and I have had to find an identical glass and then work out my own weights in ounces and grams.

In the post-war years in Moscow I sampled a wide range of dishes on a grander scale and prepared by different Embassy-employed cooks. The foreign colony of embassies and legations formed a sophisticated 'village' and invitations went round and round. Food was of the highest quality and we all put on weight as in the winter months we developed appetites like wolves.

For cooking styles and attitudes to cooking and general background information I have delved into old pre-war Russian encyclopaedias and works of an ethnological nature.

The 'uncovering' nature of this research has been a useful guide where there is proliferation of recipes for the same dish.

---

[1] Russia adopted the metric system in 1924: 1 glass=250 ml. Imperial Russia defined 1 cup (**starken**) as 273 ml. A Russian imperial 'wine glass' = 123 ml; care needed with old recipes!

Selective Bibliography

Russian Cookery books consulted

Azerbaidzhanskaya kulinariya	Baku 1981 *(Azerbeijani cooking)*
Estonskaya kukhnya	Tallin, 1984, *(Estonian cuisine)*
Kazakhskaya Kukhnya	1981, *(Kazakh cuisine)*
Khleb v nashem dome	Moscow 1982 *(Bread in our home)*
Kholodnye bluda i zakuski	Moscow, 1983 *(Cold dishes and hors d'oeuvres)*
Kukhnya narodov SSSR	V.M. Mel'nik, Kishinev, 1982. *(Cooking of the Peoples of the Soviet Union)*
Kniga o vkysnoi i zdorovoi pishche	1952 and 1971 editions, [originally published in 1939] *(The book of tasty and healthy food)*
Podarok molodym khozyaikam	Molokhovets Elena, St. P. 1861. *(A Gift to Young Housewives)*
Natsional'nye kukhni nashikh narodov	1981 *(National dishes of our people)*
Pitanie dlya vsekh	Kiev, 1983 *(Food for everyone)*
Russkaya kulinariya	various editions *(Russian cooking)*
Rybnye bluda	Moscow, 1983 *(Fish dishes)*.
Rybnaya kukhnya	Moscow, 1984 *(Fish cookery)*
Supy i tushenye ovoshchi	Tallin, 1983 *(Soups and vegetables)*
Tatarskaya Kulinariya	Kazan', 1981 *(Tatar cuisine)*
Vse iz muki	Alma-Ata, 1981 *(Everything made with flour)*
500 blud iz kartofelya	Minsk 1981 *(500 potato recipes)*

Some literary, historical and geographical works consulted

Babel' Issac (1894-1941)	works
Chekhov, Anton (1860-1904)	works
Dobuzhinsky M.	**Vospominaniya**, Vol I, New York, 1976 (memoirs)
Dostoievsky, Fyodor (1821-1881)	works
Dumas (père), Alexandre (1802-1870)	works
Gautier, Théophile	**Travels in Russia** 1866
Gogol, Nikolai (1821-1852)	**Dead Souls** and other works
Kohl, J.G.	**History of Russia**, 1842
Larousse	Encyclopaedia of Cooking
Mellor, Roy E.H.	**The Soviet Union and its Geographical Problems**, 1982
Olesha, Yuri	**Izbrannoe** (Collection of Stories) Moscow, 1974
Parker W. H.	**An Historical Geography of Russia**, 1968
Pipes, R.	**Russia under the old regime**, Peregrine Books, 1977
Pushkin, Alexander (1799-1837)	**Evgenii Onegin**
Riasanovsky, N. V.	**A History of Russia**, 1962
Tolstoy, L. (1828-1910)	works
Turgenev, Ivan (1818-1882)	works
Zamyatin, Evgenii	**Povesti I Rasskazy**, Bradda Reprint, 1969

Recipe Index ————————————————————————

248

SOURCES OF RECIPES

Principal sources of recipes: countries named in **bold**.
In addition, some recipes come from central Asia and Russia's 'Far East'.

EMBASSY DAYS

By Jean Redwood   ISBN: 978-1-870832-09-0

EMBASSY DAYS

Moscow under Stalin
Bangkok without tourists
1949-1952
Jean Redwood

Jean Floyd[1] was 22 when the Foreign Office sent her for secretarial duties to the British Embassy in Moscow in 1949, shortly after the beginning of the Cold War.

It was a time when the outbreak of World War III was regarded as a serious possibility, especially after the start of the Korean War in 1950. The use of atomic bombs was not being ruled out.

The wartime camaraderie with 'our brave Russian allies' had become a hollow memory.

In Moscow, foreigners were regarded with deep suspicion:

Diary, 11 Feb 1950 The other day I asked a woman where No.1 Shop was.... She was initially most friendly... but when I told her I was working in the British Embassy, she scuttled away in terror! And to think she might have been on the point of asking me to tea!

Bangkok was unlike Moscow in every conceivable way. Despite an occasional coup d'état *(Diary, 1 July 1951: "Whilst it was still dark, the silence was shattered by loud gunfire. I was sound asleep and nearly jumped out of my skin.")* it was a free society where Thais and foreigners met on equal terms.

Notwithstanding the intimidating character of the Soviet regime, Russia made an overwhelming impression on Jean, and one that remained for the rest of her life.

Available from: Amazon and all good bookshops.

---

[1] Jean Redwood, née Floyd

Published by: Oldwicks Press Limited

Made in the USA
Columbia, SC
01 December 2020

26039654R00143